THE EYE
OF THE VIPER

The Making of an F-16 Pilot

Peter Aleshire

THE LYONS PRESS
Guilford, Connecticut
An imprint of The Globe Pequot Press

Copyright © 2004 by Peter Aleshire

First Lyons Press paperback edition, 2005

The Lyons Press is an imprint of The Globe Pequot Press.

10 9 8 7 6 5 4 3 2

Printed in the United States of America

ISBN-13: 978-1-59228-822-9
ISBN-10: 1-59228-822-7

Designed by Stephanie Doyle

ISBN 1-59228-822-7 (paperback)

The Library of Congress has previously cataloged an earlier (hardcover) edition as follows:

Aleshire, Peter.
        Eye of the viper : the making of an F-16 pilot / Peter Aleshire.
                p. cm.
        Includes bibliographical references.
        ISBN 1-59228-260-1 (trade cloth)
1. Fighter pilots—Training of—United States. 2. Fighter plane combat—United States. 3. Luke Air Force Base (Ariz.) 4. F-16 (Jet fighter plane) I. Title.

UG703.A73 2004
358.4'383'023—dc22   2004048738

THE EYE
OF THE VIPER

DEDICATION

This book is dedicated to Frank, my father, a test pilot in World War II

who taught me to love the sky. And to these American

F-16 pilots who have died in the cockpit.

LIEUTENANT COLONEL
Dillon L. *"McFly"* McFarland
466FS, Hill Air Force Base
Reserve Unit, 2002

CAPTAIN
Mitchell A. *"Toro"* Bulmann
77FS, Shaw Air Force Base,
2001

FIRST LIEUTENANT
Jorma D. Huhtala
4FS, Hill Air Force Base, 2002

FIRST LIEUTENANT
Randy E. *"Chongo"* Murff
35FS, Kunsan Air Base,
2001

CAPTAIN
Benton Carter Zettel
522FS, Cannon Air Force Base, 2002

CAPTAIN
Luke A. *"Stiff"* Johnson
23FS, Spangdahlem Air Base, 2002

CAPTAIN
Warren B. *"Reefer"* Sneed
14FS, Misawa Air Base and
F16VPA member,
2000

MAJOR
Aaron C. *"C-Dot"* George
416FTS, Edwards Air Force Base,
2001

MAJOR
Stephen W. *"Slinger"* Simons
457FS, Fort Worth
Reserve Unit,
2000

Major
Brison *"Moose"* Phillips
78FS, Shaw Air Force Base and
F16VPA member, 2000

Major
Sammy *"Dago"* D'Angelo
93FS, Homestead Air Force
Reserve Unit, 1999

Lieutenant Colonel
Gregory C. *"Maniac"* Martineac
421FS, Hill Air Force Base, 1998

First Lieutenant
Melvin Brice *"Ronin"* Simpson
14FS, Misawa Air Base, 1998

First Lieutenant
Patrick J. *"Sherman"* Potter
188FS, New Mexico
Air National Guard, 1998

Captain
Keith *"Sandman"* Sands
36FS, Osan Air Base, 1998

Captain
Mark Patrick *"Mac"* McCarthy
510FS, Aviano Air Base, 1995

Lieutenant Colonel
John Michael *"Stewball"* Steward
184FS, Fort Smith
Air National Guard/
Air Force Advisor, 1993

Captain
John M. *"Mighty Mouse"* Barelka
USAF Fighter Weapons School,
Nellis Air Force Base, 1993

Captain
James *"Malibu"* Reynolds
414CTS, Nellis Air Force Base, 1993

Joe Bill Dryden
Senior Experimental Test Pilot,
Lockheed Martin Corp.,
Fort Worth, 1993

Captain
Robert John *"Face"* Abraham
Air combat crash, 1993

Captain
Donald E. *"Lumpy"* Leckrone, Jr.
170FS, Springfield, Illinois
Air National Guard, 1992

Lieutenant Colonel
Edward Eugene *"Indian"* Hackney
58TFTW, Luke Air Force Base,
1992

Lieutenant Colonel
Roy Allen Keyt
171FS, Selfridge
Air National Guard, 1992

Captain
Arnold Arthur *"Arnie"* Clarke
419FW, Hill Air Force Base
Reserve Unit, 1991

Michael Terrance *"Soulman"* Sowell
388FW Hill Air Force Base,
1991

First Lieutenant
Keith Gregory Nylander
34FS, Hill Air Force Base,
1991

Captain
Michael Leo *"Chins"* Chinburg
Saudi Arabia, 1991

First Lieutenant
Steve *"Sunny"* Sundstrom
496TFS, Hahn Air Base, 1989

Captain
Mike A. Crandall
313TFS, Hahn Air Base,
1988

First Lieutenant
Tom E. *"Popeye"* Doyle
10TFS, Hahn Air Base, 1988

Captain
Alex M. Rupp
USAF Fighter Weapons School,
1987

First Lieutenant
Ralph Cyr
17TFS, Shaw Air Force Base,
1986

Captain
Larry Edward Lee
3246 Test Wing,
Eglin Air Force Base,
1986

Captain
Glen *"Dupes"* Dupuis
10TFS, Hahn Air Base, 1985

Lieutenant Colonel
Yeadon D. *"Dell"* Dorn
157TFS, McEntire
Air National Guard, 1984

First Lieutenant
Steve Wallis
10TFS, Hahn Air Base, 1983

First Lieutenant
Ronald L. *"Ronzo"* Gray
430TFS, Nellis Air Force Base,
1983

Major
Pete Jones
USAF Fighter Weapons School
Instructor Pilot,
Nellis Air Force Base, 1983

Captain
Ted T. *"Gamble"* Harduvel
80TFS, Kunsan Air Base, 1982

Captain
Francisco *"Frank"* Pineiro, Jr.
3246TW, Eglin Air Force Base,
1982

Captain
S. Curtis *"Bullet"* Robinson
80TFS, Kunsan Air Base, 1982

Captain
J. Edgington Moats
388TFW, Hill Air Force Base,
1981

Jacques Olivier
Pilot of a private plane killed in
midair collision with an F-16,
2000

Lieutenant General (retired)
Eugene H. Fisher
1998

LIEUTENANT COLONEL
William Nusz
419FTS, Edwards
Air Force Base, 1997

FLIGHT LIEUTENANT (RAF)
Leigh Fox
445FTS, Edwards
Air Force Base, 1997

CAPTAIN
Dwi Sasongko
Jakarta, 1997

MAJOR
Peter Woodbury
148FW, Duluth
Air National Guard,
1997

CAPTAIN
John Kindred
1994

SECOND LIEUTENANT
Julian Beneker
148FS, 1994

FIRST LIEUTENANT
Stephen Taylor
114FS, Klamath Falls
Air National Guard, 1993

LIEUTENANT COLONEL
Ralph Earl *"Bark"* Gardner
35FS, Kunsan Air Base, 1993

CAPTAIN
Luis F. Jordan
18FS, Eielson Air Force Base,
1993

MAJOR
(Dr.) Robert D. *"Doc"* Verdone
18FS, Eielson Air Force Base,
1993

CAPTAIN
Glen Scott Porter
18FS, Eielson Air Force Base, 1993

STAFF SERGEANT
Chris Ford
148FW Duluth Air National Guard,
1991

LIEUTENANT COLONEL
Jeff Dennis
148FW, Duluth Air National Guard,
1991

CAPTAIN
Percival Taylor *"Teflon"* Gates
422TES, Nellis Air Force Base,
1991

MAJOR
Robert Dean Ashenfelter
Air National Guard, 1991

CAPTAIN
Dale Cormier
Saudi Arabia, 1991

MAJOR
Cary Carlin
184FG, McConnell
Air National Guard, 1991

LIEUTENANT COLONEL
Barry Bost
70TFS/DO, Moody
Air Force Base, 1990

MAJOR
A. *"Gino"* Stuart
347TFW, Moody
Air Force Base, 1990

MAJOR
Rob *"Pork"* Tucker
302TFS, Luke Reserve,
1989

CAPTAIN
J. Bourne, U.S. Marine Corps
Orientation flight, 1989

FIRST LIEUTENANT
Danny Ralph *"DJ"* Johnson
612TFS, Torrejon Air Base,
1989

FIRST LIEUTENANT
Josh Levin
35TFS, Kunsan Air Base, 1989

MAJOR GENERAL
Winfield Scott Harpe
16AF/CC, Torrejon Air Base,
1988

MAJOR
Willy *"Birdseed"* Kempe
302TFS, Luke Reserve, 1988

LIEUTENANT COLONEL
David F. Shontz
612TFS, Torrejon Air Base,
1988

LIEUTENANT COLONEL
Richard *"Dick"* Allain
86TFW, Ramstein Air Base,
1987

MAJOR
Michael J. Lotti
USAF FWIC Instructor Pilot,
Nellis Air Force Base, 1987

FIRST LIEUTENANT
J. Holmberg, 1987

LIEUTENANT COLONEL
Eric Oliver
33TFS, Shaw Air Force Base, 1986

CAPTAIN
Jerry Noble Allison
Fighter Weapons School,
Nellis Air Force Base, 1985

FIRST LIEUTENANT
S. Brad *"Face"* Peale
421TFS, Hill
Air Force Base, 1985

SECOND LIEUTENANT
J. *"Ned"* O'Brien
72TFTS, McDill
Air Force Base, 1985

CAPTAIN
Ed Johnson
19TFS, Shaw
Air Force Base, 1985

FIRST LIEUTENANT
Steve Vick
613TFS, Torrejon Air Base,
Spain, 1984

MAJOR
Glenn Hessel
474TFW, Nellis
Air Force Base, 1984

FIRST LIEUTENANT
Scott Trapp
613TFS, Torrejon
Air Base,
1984

LIEUTENANT COLONEL
Richard *"Dick"* Andersen
16TFTS/CC, Hill
Air Force Base, 1984

LIEUTENANT COLONEL
W. Roy Neisz
388TFW, Hill
Air Force Base, 1984

CAPTAIN
L. Christopher *"Boo Boo"* Barber
388TFW, Hill
Air Force Base, 1983

LIEUTENANT COLONEL
Bill George
34TFS, Hill
Air Force Base, 1983

MAJOR
Richard *"Dick"* Olson
388TFW, Hill
Air Force Base,
1982

CONTENTS

AUTHOR'S NOTE

IT'S HARD TO HUMBLE and inspire a writer—especially a veteran reporter.

But the six months I spent following a dozen young Air Force officers through basic training as F-16 pilots at Luke Air Force base in Glendale, Arizona did the trick.

The eager, bright, disciplined young men and women—mostly in their early twenties—have dedicated their lives to flying jets and serving their country. They each made considerable sacrifices to dedicate themselves to a daunting and dangerous task that will prepare them to risk their lives as a routine for their country and ground pounders like me.

And that wasn't the half of it. The veteran, combat pilots who served as their instructors have devoted decades to the nation's defense, in the process developing the astonishing skills needed to fly the most agile and flexible fighter jet ever built. I was moved and humbled by their courage, skill, dedication, and patriotism—not to mention their wicked humor, staunch brotherhood, and slashing sense of the absurd.

I am grateful for their trust and the chance to see them at work.

I am also grateful for the willingness of the Air Force to allow me unrestricted access to Luke. For six months, I spent several days a week at the base. I attended briefings, interviewed pilots, flew the simulator, and was strapped into the backseat of an F-16 modified to have a back seat for an instructor. The pilots were open, honest, and forthright—answering every question I could think to ask. They patiently explained things that seemed commonsensical to them, but which baffled a ground-hugging reporter.

I can only hope I have told their stories faithfully. I hope they'll forgive me for oversimplifying in my efforts to explain to a general audience what it took them years of concentrated study to master.

I agreed to let the Air Force review this manuscript to avoid any inadvertent revelation of classified information. I'd like to thank the Air Force and Luke Wing Commander Brigadier General Philip Breedlove for their unstinting cooperation and professionalism.

I am also deeply grateful to Col. Bob Egan and Major Howard Hobday, who reviewed the manuscript to avoid revelation of classified tactics and information. They also patiently tried to correct my mistakes and misinterpretations. Their help proved invaluable. However, all the mistakes that remain are my own.

In turning the remarkable six-month experience into a coherent narrative, I had to make a difficult decision to exclude from the final book some of the pilots who helped me. I spent all my time with the Emerald Knights, a training squadron in the 56th Fighter Wing at Luke Air Force Base, following a single group of thirteen student pilots through the B-course, a six-month gauntlet during which pilots who have learned the basics of flying fighter jets specialize in the F-16. The book revolves around the experiences of those students and the approximately twenty-six instructor pilots who taught them how to stay alive in the air while "killing people and blowing up their shit." I sat in on the briefings and debriefings of many different missions involving many different pilots. When I sat down to write this book, I concluded that the reader could never keep track of so many vital characters, so I decided to cut from the book five of the student pilots to make the narrative manageable. I also left out many of the instructor pilots. This sometimes required me to combine missions to preserve the narrative—principally during the large force deployment at the end of the book. It also required me to replace instructor pilots and sometimes student pilots on particular missions with different pilots once I made the painful choice as to which students and instructors to leave out. I apologize to the omitted students and instructors—for their contributions were no less vital than those of the officers I included. However, none of the biographical information has been changed or combined—for either students or instructors. The details of the training missions flown have not been altered, nor have any details of the combat missions described, although I have omitted details that might reveal classified weapons or tactics. I only hope the pilots excluded for the sake of the coherence of the book will forgive me and understand my dilemma.

Beyond that, I claim sole credit for all of the mistakes, mangled sentences, misunderstandings, dumb stuff, and oversimplifications. My long-suffering editor at Lyons Press, Tom McCarthy, did his best to help. The sharp eye of copyeditor Alex Barnett provided the proper polish. My wife Elissa put up with my endless absences and long mutterings and provided unfailing support and encouragement. And the pilots of the Emerald Knights did everything in their power to make sure I got it right. The Air Force gave me such startling access and freedom to report that they left me with no reasonable excuse for whatever flaws exist in this book.

For all of that help and patience, I'm grateful.

And finally, I would like to express my profound gratitude to the more than ninety F-16 pilots who have died flying the Viper in defense of their country. Most died in training accidents. That's not surprising. In the quarter century the F-16 and its pilots have defended the nation and won every war, the Viper has never lost a dogfight and has helped crush every air defense system it has faced. That's only possible because of the intense, tireless, and risky training this book attempts to describe. In the end, this nation's triumph in war stems directly from this triumph of training.

Prologue: Dead Heroes

———✦———

Blame it on the Blue Angels.

And Chips. Blame it on Chips, too.

First, the precision roar of the Blue Angels in their roaring Phantoms made five-year-old Howard dream of jets and yearn toward that wild blue up yonder.

Then his uncle "Chips" went off to Vietnam. Chips started out piloting a cargo jet—"hauling the mail"—but then jumped at the chance to serve as a Weapons System Officer in the backseat of an F-4 Phantom in the missile-streaked, flak-punctuated skies of Vietnam. Chips had joined the world's most exclusive and dangerous club as a hotshotting, g-turning, Red Baron, ball-busting, badass. Howard yearned for Chips's every visit back from the bewildering jungles where the world's richest, most powerful nation had hurled the most expensive military in the history of the known universe against a bunch of raggedy-ass commies in black PJs to Make the World Safe for Democracy and President Thieu's cronies.

Chips got in on the action just as the Vietnam War started turning into a genuine U.S. Air Force disaster. Even worse than Korea—which was bad enough.

Korea was the first big war of the jets. And it started off bad when the astonished U.S. pilots discovered that the cheap, mass-produced, Soviet-built MiGs could outclimb and outturn their much more expensive, loaded-up, multipurpose Sabers.

Under the spell of the Strategic Air Command, a nuke-obsessed Air Force had figured that city-destroying strategic bombing would decide all future wars, with giant bombers flying too high for the fighters to reach them. But in Korea, U.S. pilots found themselves trying to hit tactical targets like tanks and troops with planes built to bomb cities. Worse, U.S. pilots soon discovered that the cheap, nimble MiGs could outfly them in a dogfight. Only superior training and flexible doctrine saved them, coupled with the development of improved air-to-air missiles.

In Korea, the introduction of the Super Saber and superior training and doctrine gradually gave the U.S. and UN forces air superiority. The U.S. flew a million sorties and lost more than 2,000 aircraft, about half to missiles and ground fire, and half to the MiGs. The bloody, swirling clash between jet fighters drove home the air-combat lessons of World War II, which stressed the importance of the pilot. In Korea, 5 percent of the 800 U.S. fighter pilots accounted for 37 percent of the kills in the air; it was about the same in World War II. On the North Korean side, a handful of Soviet pilots, brought in when the U.S. fighter jocks devastated the poorly trained North Korean pilots, accounted for most of the air-to-air kills.

But despite the hard lessons of Korea, the brass made additional crucial mistakes before the Vietnam War. The four-stars did approve new fighter jets—mostly the muscular, heavyweight F-4 Phantom. But convinced that air-to-air missiles would end dogfighting forever, they took the cannons out of the Phantom and loaded it up with bombs and missiles. They also changed flight training for fighter pilots, stressing the use of missiles and cutting back on air-to-air dogfighting, with its inevitable crashes and collisions. Surely the U.S. edge in high-tech missiles would do away with light, nimble fighter aircraft. We don't need cannons—who's gonna get that close?

So along comes Vietnam.

And the MiGs were still faster, higher, and more nimble. And they had cannons. Lethal cannons. Worse yet, the U.S. missiles didn't work that well.

So the MiG pilots, lightly trained and tightly controlled from the ground, started shooting down Phantoms. Lots of Phantoms.

The Phantoms spent most of their time bombing—usually close air support, or attempted pinpoint takeouts on bridges, power plants, and small targets. That meant flying through the best air defense system in history, courtesy of the Soviet Union and China, who saw in Vietnam an opportunity to test their tactics and bleed dry their superpower rival. The

Strategic Air Command generals didn't really take that into account. They figured nukes would change everything—transform war. In fact, the nukes didn't do a damn thing, except rule out a direct U.S.-Soviet war. And Vietnam rapidly deteriorated into an Air Force clusterfuck.

The politicians immediately ignored the most glaring air war lesson from World War II and Korea: first establish air supremacy. Hitler had ignored this rule when he shifted from blowing up British airfields and radar installations to vent his rage on London, a decision that cost him the Battle of Britain. In Korea the U.S. modified the rule by settling for stalemate when it elected not to go after the Soviet MiGs based in China.

So every swinging dick in a cockpit knew that in Vietnam, the bombers should have immediately obliterated every runway and surface-to-air missile (SAM) site in the country, and then sunk every Soviet and Chinese ship hauling in SAMs. Instead, the politicians focused on avoiding the kind of escalation of the war they'd provoked in Korea, where millions of Soviet and Chinese troops were drawn into the struggle. That left the pilots to face the most elaborate air defenses in history. And every year the war went on, the defenses got stronger as Soviet and Chinese aid poured in. Initially, the U.S. pilots couldn't even blow up the SAMs shooting at them without elaborate permission requests up the chain of command to the nitpicking, number-toting, micromanaging White House. The politicians, all safe and cozy in their limos back in D.C., figured they could use bombing as some combination message system and aversion training. So they developed an elaborate rationale for starting and stopping the bombing to get the North Vietnamese to cooperate and play nice. Of course, the North Vietnamese had been struggling for generations and were fighting a holy freaking war of liberation; they used the bombing halts to rebuild their air defenses—with no intention of ever giving up, no matter how many high-explosive messages they received.

Moreover, the fighter pilots found themselves once again facing superior Soviet fighters, at least initially. The U.S. F-100s Sabers were built for a nuclear war with the Soviets. So was the F-105 Thunderchief, designed to drop a nuclear bomb deep in Soviet territory. They had air-to-air missiles, which the brass figured would eliminate any silly dogfighting by killing the pesky MiGs at long range. Instead, the rules of engagement, the lack of a good lookdown radar, and the lack of long-range radar planes controlling the battle made it easy for the MiGs to lay traps. Even when the U.S. pilots did spot a target on their radars, they often had to get close to within visual range to get permission to shoot. So the frustrated American pilots found themselves forced to get close to the nimble, maneuverable, hard-to-see MiG 17, and later the MiG 21, before they could shoot. And at that point, they discovered, they were too close to effectively use their air-to-air missiles, which only hit their targets about 10 percent of the time anyway. Once again, the brass had sent the pilots into the wrong war with the wrong weapons.

The F-4 Phantom illustrated the confusion of Air Force design. It was designed to fly long distances hauling bombs and dogfighting along the way, using air-to-air missiles. It was an expensive brute, with big, powerful jet engines that left a smoky trail visible for miles. That made it easy for the small, stealthy MiGs to spot and outmaneuver the Phantom. Lacking cannons, Phantom pilots relied on their air-to-air missiles—the Sparrow, with a theoretical 28-mile range, and the heat-seeking Sidewinder for close-in. But these early air-to-air missiles usually missed, which cost many F-4 pilots their lives. So they did what U.S. pilots have always done: they drew on their superior training, creativity, and initiative. The heavy, conspicuous, two-seat Phantom had one great advantage over the lightweight MiG: brute power. Moreover, the backseat bomber and navigator could keep his eyes on the enemy fighter in the spin of battle. The U.S. pilots developed a whole new method of dogfighting based on the skillful use of that power advantage to offset the MiG's turning advantage. Even so, flying level and straight for the thirty seconds needed to get a missile lock often proved lethal. In the end, the Vietnam War demonstrated the near-futility of ineptly applied air power. Despite the overwhelming U.S. advantage in the air, the North Vietnamese won the war. The U.S. dropped three times as many bombs on Vietnam as the Allies dropped on Japan and Germany combined in World War II. Nonetheless, the bombing had virtually no impact on North Vietnam's war-making capacity, in part because all of the vital factories manufacturing war material were located in China and the Soviet Union. The war embittered the Air Force, from the generals on down. They maintained that unrestricted bombing in and around Hanoi finally approved in the closing days of the war demonstrated what they could have done if they'd been turned loose in the first place—although that argument ignores the escalation lessons of Korea. By the time the U.S. turned its full attention to Hanoi's air defenses and supply lines, all America really wanted was to save face and get the hell out of there. So air power over-promised and under-delivered—as it has ever since World War I. Meanwhile, the North Vietnamese shot down 445 Phantoms, 397 F-105 Thunderchiefs, and 243 F-100s, which cost a total of $3 billion. The Air Force lost 2,118 people, plus another 599 missing in action.

Including, as it turns out, Chips.

Howard looked forward to his uncle's brief leaves from the war. He pestered him for stories about flying those awesome jets, but most of the time Chips changed the subject.

Howard drank in every word, loving his uncle's stories, his big voice, his easy grace. But Chips wouldn't talk much about Nam, the topic that most interested Howard.

In fact, many of the American pilots battled mounting, dangerous frustration. The politicians picked the targets, and the pilots often found themselves repeatedly bombing worthless targets, but forbidden from attacking Soviet ships loaded with crates of SAMs floating in the harbor. In fact, one Phantom pilot nearly got busted for bombing a SAM battery that was shooting at his wingman. Pilots also faced dangerous restrictions on defending themselves against the MiGs. The rules required them to make a visual identification before shooting down a suspected enemy. That meant they had to let the small, maneuverable, cannon-equipped MiGs get within visible range, neutralizing their advantage.

Once Chips mentioned a mission in which antiaircraft fire damaged his Phantom. "What was it like?" asked Howard.

Chips abruptly bashed the tabletop several times, startling the boy. "Like that," he said laughing.

"Two bits of advice," Chips added. Howard sat breathless, eager and dry as a sponge.

"Never fly an airplane whose wings move," said Chips. "And never fly a Weasel."

Then Chips went back to Nam.

He survived to the end of his tour, then re-upped. Soon after that, he flew a mission over Laos. An antiaircraft battery opened up on the "strike package," consisting of the bombers and the supporting fighters. Everyone started climbing and diving and bombing and gunning. Chips's

Phantom got hit, and other pilots reported seeing two chutes, suggesting Chips and the pilot got out.

After that, Chips just vanished.

Maybe he died in the crash or the jungle landing. Maybe the North Vietnamese got him. Maybe they executed him. Maybe he died in prison.

There's all kinds of ways for a pilot to die, not all of them quick.

Now here's the weird thing about this story.

It's about Howard Hobbday.

Even though his uncle died, from that day forward all Howard ever wanted to be was a fighter pilot. That's it. Nothing else. A fighter pilot.

And it gets worse. When he grew up, he flew Phantoms, outfitted as Wild Weasels. And then, in the fullness of time, he switched to Vipers. That's an F-16 to ordinary people, or a Fighting Falcon to Air Force publicists. But the pilots call them Vipers, after the fighters in *Battlestar Galactica*.

And as any Viper pilot will tell you, the F-16 remains the best god-damned fighter that's ever been built.

Single engine. Single seat. Turn itself inside out. Fighter Fucking Jet.

And there you go.

Howard—better known as "Doughboy" in the incestuous, insular, competitive world of the F-16 squadrons—has been flying fighters for most of the last twenty years. He's bombed Iraq in two different fighters; he's called down death and destruction on Afghanistan. He's careened sports cars, shredded his marriage, and risked death as a routine. And now he's at Luke Air Force Base flying across the sun-blasted, sonic-boomed desert outside of Phoenix, training brand new F-16 Viper pilots.

And the thing is, they're all just like him—kids who never wanted to do anything but fly fighters. Intense, disciplined, brilliant, obsessive, thrill-seeking—yearning to fly out there beyond the sound barrier at the edge of the envelope, loaded with death and destruction. They want to kill people and break things and be better and quicker and smarter and more dangerous than anyone else anywhere—especially the guy in the next jet.

So you've got to wonder—where do we get these guys? And what does it mean that we produce so many—so eager—so deadly?

Maybe it seems like a dumb question. Obvious even.

But after you think about it for a while, and watch them for a while longer, it seems the answer might hold the key—the Secret to Everything.

Maybe if you can figure out why Doughboy had to be a fighter pilot you'd understand all the important stuff.

You'd understand the imperatives of being a man—or a woman.

You'd understand why people get drunk, die for friends, slaughter strangers.

You'd understand war, the U.S. economy, and the dynamics of empire.

Maybe you'd understand why the U.S. spends more money on its defense than the next twelve countries combined—and still the military's starved for money.

Maybe you'd even understand Doughboy and the eight young student pilots who not so long ago showed up at Luke Air Force Base determined to become hotshot fighter pilots—in a line stretching back to the Red Baron—or die trying.

Here's their story: the costly, dangerous, demanding process of turning bright, brave American kids into fighter pilots, dedicated to "killing people and blowing shit up," and protecting their country.

It's the story of one squadron on one air base for the six months it takes to turn "punks" into no-kidding fighter pilots. It's the story of the football star, the bush pilot, the surfer dude, the insurance salesman, and the woman who could run all day and keep her mouth shut. It's also the story of Doughboy and the other instructor pilots, who have fought in every one of America's wars since Vietnam.

And whether we have the right to ask it of them.

The Eye
of the Viper

I

THROUGH THE CANOPY

JUST LIKE DOUGHBOY, CHRIS PERKINS spent his whole life dreaming about being a fighter pilot.

So he learned to fly little planes in the Alaskan bush, got a degree in aeronautical engineering, signed up for the college campus training ground for officers, the Reserve Officer Training Corps (ROTC), and so joined the Air Force.

Heavy-jawed, dark-browed, easygoing, bright, quick, and unflappable, he loved to fly—but he didn't particularly enjoy the abuse, pressure, and relentless criticism of basic pilot training, which seemed designed more to drive him out of the sky than to perfect his flying skills.

But basic training was tough.

And sometimes he wondered whether he had the "right stuff" after all.

That is, until the night he nearly died.

He is inbound from a night mission during basic pilot training in New Mexico. He has too much gas in the tank for a landing, so he is flying around burning up gas near the airfield. He climbs a little, then "unloads" the jet, reversing his climb to descend; this creates a cool moment of zero gravity, like the moment at the top of a roller coaster before the plummet. Pilots love this. Pens float in the cockpit. Of course, you're not supposed to let pens go floating around the cockpit, but you get the point. So Perkins pulls the nose up 15 degrees, hits the speed brake flaps, and then hits the the full-throttle engine surge of the afterburner to consume the extra 400 pounds of gas. He only means to go to .5 g's, not zero gravity. But he overshoots a little.

Next thing he knows, he's rising upward in the cockpit. That's not right. Then he hears a crash, and shards of the canopy start falling down around him. Somehow his oxygen mask is pushed aside and there's some kind of fluid or something running across his face. He's hanging onto the control stick for dear life, looking down at it and feeling like he's about to shoot up out of the jet. Very strange. Later, he discovers that someone on the ground crew forgot to bolt his ejection seat to the floor; when he shifted to 0 g's, the seat shot up along its railing and his seatback and helmet broke through the canopy. The shards cut his face, which is now sheeted in blood, obscuring his vision.

Fortunately, his instinctive pull on the stick brings the nose up, restoring g-forces, and the seat slides back down the railing to the cockpit floor.

But his problems have just begun. First of all, a chunk of the canopy of the T-38 got sucked into the left engine, and now that engine shimmies violently, shaking the plane like a jeep doing 60 on a washboarded dirt road. The wind is roaring past his face and he's thinking, "Holy shit, my canopy is gone." He still can't figure out what happened. He thinks maybe he hit a bird. "It was total time compression," he recalls later. "Everything that seemed to take two minutes actually took like two seconds."

He shifts into a disaster reflex thanks to a combination of training and temperament. He slows to 300 knots, drops to 12,000 feet, and checks the engines. The left engine's basically shut down, but he doesn't want to actually turn it off because he remembers the lights run off that engine and so he might lose them altogether if he shuts it down. He could throw the crossover relay, but he's afraid that might trigger the same result.

Instincts take over. "I will maintain control, I will analyze the situation, take proper action, and land as soon as conditions permit," he tells himself, repeating the mantra of his training. "So you maintain control and figure out what's happening. It's vibrating—the engine is fucking itself. So you pull back on the throttle. The vibration goes away. But I'm now on a single engine, and I'll fall out of the sky if I go less than 250 knots, so I push the right engine back up until I'm just over 250. Make an emergency call because I don't have a canopy anymore."

Only when he goes to make an emergency call does he realize that his mask is gone. He can't radio. Later, he finds a deep scratch on his helmet that suggests a shard from the canopy ripped away his mask, although he has no clear recollection of the moment. He gropes about and finds the dangling mask and holds it to his bleeding face to make the transmission, calling for emergency clearance to land. Next, he pulls out his flashlight to figure out why he's short of breath. Obviously, his oxygen isn't working. He sees his sunglasses on the floor. He can't figure out how they got there. But in thinking about that, he realizes that his visor has also gotten ripped away. He puts his glasses on to mitigate the windblast through the shattered canopy, but for some reason can't see through them. So he puts them in his pocket and fumbles for his emergency checklist.

Now alerted, the air controllers clear the airspace around the crippled jet, waving off other landings and giving him a clear path to an immediate landing. "The radio was going nuts the whole time I was flying back," he recalls. Except for some reason, he can't communicate with the tower. He describes everything he's doing, but gets no answer; he can hear other traffic, but nothing directed to him.

So he lines up on the closest runway, although it isn't the runway he had been briefed to land on. As he gets closer, he can see the lights of the fire trucks to the side, and he figures they know he's coming. But he doesn't have the steady green light at the end of the runway that tells him he's cleared to land. "It doesn't really matter," he's thinking, "no way I'm taking this airplane around. Ain't going to happen."

Then he remembers he still has an extra 15 knots of airspeed—and only a 1,000-foot margin of error for coming to a stop on the runway. But he's afraid to pull back the throttle to slow down, knowing that if he starts to stall he doesn't have that second engine to speed up again. He'll have to risk coming in a little too fast. As he nears the runway, he finally gets the green light, and sets down in a textbook landing. He can barely remember the moment the wheels actually contacted earth—just as he can't remember going through the canopy.

"As soon as my wheels touched down, I went, like, on emergency ground egress. Roll flaps down to full. Trying to stop the airplane. Stomp on the brakes. The left engine is cooking off again, because there's no air going through to cool it off. I'm standing on the brakes so hard, thinking if I shut down the left engine now, I won't have any nose wheel steering if I blow a tire. I have my ejection seat pin in and I start to pull it out, but then I think, 'I just hit my head on the canopy, do I really want to jump out of this airplane?' So I'm just going to sit here. Fire engine comes up and shuts me down. You see these firemen come walking up to the jet, and their eyes are like this big around. Here's this jet, and there is no canopy—just the frame. Visor is down, and blood all over my face and shoulders. I didn't even know I was bleeding."

The fire crew helps him out and checks him out. He spits out little bits of Plexiglas; he's bleeding pretty good. He's got a big gash in his shoulder and is turning black-and-blue from elbow to collarbone. He's a little disoriented now, already wondering what he did wrong, thinking they'll boot him out of the program. So they load him into the ambulance for a dash to the hospital. On the way, the driver suddenly slams on the brakes, and the ambulance fishtails across the road, swerving, nearly rolling over—just missing a terrified deer in the middle of the road. Great. What a night.

Next thing he knows, he's getting stitched up and x-rayed, his eyes flushed out.

And then the wing commander's standing there. Jesus Christ. The freaking wing commander. Perkins must have screwed the pooch royally. Jesus. He probably did $250,000 in damage to his plane. Some bonehead mistake. He's toast. Kicked out, four rides from graduation. Suddenly, the group commander's there as well. Freaking great. "It's like two in the morning, and there's the wing commander," groans Perkins.

Then the colonel sticks out his hand. "How you feeling, son?"

"Well, sir, considering, I guess I'm doing all right," gulps Perkins.

"I just want to shake your hand and thank you for bringing the airplane back—and tell you I'm glad you get to call your folks back and not me."

Oh. Damn. He's got to tell his mother.

So he calls them.

And his mother cries.

But it's a funny thing. In a weird way, she worries less after that happened. Like it had reassured her that even if something bad happened, her boy could get the plane home.

And here's the thing. It also reassured Perkins.

Suddenly, he isn't just a mediocre student bucking a washout.

It's like combat. Every unbloodied soldier wonders what he'll do when the bullets fly. He can train. He can practice. He can psych himself up.

But he never knows until the shooting starts. Then he's either got it, or he doesn't.

Now Perkins knows that when everything goes wrong, he won't panic. He might make mistakes. The engine might blow up. Some frigging MiG might kill him from behind. A buzzard might fly into the intake. He might crash and die. But it won't be because he doesn't have the nerves or the guts or the instincts.

And everyone else knows it too. It's the same reason the guys with combat stories always get the most deferential hearing in the fighter bars—even if the story revolves around some Air Force clusterfuck. They've seen the elephant—and come back with a story.

It starts later that morning when he drives in, still shaken, with his face bandaged. The private at the gate says, "Hey, you're the guy."

"Yeah, that's me," says Perkins, still feeling like he fucked up.

"Hey, that's awesome," grins the airman.

Everywhere he goes it's, "Hey, are you the guy?" So even though he finishes basic pilot training somewhere in the middle of the pack of young hotshots who might someday become honest-to-God fighter pilots—one screwed-up ride away from washing out—Chris Perkins finishes with a certain cachet.

Truth be told, in their heart of hearts the other students envy Perkins for the night he nearly died and instead won a gruff compliment from the wing commander, who normally dices up students and sprinkles them on his corn flakes.

So Perkins feels almost confident when he gets his orders to report to Luke Air Force Base, where drooly, diapered, dumbass, would-be fighter pilots get stripped down, disassembled, spun, bounced, and stress-tested—before being reassembled into Viper pilots—slit-eyed, ice-cold killers. He has that one slender edge on the other students about to enter the cocoon of the fearsome Emerald Knights training squadron for the six-month F-16 B-course, where they will hopefully metamorphose into Viper pilots.

He even has a funny story to tell at the bar.

Unless, of course, Doughboy or one of the other instructor pilots happens to be talking about combat. You know, a real war story. A fighter pilot story.

2

✦

THE MAKING OF
AN INSTRUCTOR

ABOUT THE TIME PERKINS started having his first childish fantasies about flying jets, Doughboy was getting ready to bomb Iraqis—the first time.

He was about to enter combat—the place where instructor pilots (IPs) are created to mold future generations of clueless, would-be MiG-killers like Perkins.

Combat. The be-all of being a fighter pilot—the secret handshake and maker of men—the very thing Doughboy had set his childish heart upon in the fear and disbelief of his uncle's death.

After Chips died, all Doughboy ever wanted to do was fly a Phantom. "That was my whole mission in life—to fly F-4s." His dad was a ship-yard worker, then a city inspector. His mom was a bus driver. And Doughboy grew up near a Navy base in Virginia. He didn't really want to live far from home, so he went to Virginia Tech, enrolled in ROTC, and signed up for the Air Force. He served a stint as a pilot of lesser jets, but finally drew the Phantom, an aging workhorse that was being eclipsed by the newer F-15s and F-16s. "I loved it, those Barney Rubble F-4s," he recalls. He trained at the same base in California where Chips had. The Phantoms had been reduced to the Wild Weasel mission, because they had a backseater to handle the electronics. Despite his uncle's advice, Doughboy loved Weasel school. "It was awesome. It's a high-speed chess game—you against the surface-to-air missile. A great blast—lots of hard flying."

They shipped him to West Germany in 1989 for the final days of the Cold War. When he got there, he could see the tanks clanking through the streets. By the time he left, they'd pulled the wall down—he left with chunks of the Berlin Wall. In substantial measure, the Soviet Union had simply collapsed under the cost of keeping up with the United States militarily—the cost of putting all those MiGs in the air for Doughboy to worry about.

The USAF had undergone dramatic changes since Vietnam. The brass had adopted the doctrine of unflinching air supremacy: a determination to obliterate opposing air defenses in the first moments of any conflict. The USAF had invested heavily in a fleet of radar-wielding, central air controllers called AWACS planes (for Airborne Warning and Control System). The AWACS planes are converted airliners that can sweep the skies for hundreds of miles in every direction and direct fleets of bombers and fighters. In addition, the USAF had a host of midair refueling tankers, which allowed the short-range fighters to operate indefinitely anywhere in the world.

A whole new generation of fighters and bombers had taken to the air. A brilliant, subversive group of fighter pilots known as the "Fighter Mafia" had waged a determined, resourceful bureaucratic war from inside the Pentagon to shame, trick, and manipulate the generals into building a plane designed for pilots. As a result, two nimble, flexible, and lethal planes now dominated the fighter force: F-15 Eagle and the F-16 Flying Falcon—the Viper. Even more revolutionary, the woefully inaccurate gravity-driven "dumb bombs" of Vietnam and earlier wars had given way to the first generation of "smart bombs": bombs guided by lasers, GPS coordinates, or TV cameras.

The new era in air power dawned in the closing days of Vietnam, with the destruction of the Paul Doumer Bridge over the Red River near Hanoi, as well as the Thanh Hoa Bridge over the Chu River, both vital links in North Vietnam's supply chain. In 1965, about 70 planes supported by 10 air tankers in two days dropped about 500 bombs and shot 32 missiles at the bridge, losing five jets in the process. They inflicted only minor damage. Similar efforts over the next seven years had little impact. Mission planners calculated that keeping these two vital bridges shut down would require the full-time efforts of 250 jets.

Then came "smart bombs," including one variety guided by a TV camera and another guided by a laser. The TV bomb was a "fire and forget" bomb—a lifesaving quality for a pilot zigging and zagging for dear life. The more accurate laser bomb required the pilot to keep a targeting beam on the target as the bomb fell. A small flight of jets finally knocked out the Thanh Hoa Bridge with five 2,000-pound smart bombs. None of the attacking jets was shot down. A month later, 40 jets attacked the Paul Doumer Bridge. Most attacked the air defenses as 16 Phantoms delivered 29 2,000-pound bombs. Half hit their targets, knocking out the bridge. All told, 37 tons of bombs accomplished in 1972 what 200 tons of bombs could not in 1965. In another striking contrast, 91 percent of the planes attacking in 1965 dropped bombs. In 1972, only 37 percent dropped bombs—the rest targeted the air defenses. As a result, the attackers in 1972 suffered no losses.

The development of such precision munitions came too late to stave off defeat in Vietnam, but transformed USAF strategy and the role of fighter pilots in subsequent decades.

The Gulf War provided the first real test of whether the new technology could finally deliver on the promises the Air Force generals had been making for fifty years. And Doughboy would get his chance to make the delivery—in the same type of plane Chips had flown—transformed by nearly two decades of technological upgrades.

Doughboy's Wild Weasel Phantom squadron is dispatched to the Middle East as the Coalition gathers itself for the first war in Iraq. He leaves behind his pregnant wife and toddler—the first of many such forced absences. Fliers' wives have to work out their abandonment issues and learn to raise their families alone during the frequent, long deployments—even in peacetime. Some never adjust.

But Doughboy is having a blast and getting ready for his war—the war every pilot dreams about during the endless mock dogfights of his career. The base has no bar, so they build a beer tent for the Air Force guys. The military thoughtfully provides Marine guards for the tent, but won't give the Marines those three beer chits a day. So the pilots take to sneaking the Marines into the beer tent—a potentially career-stunting prank. Of course, no one has time to go to the beer tent once the war starts, because they're flying around the clock. The only diversion then is to periodically go out and watch the SCUD attacks, as the Iraqis lob their uselessly inaccurate missiles in the general direction of the U.S. forces. "We'd go up on the roof and watch the SCUDs land in the Gulf, and we'd be clapping, 'A little off, Saddam.' "

On his first combat mission, Doughboy has to choose between following orders and making Air Force history.

He takes off as the number two jet in a Weasel four-ship (a formation of four planes) providing cover for a flight of F-16s bearing bombs. The F-16s end up aborting, so the Phantoms fly around in a big circle, looking for a surface-to-air missile (SAM) site to kill. After a while, two jets head back to refuel, leaving two Phantoms on patrol. They are just about to call it quits when the AWACS plane directing the action warns them of the approach of two "bogeys," most likely Iraqi Mirage F1s, one of the better planes in the Iraqi inventory. An actual dogfight looms, although the Weasels are outfitted for killing SAMs with high-speed antiradiation missiles (HARMs) missiles. Usually the F-15 Eagles, with their specialized air-to-air missiles and oversized radars, enjoy the macho glory of killing enemy fighters.

Doughboy has been dreaming of such a kill for most of his life, although at the moment he's too busy with the radar, weapons systems, radio, and demands of flying to even register fear.

"They split, so we split one-versus-one," says Doughboy. The Iraqi pilots were flying the classic combat strategy for two-ships, trying to flank the enemy. If the maneuver works, the enemy jets must pivot to face one of the approaching jets, turning their backs on the wingman. Instead, Doughboy and his flight lead also split and hurtle toward the approaching fighters. Of course, this exposes them to a possible ambush from some other, undetected pair of Iraqi jets—but they trust the AWACS to warn them.

Besides, the Iraqis are probably flying blind, crippled by the all-out attack on the Iraqi command and control structure. The Iraqis probably think they're sneaking up on some fat American bombers they can backstab in a classic fighter maneuver. The Iraqi air force has been trained to fight Soviet style—with flights of fighters rigidly controlled by the ground-based radar. That kind of system can coordinate large numbers of planes flown by even lightly trained pilots. By contrast, the USAF builds its strategy on two-ship units given great autonomy and flexibility. It costs about $4 million to train a pilot to fly effectively in such a forma-tion, when you include the instructors and the flight time in the jet—which averages about $15,000 an hour in the F-16. But it has enormous benefits—as the lopsided air war over Iraq quickly demonstrates. Once the U.S. air strikes cripple the ground-based radars and command system of the Iraqis, the otherwise up-to-date MiGs and Mirages of the Iraqi air force prove all but helpless.

"Skippy," the navigations and weapons officer in Doughboy's back seat "pit," fires up his air-to-air radar and pings the approaching Iraqi fighter.

As soon as Skippy's ping hits him, the Iraqi pilot goes into violent defensive maneuvers. At this moment, Doughboy looks at his gas gauge for the first time. He's already 2,000 pounds of gas below the level that should have triggered a return to base. Now he's chewing rapidly through his margin of safety. "So now I'm already eating into my divert fuel. That doesn't worry me too much—but as I go diving down to follow the Mirage I can see that I'm 20,000 feet above the whole Iraqi Republican Guard."

Bad place to run out of gas.

"The Iraqi guy realizes this is not a good place to be, and he's leaving. I should have shot him. I could have shot him."

But Doughboy has another problem. A general on the watching AWACS plane wants to save all his precious Wild Weasels. He doesn't want them playing with enemy fighters—let the F-15 Eagles do that. The general needs all the SAM killers he can get. So the general tells the AWACS controllers to order Doughboy and his flight lead to knock it off and break east.

Doughboy's flight lead, "Stick," protests. They can make the kill, he says. But the general insists—as generals tend to do. The AWACS orders them to "turn east immediately," adding "Hammer directs," which is the call sign for a general on board. Stick and Doughboy turn east just enough to comply, fighting temptation.

"Easy shot. I just never got permission. Would have been the last F-4 air-to-air kill. I regret it to this day," says Doughboy.

All told, U.S. fighter pilots shot down twenty Iraqi fighters in the opening days of the war. In most cases, the AWACS warned the Ameri-can fighters of the approaching Iraqis, which gave the Eagle and Viper pilots time to split and stalk and kill the MiGs before the hapless Iraqis ever knew what hit them. Only a few Iraqi pilots took the fight to the Americans—and none of them survived long. With their ground-based command structure crippled, the Iraqis couldn't match the initiative and flexible tactics of the U.S. pilots, instilled through hundreds of hours in the air at places like Luke.

The U.S. lost one fighter in air-to-air action, the last F-18 Hornet in a four-ship formation on a bombing run. Flying in the rearmost spot of the formation, in the blind spot of the other jets, he simply dropped off the radio check. They never figured out what happened to him, although one unit on the ground reported seeing a fireball. Maybe a SAM killed him, drawing a bead based on the path of the first plane in the element. Maybe a bold Iraqi fighter slipped in behind the formation and killed him.

But after the first week, the Iraqi fighter pilots either hid or fled.

Which left Doughboy and his friends to attend to the important business of blowing the hell out of Baghdad, or at least the key military targets ringing the capital.

"One night over Baghdad," he recalls, "we were escorting F-111s," a costly and controversial swept-wing bomber given a new lease on life as a result of smart bombs.

Suddenly, one of the F-111 pilots calls out, "We have a MiG 29 in our formation."

A MiG? In the formation? So everyone is frantically looking around trying to spot the MiG. The F-111s are flying strung out in the darkness, lights off so as not to bunch up and invite a volley of SAMs. The MiG pilot has wandered into the middle of the formation, obviously clueless in the dark—or he has slipped up from the rear and is waiting to pick them off from behind. "We've got so many planes trying to get to this one spot from everywhere—so the sky is just covered with planes," says Doughboy to Skippy, the weapons officer in the backseat.

The F-111 pilot yanks the throttle back, so as not to overrun the MiG, which has now disappeared. "Everybody's in a line, and now they're yanking around," says Doughboy, "and I'm thinking, we're going to have a midair collision in a minute here."

Moreover, even if they can get a lock on a suspected MiG, launching an air-to-air missile in the middle of the formation could be disastrous. Fortunately, the MiG simply disappears without taking the easy shot.

The Iraqi pilot was probably unnerved to find himself suddenly in formation with a host of American warplanes.

On the whole, the fog of war probably posed the greatest danger once the early onslaught had scared off the Iraqi air force and crippled the air defenses. As a result of friendly-fire incidents, the USAF inflicted more casualties on ground-based American forces than did any Iraqi jets.

On the fourth night of the war, Doughboy's four-ship formation got screwed up on its tanker track. The largely unheralded tankers are a vital and vulnerable element in USAF strategy in a world where U.S. pilots never fight anywhere near their home bases. Fighter jets need gas about once an hour, which means even a normal mission requires four to six midair refuels via a boom trailing behind the tanker. The air tankers, which wouldn't have a chance against the most pathetic of fighters, orbit at the edge of the battle, protected by F-15s. During the Gulf War, the tanker fleet orbited along set tanker "tracks," which were burned into the pilots' brains during the briefings.

"In the beginning, we really hadn't figured out the whole tanker issue. So I'm going to the boom to get more gas. It's pitch black and you've never seen so many stars. When the tanker just pulls up the boom, which means we are out of gas."

The four jets split up, with Doughboy and his flight lead heading for another tanker track.

Suddenly, out the window it looks like every antiaircraft gun in the sector is shooting at them. "Skippy, look out the window," Doughboy says.

"There's nothing but tracers—red and orange tracers—from horizon to horizon, with an occasional missile coming up out of it. At 25,000 feet, you're above most of it—but there's still the stray magic BB. They're just throwing up bullets, hoping you get in the way. They had a couple of radars on and we're just grossly out of gas. But we're carrying two HARMs and three empty gas tanks. So we find a radar and launch a HARM. I have no idea if it hit. Then I punch off the tanks."

When Doughboy punches off the empty fuel tanks, there is a bright flash from the charges that release them. Abruptly lighter, the jet surges.

"We've been hit! We've been hit!" yells Skippy.

"I blew the tanks! I blew the tanks!" screams Doughboy.

"Jeez. Tell me before you do it," grumps Skippy.

"I did. I did," says Doughboy.

"Hell you did," says Skippy.

This goes on for several minutes as they flew further and further into the antiaircraft artillery (or triple-A) coming up from the ground.

Doughboy flew twenty-eight combat missions in the first Gulf War.

One of the most memorable came during a night mission over Baghdad, escorting B-52s, flying down below the bombers to draw missile fire so they could kill the SAMs. "We were leaving, crossing over near Baghdad Airport, when I realize they seem to be shooting in my direction more than a generic up-and-down."

Looking out, he sees a roiling orange fireball stationary in the canopy, getting steadily bigger. From the backseat, Skippy says, "Didn't they teach you that things that don't move in the canopy are coming up at us?"

"Yeah, well," says Doughboy, checking the altitude and trying to decide if he can outclimb it.

"Don't you think you ought to be doing some of that pilot stuff up there?" says Skippy politely.

"Dude, what do you want me to do?" says Doughboy, laughing at Skippy's twisted sense of humor as he starts to climb.

A small caliber shell explodes beneath them. "If it had been a bigger shell, it would have killed us," Doughboy recalls. "But I'm pulling the stick, looking around, and realizing that we're the last guys out of Baghdad. If you're the last one out, people get very interested in you."

Sometimes the war seems surreal. He remembers another flight, escorting B-52s along the Iranian border, over the oil fields the Iraqis set on fire as they retreated. "Looking down, I could see the silver outline of the Phantoms against that boiling black smoke. It was a vision of hell."

Ironically, the second-closest he comes to dying was the night he gets bombed in midair by the B-52s he was protecting. He is flying offset and below the B-52s, watching for any foolhardy SAM operators tempted by the big fat bombers.

But the bombers have changed targets—without telling the fighters flying cover. Stick, the flight lead, notices that the bombers have veered from their expected path. Any minute now, they'll be directly over Doughboy. So Stick tells him to come right pronto. Reacting instantly, Doughboy rolls right, looking back as he moves. A moment later, he sees the bombs exploding on the ground directly below the patch of sky he'd occupied the moment before.

That wasn't the only time the Americans nearly killed him. Couple of nights later, his flight lead shot a HARM at him. He didn't mean to. He was shooting at the fleeting signal of a SAM site directly below Doughboy, who had just turned into the path of the missile. "I could see the missile come off his jet—I could read the lettering. And it goes right over my canopy."

"Confirm that's a HARM," says Doughboy, his mouth as dry as his humor.

"Affirmative," says Stick.

"Yeah, well, look where you're shooting."

"Where are you?" asks the bewildered Stick, who thought Doughboy was behind him. Instead, Doughboy had steered straight toward the next steerpoint programmed into the jet's navigational computer.

"I'm in front of you," deadpans Doughboy.

Fair's fair, though. Doughboy himself nearly shot down an F-4.

He's flying through scudding clouds, when he picks up a solid contact from an Iraqi SA2 SAM site that had risked turning on its radar. Doughboy and Skippy launch a HARM. The missile comes off the underside, hangs for a moment seeking its target—then pulls a 90-degree turn and hurtles itself at a cloud.

A moment later, two Phantoms come flying out of the cloud Doughboy just missiled. Turns out, an SA2 shot a missile at the Phantoms just as Doughboy locked up the same site, with the Phantoms caught in the crossfire.

Doughboy shot only eight HARMs in his twenty-eight missions and has no idea if he destroyed any SAM sites. The pilots rarely see the missile hit; they just infer success if the SAM radar never comes back on the air. On the other hand, they clearly succeeded because the SAM operators rarely dared to even turn on their targeting radars. "The Weasels all had beer call signs. Sometimes other planes would pretend they were talking to Schlitz 4 or Budweiser 3, just to scare the Iraqis."

Many of the fighter-bombers were assigned to kill boxes, certain areas where they had clearance to kill anything that moved. But they were often vulnerable to hidden mobile missile sites that could calculate their patrol path. So they always hoped for a Weasel for protection. "Guys would check in for their kill boxes, and say, 'Is there any beer in Iraq tonight?' And we'd say, 'Yeah, Michelob.'"

Two decades of risk, innovation, and pilot deaths had perfected the Weasel system. Each new generation of air-to-ground missiles posed a deadly threat until the pilots developed new strategies and electronic countermeasures. Generally, pilots learned they could outfly a missile if they could pull one third as many g's in a turn: a 9-g turn could frustrate a missile capable of about a 27-g turn. That proved enough to elude earlier generations of SAMs. Unfortunately, the newest SAMs can make 90-degree turns and pull 50 g's; a trained pilot can withstand a maximum of about 9 g's without passing out. As the guidance systems and onboard computers in the missiles improve, the manned jets will face ever-steeper odds. "I guarantee you, fly into the range of a Patriot battery, and you're going to die," says Doughboy, referring to the American SAM system.

In the course of his missions, Doughboy discovers the personal cost of even a war you win—the realization that settles in once the novelty of combat has been sandblasted away and the warrior has answered those dark, inchoate questions about courage. Back home, Doughboy's wife is about to have his second child, a son. "I knew that no matter what, I was going to get back to see my wife and kids. We're going to fight for each other—no one's going to shoot down a B-52 when I'm capping. But I'm not going to go out there and do something crazy."

The U.S. pilots also learned startling lessons from the Gulf War that dramatically accelerated the transformation of Air Force doctrine and the role of fighter pilots. Before the war, U.S. planners predicted as many as 10,000 Coalition casualties in ten days of fighting. Some analysts predicted a two-year war with 30,000 Coalition casualties—based mostly on the relative sizes of the contending forces. Iraq, after all, had one of the world's largest armies, hardened in the horrendous Iran-Iraq war. But those estimates failed to consider the transformation of air power wrought by smart bombs and strategy. The six-week air assault that destroyed Iraq's air defenses and routed its sizable air force made possible the war of maneuver that swept around Iraqi defenses and destroyed the blind, immobile, demoralized, bombed-out Iraqi army. The emphasis on air supremacy, intelligence, and maneuver grew out of a transformation in military doctrine—in some measure spurred by the "Fighter Mafia" led by the remarkable and often despised fighter pilot whose ideas drove the design of the F-16, Colonel John Boyd.

The Coalition air forces suffered only modest losses, although Baghdad's air defenses were seven times as dense as Hanoi's, and the Iraqi air force boasted 700 aircraft, about half of them comparable to the F-4s and the F-16s they confronted. But the Coalition forces lost just fourteen aircraft—some to friendly fire. In fact, the Gulf War continued a decline in losses stretching back to the already modest 1 percent per sortie loss rate among U.S. pilots in World War I and World War II. That loss rate declined by 83 percent in Korea, by another 46 percent in Vietnam, and by a further 59 percent in the Gulf War to .048 percent per sortie. In the meantime, the number of bombs dropped per mission declined by nearly one third between Vietnam and the Gulf War—to 2 tons per sortie.

In *Storm Over Iraq,* John Hallion calculated the dramatic change in the number of bombs it took to deliver 2,000 pounds of explosives to a roughly 100-square-foot target. In World War II, it took 9,070 bombs and 3,024 airplanes to destroy a 100-square-foot target, which would also incidentally destroy everything within 3,000 square feet. In Korea, it required 550 planes and 1,100 bombs to kill that same target, plus everything within 1,000 feet. By the end of Vietnam, the figure had plunged to 176 bombs delivered by 44 planes. In the Gulf War, 8 planes dropping 30 bombs could destroy that same target and limit collateral damage to 200 square feet. That sharp decline in the number of planes needed to destroy a given target largely accounts for the sharp reduction in losses, concluded Hallion. In Desert Storm, smart bombs accounted for 11 percent of bombs dropped. But the 17,000 smart bombs did as much damage to a given target as 500,000 conventional bombs would have, argue George and Meredith Friedman in *The Future of War.*

On the other hand, the Gulf War also dramatized a worrisome trend, with portents of doom for manned fighter jets. The Air Force calculated that getting thirty-two fighter-bombers to the target to deliver their bombs requires a huge fleet, including fifteen tankers, sixteen jets to watch for enemy fighters, eight jets like Doughboy's to deal with the air defenses, and four search and rescue helicopters—not to mention coverage by AWACS planes. That means it takes some forty-one support aircraft to cover thirty-two bombers. Militarily, when you spend most of your effort protecting the tactically relevant weapons, you're in trouble. Such trends doomed knights in armor and the battleship and now threaten core weapons systems like the aircraft carrier, the tank, and even manned fighter-bombers.

That grim reality—and the lurking suspicion that the last generation of manned fighters is already on the drawing board—has required changes in strategy and training for would-be fighter pilots.

But Doughboy wasn't too much worried about the big picture.

He was just glad to have survived.

He finally headed home to his family, although the strains of his deployment and his obsession with flying had begun to wear through the link that bound them.

And in the course of all that death and destruction and confusion, he picked up the instincts, reactions, and habits necessary to stay alive flying a single-seat, single-engine fighter jet.

Every air war so far has underscored the lesson of the Red Baron in World War I: a handful of fighter pilots on each side make most of the kills. And that means the knowledge and experience of veteran pilots like Doughboy are crucial to maintaining an effective air force—and turning bright kids into lethal pilots.

So now Perkins and all the other young, inexperienced, pathetically easy-to-kill would-be Viper pilots are converging on Luke Air Force Base in the hope that Doughboy and two dozen other veteran pilots will somehow teach them how to stay alive when their own war comes.

3

⚉

THE PUKES CONVERGE

THE TWENTY-SOMETHINGS CONVERGING on Luke Air Force Base for a transformation into Viper pilots have already been worked over pretty good during two previous rounds of pilot training on less specialized planes. They're the best and the brightest—quarterbacks, star runners, professional skiers, outstanding students, engineers, math majors, natural leaders. They're all officers and college graduates, many from the Air Force Academy. They've all passed through the fine mesh—the ever-tighter screens of the selection system. They excelled in high school, aced college, won a pilot's spot, survived basic pilot training (undergraduate pilot training, or UPT), endured Introduction to Fighter Fundamentals (IFF), and each dreamed of flying the F-16—perhaps the most agile, deadly, and graceful jet fighter ever built—good at dogfights, laser bombing, and killing SAMs. Vipers even carried nukes in the bad old days.

Most of them, like Perkins, never wanted to do anything else—least-wise, not that they'll admit now. Perkins says he was hooked on his first flight, when he was four and his dad took him up in a Cessna. "I could barely see over the dashboard," he recalls. "But I was hooked."

His first word was "mom."His second word was "dad." His third word—and he swears this is true—was "airplane."

Maybe it was growing up in Alaska, a state one-fifth the size of the continental U.S. with 4,000 miles of paved roads, which reach only 30 percent of the state. Only the bush pilots can go wherever they want, landing on lakes in the back of beyond. His dad was a doctor, his mom a beautician, but all he wanted to do was fly airplanes—even though the family had little military background.

When his family moved to Nome in 1986, his dad did the "bush doctor thing" and bought a plane in partnership with his best friend. Perkins grew up around airplanes, hitching rides, despite his mother's deep misgivings. Her brother had died as a result of a plane crash in the bush. Her brother and another man landed alongside a deep, fast river; then the other guy took off to land on the far side of the river, leaving Perkins's uncle behind. When his friend crash-landed on the opposite shore, Perkins's uncle died trying to swim across the river to help him. There's some kind of moral in there somewhere, but Perkins just shrugs. In fact, that element of danger attracted him to flying.

Perkins got his pilot's license at seventeen and started racking up the hours in the air. He figured maybe he'd design airplanes, so he went to Embry Riddle University in Prescott, Arizona. He loved it there—hiking down into the Grand Canyon and looking for the wrecks of World War II bombers and fighters. Most of the nation's pilots learned to fly in Arizona during World War II, many at Luke Air Force Base, which trained 15,000 pilots during World War II. The resulting influx of military trainees spawned modern Phoenix after the war. Every summer, Perkins worked as an Alaskan wilderness tour guide. He used to guide hunters until the day the guy he was guiding hit a charging bear in the neck at 150 yards. Although the bullet shattered the bear's spine, that bear kept blindly charging for another 50 yards—dragging his head along the ground. "That was enough for me, I don't hunt anymore," says Perkins. That bear was so big you could stick a basketball in its mouth—inside—and still close the mouth shut around the ball. Monster.

His dad wanted him to be a doctor, but then someone at school suggested Perkins join ROTC so he could fly fighter jets. That sounded good. He was already starting work on his own airplane from a kit. He found that being a pilot also impressed college girls. He impressed the hell out of one girl, taking her for a picnic lunch in a little meadow on a mountaintop in a rented plane. Brave girl.

On the other hand, he notes, lots of girls don't know quite what to make of military pilots—bomb-droppers and nuke-haulers. "It's a little tricky in a college town. The girls figured we were all hippie-hating war-mongers, and they're leaning more towards being granola munchers. But I had a lot of good times."

So he set off for the Air Force as his parents shook their heads. His father reluctantly gave his blessing, but his mother couldn't get her dead brother out of her head. Of course, as he progressed through training they warmed up to the idea. Now his dad figures being a fighter pilot is the coolest thing in the world. And his mother basks in the buzz about her heroic young son down at the beauty parlor.

He did pretty well in basic (UPT), a nine-month course focusing on basic flying—especially after he stuck his head through the canopy.

But his life turned to hell when he got to Introduction to Fighter Fundamentals (IFF), designed to weed out the unworthy. There they flew the T-38, a cranky, sensitive, powerful training jet. He'd lost his pilot's edge during the three months he waited to start IFF, and the instructors treated all the student pilots like boot camp dumbshits. Many of those IFF instructors are fighter pilots pissed off at getting shuffled back into training jets.

Perkins, a proud, independent, low-key, easygoing guy, put his head down and ignored the harassment. He just concentrated on the misery-loves-company camaraderie of the other students and the chance to fly a kick-ass, screaming muscle jet. Of course, the T-38 has a tendency to suddenly squish out of control at low speeds if you misjudge your landing. But that just gets the adrenaline pumping.

He nearly washed out, a shock for a guy who'd aced every test in his life. He busted three rides. He took a turn too fast and pulled 6.4 g's—.2 g's over the limit. He got too close to an instructor's jet on a merge. He maneuvered badly in a dogfight.

"In IFF, they pretty much treat you like shit. The party line answer would be, 'Look, anybody can fly an F-16. We're here to teach you to be single-engine, single-seat fighter pilots.' But do they have to be such assholes?"

But now he's at Luke.

Maybe it will be different.

Like Perkins, Julie Moore can't remember when she accepted her destiny—flying fighter jets. But it was early. Way back.

Her dad was in the Air National Guard, flying F-106s, then airliners for United Airlines. After he put in his retirement papers, he flew his monster F-106 over the house while his skinny, deep-eyed, eight-year-old daughter stood on the front lawn, her face upturned to the cascade of wonder as her daddy twirled the jet over their house. "I thought, wow, that's pretty cool," she recalls.

She adored her dad—bragged on him to the other kids. "When I was five, I'd ask him, 'How'd the plane fly?' And he'd talk and talk and talk and get into the hydraulics system. All I wanted to know is whether it had strings attached like at Disneyland. But I always got more detail than I was expecting."

Her older sister became a flight attendant for United—like her mom.

Maybe it was that flashing roll of her daddy's jet when she was eight. But after that, she knew she'd be a pilot, without ever thinking it all the way through. In high school she went to a summer camp at West Point intended to lure the best and the brightest. "It was this kind of academic nerdy thing, a little bit of a recruiting trip, I guess. They took a couple hundred students and brought them to West Point. But I didn't want to go to the army. I wanted a pilot's slot—which meant the Air Force Academy."

The Academy remains a tough, grueling, macho, masculine environment—sometimes to the point of dysfunction, as the recent revelations of rape, harassment, and cover-up have shown. The institution insists on a rigorous, often outdated, deeply traditional academic course. It also relies on systematic and demeaning hazing administered mostly by upperclassmen, exacting revenge on the next generation of cadets for their own recent debasement.

It's worse for the women, excluded from the rough fraternity that offers the only solace in the face of the hazing. Everyone assumes they got in on some kind of exemption. So they're resented—for their very existence. Moreover, the Academy stinks of testosterone—it's a fraternity of Type As, aggressive, driven, macho guys so eager to prove themselves that they've signed up to be underpaid warriors in the richest society in the history of the world.

But Moore won't tell any tales of her time in the academy—or even admit to seeing any harassment.

Instead, she fit in. Lean, conditioned, and taut as rawhide, she played forward on the Academy soccer team. She'd always been a jock—a standout in soccer, volleyball, and cross-country. Ironically, she almost got barred from the Academy when her physical revealed a heart murmur. Frantic, she applied for a waiver—or another exam. Her doctor told her that if she stopped running her typical 5 miles a day, the murmur would go away. She stopped running and retook the physical. The murmur was gone.

One thought got her through—flying F-16s. She can't tell you exactly why she had to be a Viper pilot, except that the F-16 is beautiful and sleek and you're all alone in the cockpit. You do everything. You screw up; it's all on you. It's like running—it's all on you.

Her dad was overjoyed. Her mom was dubious—hung up on the single engine.

"But I love the F-16," Moore says. "I like the idea that it does everything—kind of a jack of all trades. I like to do a little of this, a little of that."

She didn't worry about being one of the few women fighter pilots in the world. "I think I came from a really strange time. All my girlfriends were the same way. We all played soccer. We seemed normal to ourselves. Until I got to pilot training, it never even occurred to me that usually I'd be the only woman around."

She says she's always been treated with respect—and been offered no special treatment.

"At the Academy, I didn't experience anything like what's coming out now and to my knowledge, none of my friends did either. It kind of surprised me a little bit. I was probably less prepared than some of the kids there. My dad was in the Guard—not in active duty—so I didn't have a military upbringing or anything like that. I didn't really understand how it worked. It took a while to figure and get and I messed up a lot—with everything, the whole culture. But if you don't wonder about yourself— don't struggle a bit to adjust—there's something's wrong with you. A lot of people were unhappy with how that system worked."

For Chris Gough, flying Vipers wasn't so much ego as tradition.

He followed a long, roundabout path to what now seems inevitable— following in the slipstream of his father and grandfather. His grandfather flew Thunderbolts in World War II, providing close air support for tanks rolling into Germany. His dad was a fighter pilot and has flown F-111s, F-105s, and F-16s. His dad spent thirty years in the Air Force and came out a full bird colonel after flying in Bosnia and other combat situations. Now he's an airline pilot. His mom's a flight attendant. So Chris grew up as a military brat, knocking around the world. He's got two brothers; one's a lawyer and the other's training to fly B-52s.

At first, Chris resisted the family calling. He enlisted in the Reserves—the Marines for Christ's sake. He spent eight years in the Reserves as an avionics technician right out of college, working on F-18 Hornets and C-130 cargo planes.

Perhaps he had too much information about the toll flying takes on a family—the long hours and the long deployments. He remembers watching his father struggle with his relationship with his grandfather. "They didn't get along that well. They went through phases, I guess, but I think my grandfather was kind of a jerk—and wasn't real good to his family."

In fact, fighter jets chew up marriages. Divorce is common as families struggle to adjust to the near estrangement from normal civilian life many fighter pilots suffer. Inevitably, F-16 pilots also have to serve a year or more away from their families in Korea—famous for its parties and intense flying. The F-16s patrol the demilitarized zone between North and South Korea, death-dealing hostages to the continued U.S. commitment to the south. Their role as both dogfighters and bombers gives them great flexibility.

Sure enough, Chris's own parents split up in 1979 when he was a kid. "It was the standard military husband-wife stuff," Chris recalls. "He was gone a lot, she was home taking care of three kids. She wanted to work—but that's tough to do when a guy's on active service, since they're moving around all the time."

Realizing the stark choice he faced, his father retired soon after the divorce and got a job as an airline pilot, although he remained in the Reserves. Chris's mom worked a while as a nurse, then as a flight attendant. His parents drifted back together and remarried, the rare case of a riven military couple that gets a second chance.

But Chris grew up seeing his dad once a month. He silently resolved not to sacrifice his own family on a military altar, although he couldn't help but envy the easy camaraderie of his father's fraternity of pilots.

"He'd give you the shirt off his back—and has always been like that with all his military buds. Sometimes he's hot tempered, but then he'll see that and chill out. I did a lot of stuff growing up to make him mad—like getting tickets and rolling the Blazer from driving too damn fast then getting a blowout. But we worked it out."

At first, he was determined not to follow in his father's footsteps. So he went to Texas A&M and got a degree in Animal Science. He got out and got a job in the commodities business, selling futures for soybeans and sunflowers. After six months at his desk, he hated it. So on impulse, he and his younger brother both took the entrance test for Air Force Officer's Training. His brother was an auditor—and hated his job as much as Jack did. "He brought it up and I said, 'That's a fucking great idea,' " recalls Chris.

So Chris quit the Marine Corps Reserves and signed up for the Air Force Reserves, on promise of a pilot's spot.

"A lot of guys I knew made a lot of money in the commodities business, but that wasn't making me happy. I wanted to be part of something bigger."

He figured that the slot in the Fort Worth, Texas Reserve unit flying Vipers would offer the best of both worlds—serving his country by flying the world's coolest fighter jet and still going home to his family every night. The modern Air Force has become critically dependent on Reserve units, which face frequent, often extended deployments in unofficial wars and police actions, but still it seemed a good compromise.

Besides, he wasn't sure his wife would go for the constricted lot of a military wife. When she met him, he was making money in commodities. He was a nice young man, likable, gentle, and funny, with a promising future. Two weeks after they were married, he quit his job and joined the Air Force Reserves. "She appreciated that about me—that I was willing to quit this job and totally pursue a job as a pilot." So she quit her job to move with him to each of his pilot training assignments. It was a culture shock for a modern, career-oriented woman. "She gave up a lot to go with me, it's tough for her. Now I can identify with the parallels with my parents—why they split up. I can imagine a woman like my wife who is career-oriented, with three kids, finding herself suddenly ten years down the road realizing this isn't what she had planned for herself."

But maybe in the Reserves he can stay close to home in Texas, with only intermittent overseas deployments. Maybe he'll end up with a good airline job and put in eight days a month for the Reserves. She can get a job—maybe interior design sales.

Maybe—although it's been unexpectedly rough so far. During pilot training he got pulled out of the jet on the runway and rushed to the hospital when Jane started bleeding twenty weeks into her pregnancy. She nearly died, but pulled through and ultimately had the baby. He doesn't even want to think about something happening during a deployment. "It was tough. It's hard when you take your wife to the emergency room and go in and perform a sortie the next day. I did the best I could—to compartmentalize."

Lots of pilots get very good at "compartmentalizing." Could explain the divorce rates. Could also be why so many pilots come from military families, where everyone understands the arrangement and the wives value the independence that comes with their functional widowhood during deployments—the upside of the trade-off.

That distracting fear might account for the thread by which Gough hung during pilot training. He was stressed and distracted by the pregnancy and the ongoing health problems. Then he got a four-month pause between basic and IFF, which meant he was rusty when he started the boot-camp abuse of IFF. He barely hung on.

"It's all that little stuff that rears up and bites you. You just can't find the right position. You're too close, or too wide—you're getting behind the jet. You're late in your cross-check. I didn't have any problems with the meat of the maneuvering—it was just the crummy formation flying, setups, and stuff like that between engagements—just getting kind of task-saturated," he says, with his charming, apologetic, lopsided grin. He has a modest, instantly likable face beneath a tousled, receding hairline. "So you just try to keep your head in the game and not do anything stupid out there."

Greg Newlin, a tall, mild, handsome man with a tentative air, seems more like a genial, small-town insurance agent than a fighter pilot—maybe because he's older, married, devoted to his fledgling family, and in the Air National Guard. Newlin, twenty-eight, doesn't quite fit in with the swaggering, salacious, wisecracking, confident, macho gaggle of B-coursers, all jostling like racehorses in the starting gate. He's gentle, with a diffident air of apology. He has thin features and a receding hairline, with a charming, low-key, slightly gap-toothed grin that invites you to underestimate him. A devoted family man, he's got a six-year-old and a three-year-old and always seems to be getting calls from his wife. When he gets on the phone with her, his voice softens so you can hardly hear him. Partly that's because he misses her during the day. But partly it's because he doesn't want to sound like some kind of romantic, mush-brain in front of the other B-coursers, most of whom are still making the most of the single life. He hurries home. On the weekends he takes his family jeeping, or builds furniture. They don't have the money to do much else, but that's all right, since they love camping. He's the son of two nuclear scientists who worked at the Los Alamos labs in New Mexico where the atomic bomb was born. His dad was in the Navy—submarines—but always wanted to fly. Newlin saw his father's yearning and took it upon himself, like a debt. They used to go down to the airport and watch the planes take off. Greg was a good boy—kind, dutiful, hardworking. He was going to make his dad proud. Although—let us be honest—he doesn't act like a fighter pilot. The fact that Newlin is just Air National Guard is significant. Granted, the Air Force would come apart under the stress of an increasingly unremitting, global responsibility without the Guard. Still, you can sense the caste differences—with the Academy hard chargers at the top, then the ROTC (to train officers for the reserves) and Officer Training Corps (to train officers for the regular Air Force) full-timers next, and the Guard guys at the bottom. In theory, the Guard guys are supposed to just wait around for the Big One, when the North Koreans flood across the DMZ and we're throwing every goddamned sack of sand into the breech. The Air Force concentrated a lot of its all-out-war specializations in the Air National Guard. But then the U.S. turned into the only superpower still standing, in a world of smoldering brushfires. Suddenly we've got all these little wars and a seemingly limitless number of new places to bomb. So the National Guard units get called up every year or two or three—especially the F-16 squadrons, with their $6 million pilots who thought they were going to have a normal life and still get to fly Vipers.

But Greg got the flying bug watching Thunderbirds split across the aching blue sky when he was seven. He didn't have the grades for the Air Force Academy—not that he would have gone for all that gung-ho, biting-the-heads-off-rats stuff anyway. So he went to a small engineering school in central New Mexico—close to home. He took his degree in electrical engineering and then worked at the White Sands Missile Range for about three years, hoping a pilot slot would open up in the New Mexico Air National Guard unit in Albuquerque. He got his civilian pilot's license and started practicing. Another kid might have given up his fighter pilot fantasy by then, with a good job and a family. But Greg has a certain dogged persistence. He's not flashy. He fades in a crowd, watching people with his soft, thoughtful, dark eyes. But he's no quitter. He's like a bony bloodhound trailing the yapping pack and hanging onto the scent through the darkness when others have fallen to the side, panting.

He applied to the Guard when he was twenty-four—and didn't get selected.

He tried again the next year—and got a slot as an alternate.

Then the first-choice guy developed an eye problem. Greg was in.

His parents are terribly proud—although his mother is frightened.

He loved pilot school in Texas. That was the first time he'd lived in a town with its own Wal-Mart.

IFF, on the other hand, was a nightmare. "I almost washed out there," he says with his typical, unaffected candor. "Had a rough go with the defensive BFM [basic fighter maneuvers]. Just couldn't get comfortable looking over my shoulder fighting the guy behind me. Busted five or six rides—one more and I was out. I had a couple of mistakes early on—just silly ground operations type mistakes just getting ready to take off—and that set the stage. So when I started having flying problems, I didn't have anything to give." Besides, he ached for his family. He missed Halloween. He missed his daughter's birthday. "In UPT, you got to go home every night, and that definitely helped." But IFF was three months away from his family—like going to war.

"I wasn't seriously thinking about quitting, but I remember thinking, this needs to get better," he recalls.

Even so, he nearly washed out again when they sent him to the centrifuge to prepare him for the 9-g turns of the Viper. The T-38s only pull 6 or 7 g's—usually not enough to make a pilot black out. The Viper pushes the envelope, although the computer that actually flies the plane is programmed to never let the pilot pull more than 9 g's—lest he pass out and fly straight into the ground. So all the would-be fighter pilots have to survive the centrifuge. But every time they got the seat on the end of the spinning arm revved up to 9 g's, Greg just blacked out. It was brutal—a swirl of full-body pain. So they sent him to the flight surgeon.

Turns out, he wasn't doing his g-force breathing and tensing up properly. The doctor explained it carefully, Greg changed his breathing and sequential muscle tensing, and he quit passing out. It was a painful three days. Maybe it was even a portent.

Physical conditioning and training remain essential to retaining consciousness in high-g turns, when the enormous force of the turn drives blood into the arms and legs and away from the brain. The pilots all wear flight suits lined with bags that inflate automatically in such turns, so the air pressure will keep the blood from hurtling to the hands and feet. Moreover, pilots must constantly tense and release their muscles throughout high-g maneuvers, straining against the inflated bags to make sure the blood still reaches their brains. Even with the pressure suit and muscle tensing, few pilots can function in turns greater than 9 g's, which would make a 200-pound man effectively weigh 1,800 pounds.

"That was about three days of my life I'd rather forget," says Newlin.

So he's on CAP coming into the B-course at Luke, which means he flies with a smaller group of IPs so he'll have more supervision and more consistent instruction.

All of the setbacks should have discouraged him, but he's clamped down on making it through—like an eel with his teeth locked. "That desire maybe gets eroded some by the problems, but in the long run it makes me want it more because I've had to do so much more. Initially, maybe you wonder if it's worth it. But then you want it all the more because you have had to fight for it so bad. I've never had to fight for anything so hard."

In the meantime, he has at least a shot at being a fighter pilot. "I just value the chance to live out a dream. I'm one of those fortunate few, so it's worth it."

And then there's his son, Vance, who is three. The other day they were in the backyard when a pair of Vipers went hurtling past overhead. Vance tilted his head back to stare at the roaring jets, nearly toppling over backward. He pointed a pudgy three-year-old finger at the jets and said distinctly, "F-16. F-16."

Kevin Quattlebaum, one of two captains in the B-course, also took the long way round to F-16s. He had no military background: his dad managed a small business and his mom taught elementary school. He had a conventional, low-key childhood, shadowed only by the long, slow deterioration of his parents' marriage. He's a good-looking redhead with thinning hair and a continual flush. Quiet and disciplined, he has a sly, almost secretive smile and an air of sturdy reserve. He loved going fast and being outdoors, so originally he wanted to ski professionally. He got into the University of Colorado at Boulder and made the ski team. "I wasn't focused on school much," he recalls, "just going to school to ski."

Eventually he dropped out of school and spent a year on the professional skiing circuit. He was in the top 100 nationally—but never the top 10. "I got to a certain level—I'd hate to call it failure—but didn't get as far as I wanted to go. At some point, you're spending a lot of money and training all the time and you realize that you're just not getting to the next level."

So at twenty-two, he gave up competitive skiing and took up engineering, intending to become a pilot. "I had always dreamed of doing it. But I'm not the type of person who can do two things at once, and flying takes your full attention."

From the start, he hoped to fly Vipers, but was tempted by the dogfighting F-15s. Eventually he decided he'd rather fly a fighter that could also drop bombs and kill SAMs. Besides, he loved the looks of the F-16—with the pilot up there on top of the whole freaking world. "You tell me, would you rather drive a Lamborghini or a minivan? Just go out there and look at it. Stand 10 feet off the nose and look straight at the airplane." It's a spear point, a single line of aching grace made in a single slash.

His parents backed his decision—although his mother's a "far left," reflexively antiwar liberal. "Some people believe there's no cause bad enough for us to go to war and kill people," he says delicately. "But she knew I wanted it pretty badly. She just says she hopes that I won't get hurt and I won't have to kill anybody." But his dad's gung ho. "He realizes there's times when you need to go to war. Of course, once you're in the military, it's not really your role to decide that anyway. But it's important that we have people like that—who will go to war when we have to. My dad and I understand that we need people in the military willing to give up their own political ideas and to go when called. My mom thinks I should be able to say, 'Wait, in this case I don't want to go. I think this is wrong.' But you can't. That's your job once you sign on."

After college, he went through Officer Training School, the third major route into the Air Force as a pilot. Quattlebaum signed on for OTS at Maxwell Air Force base in Montgomery, Alabama, a sixteen-week course that would qualify him for a shot at flying.

He went through UPT in Laughlin, where he met his future wife, a nurse. They married two years later. She already had two kids—ages nine and seven—and they soon had a baby, now three.

But in the meantime, his quest for his own Viper got sidetracked. He didn't rank high enough in pilot training to get a fighter, so he became a T-37 instructor. He spent the next three years—and 1,300 hours in the air—teaching basic flying to young pilots who, class after class after class—left him behind to go fly Vipers and Eagles.

He longed to move on—to fly a Viper. "We'd watch our students go to Germany, go to Southern Watch [over Iraq], and we're still there at Laughlin flying T-37s over and over again. We take what we'd always call shoe salesmen and turn them into pilots. And then they'd end up combat-rated fighter pilots and I'm still training another shoe salesman."

So he jumped at IFF and the chance to earn an F-16. But despite his experience in the air, IFF proved a tough grind. "I didn't do stellar on all my missions and had plenty of negative comments on my grade sheets, but at least I didn't bust any of the missions. I probably should have—some of them were pretty ugly. My only claim to fame is that I was the only guy who didn't bust any missions in IFF."

He was deliriously happy when he got assigned to F-16s.

Already he understands how remote the qualms of his mother will become should his squadron ever go into combat—with all of their lives hanging on the details of planning and execution. "I've read a lot of books written by pilots and they all say, 'I don't care if I die, just don't let me screw up something and cost someone an airplane or their life.' To me, even now, if I crash my plane and die, I don't have to worry about it—I'll be dead. But if I screw up—and there are so many ways to screw up—then I have to live with that. You go into combat and you're thinking about dropping [bombs] at the right altitude and heading and air speed and keeping visual support and clearing the area for bandits—and fifty other things. So the last thing on your mind is whom you might be killing on the ground—unless you screw up and hit the wrong target. Maybe you think about killing people when you take your oath, but it's too late to worry about that when you get into combat. I know some of the guys talk about having a hard time dropping on Iraqis—they're human beings—but I don't think I'd have any problem with that. Of course, dropping on your own guys—even if it wasn't your fault—that would be bad, man. That would be difficult at best. I can't imagine what that would feel like. Of course, I almost feel goofy even saying this stuff—I'm not even through the B-course yet. But I'm a professional F-16 pilot. I'm just trying not to screw up—and I'll just assume that the presidents and generals and whatnot are trying just as hard as I am not to screw up their end of it."

Chris Lehto also wandered into the B-course by the backdoor.

His parents were hippies, for Christ's sake—or if not technically, card-carrying hippies, they were certainly in the same zip code. Granted, his uncle was an army colonel. But his parents both programmed and sold computers until they had enough money to drop out—whereupon they bought a sailboat to bum around the Bahamas. His sister is some kind of brilliant, with a Fulbright Scholarship to go down to South America and study the cultural aspects of Shamanism. Shamanism. Jeez.

It's like he hastily clipped out an ad for "pot" and ended up in freaking "pilot" school. He's handsome, in a laconic, square-jawed, laid-back, shrug-and-grin kind of way. He has mild, light eyes, always twinkling with some inside joke. He grew up in the suburbs of Houston playing computer games, having a good time, and getting by. When it came time to think about college, he had a buddy in Annapolis who promoed the value of a free education. That's a hell of a reason to go to the military academy. Curiously enough, his parents were cool with that. Do your own thing and all. Moreover, the "free" appealed to them. They could accelerate their master plan by five years and get the sailboat all the sooner. So. Cool. Go for it, dude.

He started shopping for military academies. Turns out, not only does the military offer a free education—but they've got great retirement benefits. So he could like, be a pilot, see the world, get paid decent—then retire at 50 percent pay after twenty years, complete with lifetime medical benefits. Then he could maybe get a sailboat and take it easy. Cool. At this point, you begin to entertain small suspicions about Lehto's version of his life—the son of hippies, playing computer games, looking for a free school to chill, dude. Come on. The academy? More to this than meets the eye, maybe. File that. His sister says he's a very competitive guy—bright, quick, flies under the radar. So she wasn't all that surprised that he wanted to subject himself to the academy. He always had to be the best—although it takes you a while to figure out that he's even paying attention to the standings. Anyhow, Lehto figured if he was going to get one of those free academy educations, might as well do something fun—like fly jets or something.

"I didn't want to just go to college, get married, have a family—and wind up working nine-to-five at some desk job."

So he got into the Air Force Academy—which was, as advertised, free. But it was also a major culture shock. All of a sudden he's got people yelling at him all day long—and he has to, like, memorize the dictionary in Pig Latin—and then recite things while jogging in place on a bed of nails. But Lehto shrugs and grins and says it was tough, but interesting. "It was hard. It sucks, really. But you just want to do your best, you know."

He figured that he'd be a cargo pilot—something interesting, but not too demanding. Didn't want to blow up innocent women and children and such—not to mention getting shot at all the time and shipped off to Iraq at unpredictable intervals. So cargo planes sounded cool. You could be a pilot and get all the perks, without the downside. But then he got to talking to some crazy son-of-a-bitch instructor who had been a Marine pilot in Vietnam, bombing the hell out of downtown Hanoi and barrel-rolling over the prisons holding all the other poor, dumb, son-of-a-bitch pilots who got themselves shot down and beaten and brainwashed. "I said, 'I want to be a C-130 pilot,' and he said 'Why the fuck would you want to do that?' " The crazy-assed fighter pilot took Lehto to the simulator and gave him a taste of shooting down the computerized blips of MiGs.

"There's only two kinds of planes," the crazy Marine pilot told Lehto. "Fighters and targets. And if you're not a killing machine, then you're just shit—and any swinging dick up there with a missile owns you."

Well. Now. That made a certain amount of sense.

So Lehto figured he'd give fighter pilot training a go. Hey. Why not? What could it hurt?

"I mean, I'm not like, 'I want to bomb shit and kill people,' but I'll go to combat if I have to. As a fighter pilot, you know the guys who have been in combat. They've been shot at—combat-proven. And you know that your whole environment is just blowing shit up and killing people. But that's not why I'm in. I mean, I'd like to shoot down a few planes—but I don't figure I'm missing anything if I never get to drop bombs on people."

Bright, quick, charming, Lehto has always risen to the top with non-chalant ease—so he could cover his competitive nature with surfer dude charm and make it look like he's excelled by accident. But that facade got beat to pulp in Introduction to Fighter Fundamentals (IFF), the emotional equivalent of the first full night of getting shelled while cowering in a fox-hole. He busted rides right and left. Twice, he came in for a landing 10 miles per hour too slow—a dangerous lapse in the hard-to-land, stall-prone T-38. That was a bust. Once he whipped the jet into a 7.3-g turn—well over the 6.5-g maximum. That was a bust. Once he dropped a simulated bomb diving at a target at too steep an angle, and on the same flight got too close to his flight lead while flying formation. That was a bust.

His fourth bust involved four jets flying formation to bomb a target. He was the third jet in line. But as the second jet in the sequence rolled up and away from the target, he lost sight of the other planes and called out a warning. The flight lead called "knock it off," so everyone would level out and get their eyeballs on everyone else so as not to have some unpleasant midair death situation, with all the resulting paperwork. But Lehto was on a perfect dive to the target when he dimly heard the "knock it off" call. He was lined up perfectly. So he went ahead and finished the dive and hit the button anyway before he pulled out. "I just pickled," he sighs. "It seemed like a good idea in my brain at the time." He might have gotten away with that and not busted the ride, but he got to worrying about whether he'd busted that ride on the way back, so he screwed up his landing—came down about 10 feet early in the "overrun" portion of the runway they weren't supposed to use—as it constituted the safety margin that would prevent them from killing their damn fool student selves and wrecking a bunch of perfectly good taxpayer-owned equipment.

One more mistake and he would have washed out—in which case maybe they would have sent him back to fly cargo planes. Dude. It was rough. He damn near FAILED. Like, he'd never failed at anything he'd actually tried to do, in his grinning, joking, laid-back, charming, surfer dude way. Now, suddenly, it was a challenge just to survive. Now, suddenly, he was just that little bit away from earning the contempt of that crazy Marine pilot. He was just one bust away from conversion to a freaking target—or worse, a cowering civilian.

But he scraped through—his grade sheet spotted and stained—but a punk and a B-courser nonetheless.

Still, the instructors at Luke took one look at his grade sheet and decided they'd better put him on the extra supervision of flying CAP, which meant he would only have to deal with one or two different instructors until he caught up to the jet—trimmed his flaps and all.

Because now—finally—he was ready to try to squeeze through the finest mesh of all—the B-course at Luke Air Force Base, where they make fighter pilots out of the humbled hotshots who survive IFF.

Now they've got to squeeze through the mesh held tight by the Luke IPs, some of the best fighter pilots on the planet. These guys have got medals and combat decorations. They've dodged missiles. They've bombed Baghdad. Obliterated forests full of tanks. Chased MiGs. Rescued wingmen. Bombed terrorists at the direction of ground grunts on horseback calling in coordinates. They've ejected, crashed, and flown upside down through flak in the utter dark.

Among themselves, the IPs have a wry shorthand for dogfighting people like Perkins, Newlin, Moore, Quattlebaum, Lehto.

They call it clubbing baby seals.

But you just have to crush their little skulls.

Because you don't want to send some punk wingman out into the world whose thick hands and bad judgment will get his flight lead killed.

Besides, they owe it to the F-16.

It is—after all—the best frigging plane in the whole history of the world. A miracle of technology. The tip of the spear. A reason for living. An addiction. A lover. One of the most maneuverable, beautiful, heart-stopping fighter jets ever built. A jet dreamed up by a fighter pilot and slipped past the grumbling, quarreling, quivering generals.

In fact, the Viper's just like a fighter pilot—clever, resourceful, and lethal. It shouldn't exist. The brass hated it. They tried to kill it a hundred times. But it triumphed—against the odds.

So if you're an F-16 pilot and you love the Viper like a mistress who offers soul-destroying sex, then you're very particular about who you let fly your Viper.

4

The Making of the Viper

The Viper—arguably the best fighter jet ever built—originated with a mystery plaguing the fevered brain of a fighter pilot named John Boyd—arguably the best fighter pilot who ever lived.

Of course, such superlatives will naturally upset other fighter pilots—especially the many who consider their own silly selves the best fighter pilot who every lived. And it will definitely upset a lot of generals—especially the ones Boyd humiliated, mocked, got fired by, and actually set on fire. But God damn it, it's true. At least, it ought to be.

Boyd's brilliance, impact, and dysfunction are captured in Robert Coram's wonderful 1997 biography, *Boyd: The Fighter Pilot Who Changed the Art of War,* which documents Boyd's largely unheralded but vital contribution to fighter jets in particular, and U.S. military tactics in general. It was published shortly after Boyd's death from cancer in 1997.

Boyd had just barely earned his fighter pilot wings when the dogfighting fiasco in Korea erupted. He flew dozens of combat missions, but to his everlasting irritation never actually shot down a MiG. Still, he had killer instincts, brilliant skills, and that astonishing, three-dimensional situational awareness (SA) that distinguishes all the great fighter pilots. Moreover, he was fearless in the air—reckless even—pushing his jets just past the limits of their design specifications. Creative, obnoxious, and compulsive, he improvised tactics in the air, born of his uncanny connection to the jet, to the sky, to the enemy.

So he was naturally obsessed with the central air combat mystery of the Korean War. The MiG 15 was faster and more powerful than the American Sabers it faced, and could hold a sharp turn longer. So how did the American pilots rack up a ten-to-one kill advantage?

The question obsessed Boyd, engaging his voracious intellect until he hit upon the answer: quick turns and good visibility. Although the MiGs could fly faster and hold their speed longer in a turn, the Sabers could turn more quickly. So every time the two jets matched turns, the Saber gained about half a second. Moreover, the MiG pilots had a large blind spot to the rear, even if they twisted around in their seats. The bubbled canopy of the Saber gave the American pilots a 360-degree field of view—so they could keep the enemy in sight throughout a dogfight. Moreover, the Saber pilots had hydraulic controls that enabled them to control the jet with one finger on the stick. By contrast, the MiG pilots had to wrestle with their nonhydraulic controls so forcefully that extended maneuvering exhausted the pilot. As a result, the Saber pilots would outmaneuver the technically superior MiGs and move into the lethal six-o'clock position—directly behind the jet—for a kill. Moreover, the rapid spread of these turn-based tactics among the innovative, well-trained, and aggressive American pilots quickly nullified their technological disadvantage.

The insight spurred Boyd to develop a whole new theory of maneuver and dogfighting, which he dubbed "Energy Maneuverability," based on designing a fighter jet to fly along the knife-edge between massive thrust and sharp turns. A blazing fast fighter jet that can't turn quickly because it has a big, heavy engine just makes a slightly harder target. A nimble jet that can turn itself inside out, but doesn't have the thrust to accelerate instantly, will run out of energy after a couple of turns. The ideal jet should quiver right on the edge of control—with enough power to leap out of any difficulty. Boyd's insight—so profound that it seemed obvious after he stated it—turned designing and flying jets into a physics problem. Boyd's transformative Energy Maneuverability (EM) theory provided a set of formulas to ruthlessly evaluate the dogfighting capability of any jet design based on a combination of thrust and turning radius.

But he didn't stop there. Boyd seized upon the ideas of the fourth-century B.C. Chinese military strategist Sun Tzu, who wrote *The Art of*

War. Sun Tzu advocated a war of maneuver, intelligence, deception, and innovation that relied on confusing the enemy, concentrating forces, and controlling the place, timing, and tempo of the fighting. The victor must start with better information than his enemy, and then make decisions more quickly and adroitly. Boyd's update of Sun Tzu, developed obsessively in the 1950s, cut sharply against the grain of twentieth-century military thought, which emphasized industrial capacity, massed forces, and the throw-weight of munitions. However, the German high command employed Sun Tzu's principles when Hitler unleashed blitzkrieg to conquer all of Europe while larger armies were still massing and marching in confusion. Because the Allies had eventually overwhelmed Germany by the weight of American industrial output and sheer Russian numbers, this industrial massing of resources dominated postwar military thinking. Because they exaggerated the impact of strategic bombing on the war's outcome and remained hypnotized by the power of nuclear bombs, the air power theorists stressed tonnages of bombs and overlooked the power of Sun Tzu's ideas and close air support. Why worry about dogfighting and hitting bridges if you can bomb enemies "back to the Stone Age"?

In fact, Boyd's application of Sun Tzu's adages captures perfectly the fighter pilot's art of killing his enemy—preferably before the enemy even knows he's there. The great fighter pilots quickly learn not only to make instant decisions, but to throw in feints to fool the enemy. The flash of a wing edge thrown in before a roll to the opposite side can cause that fatal, split second of indecision on the part of the enemy pilot. Boyd took the instincts of a fighter pilot, combined them with Sun Tzu, and revolutionized U.S. military strategy with 1,500-year-old ideas. As Sun Tzu observed, "All warfare is based on deception . . . Offer the enemy a bait to lure him; feign disorder and strike him. For if he does not know where I intend to give battle he must prepare in a great many places. For to win 100 victories in 100 battles is not the acme of skill. To subdue the enemy without fighting is the acme of skill. Thus, what is of supreme importance in war is to attack the enemy's strategy."

Seized with a zealot's passion, Boyd launched a crusade in the 1960s to apply his theories to the design of a new generation of fighter aircraft.

This royally pissed off the be-ribboned, be-starred Blue Suits in the Pentagon, embedded in the heart of the "military-industrial-complex," driven by the pork barrel dynamics of the billion-dollar defense contracts unleashed by the Cold War.

Of course, Boyd himself was a very irritating guy—the quintessential fighter pilot from the days before graduate degrees in engineering and $100 million jets you can't be using to buzz your girlfriend's house. Boyd talked nonstop, called friends in the middle of the night to deliver hours-long monologues, ridiculed generals, cultivated congressmen, and operated flagrantly out of the chain of command. He disdained enemies and gloated over his victories. He would gesture wildly, shout in his opponents' faces, and poke them in the chest while holding a cigar. Once he set a general's tie on fire with his cigar as he screamed in the man's face. In the process, Boyd earned a devoted following, known as the "Fighter Mafia," willing to use leaks, briefings, and an avalanche of irrefutable research to humiliate, maneuver, and manipulate the brass into adopting Boyd's ideas.

The F-16—and to a lesser extent the F-15 and the cheap, invaluable workhorse, the A-10—are Boyd's enduring contributions to aircraft design—a brief, glorious rebellion against the Air Force's nearly irresistible addiction to unwieldy, ruinously expensive airplanes designed by committee more to win an unending stream of appropriations than to perform a clear, well-defined mission in the air.

The power of his ideas and his obsessive pursuit of them made him the most influential fighter pilot in history—but it also stunted his career. Boyd never rose beyond the rank of colonel, thanks to the host of implacable enemies he earned with his arrogance, single-mindedness, and contempt for his opponents. He retired from the Air Force in 1975 but continued to influence U.S. military strategy through his famous daylong briefings, which he refused to condense. His career culminated in a 1977 briefing detailing the OODA Loop: observe, orient, decide, act. The briefing detailed how to get inside the decision-making loop of the enemy, like a fighter pilot pivoting inside the opponent's turn circle. A parade of congressmen, policymakers, and generals heard the briefing. Boyd's theories prompted then Secretary of Defense Dick Cheney to reject the initial plan for the Gulf War—which Boyd would have derided as "Hey diddle diddle, straight up the middle." Instead, the U.S. plan called for an air campaign to destroy the Iraqi army's command-and-control system, cut off the frontline commanders, and blind the generals in Baghdad. Only then did the Coalition forces attack, sweeping around the flanks of the entrenched Iraqis in a bold war of maneuver—a blitzkrieg that adhered perfectly to Boyd's OODA loop.

Of course, Boyd's personal life was a disaster—again the quintessential fighter pilot. He grew up working three jobs to support his mother and four brothers and sisters after the death of his father, and escaped as soon as he could by joining the Army Air Corps at eighteen. He raised his own family, but all his life sacrificed them to his career and his obsessions.

When the Army wouldn't let him fly, he left to get an economics degree and joined ROTC at the University of Iowa. He graduated in 1951. After Korea he became a flight instructor. In the heyday of the Air Force culture of tough love and instruction by humiliation, Boyd offered all of the incoming students a standing bet. If they could stay alive against him for forty seconds, he'd pay them $40. He never had to pay—and savored the nickname "Forty-Second Boyd."

Boyd eventually shifted his crusade to the Pentagon, determined to force the Air Force to design a jet for fighter pilots rather than defense contractors and pork-barrel-rolling congressmen. Convinced the generals would always screw up aircraft design with political considerations and the absurd piling-on of gadgets and systems, he set out to get inside the decision-making loop of his own superiors. As a result, he narrowly averted two court-martials.

But he also enlisted a core of true believers. He insisted that the Air Force would always make them choose between being someone and doing something. If their ideas were good, their motives pure, and their tactics sound, they could win—even in the Pentagon. But they could not both win and rise to the top of the bureaucracy to wear a general's stars on their collars. It's like a designing a fighter jet—you have to choose.

So he went to war with the bureaucracy to force the Air Force to design the perfect fighter jet based on his EM calculations. His enemy was a deeply entrenched bureaucracy that produced expensive, high-tech, heavily loaded designs. Jets designed as air-to-air MiG-killers inevitably started acquiring add-ons—landing gear for an aircraft carrier, more room for gas tanks, more room for bombs, a second engine for more speed in a straightaway. Boyd pushed hard, enlisting both bureaucratic and congressional allies to avert design disasters like the scandal-plagued F-111, an 85,000-pound fighter-bomber that was supposed to land on carriers, fly long distances, and dogfight MiGs. Desperate to gain buyers by offering everything, the designers embraced movable wings and an untested engine. The wings were supposed to slide in and out, changing the jet's configuration for takeoffs versus supersonic flight. In theory, the moveable wings let you have a jet that's both fast and heavy. Fixed wing designs like the F-16, must choose: in the F-16's case, the design maximized maneuverability—even at the cost of carrying capacity and top speed. However, in the F-111 both the swing wings and the untested engines proved a disappointment and a source of grave difficulties in the air. Boyd's formulas correctly predicted a fiasco—an unwieldy, over-budget plane that could do none of its contradictory missions well.

So when the Air Force put out a call in the late 1960s for a competition to design the "FX" fighter to replace the Phantom and smite MiGs, Boyd and his acolytes invoked Sun Tzu and went to war with the generals. When the prototype's design specifications called for a weight of 65,000 pounds, Boyd pushed for 35,000—prompting the Air Force to finally compromise at 40,000. Next the Air Force decreed the new fighter should reach speeds of three times the speed of sound (Mach 3). Boyd fought that too, arguing that designing a fighter to reach those speeds would ruin its agility—as the muscle-bound jet went screaming past a quick-turning adversary, it would offer the slower jet a free shot.

Boyd suffered repeated defeats. The top speed dropped to Mach 2—still too fast for the perfect fighter. The width of the fuselage increased to accommodate a larger radar. The weight crept up to 43,000 pounds. The brass insisted on an internal ladder to climb into the cockpit and other extras that added weight and reduced the turn rate.

In part the brass fought Boyd's efforts to cut the size of the fighter because the Navy promised to buy the same jet if it had the heavier structure and gear needed to land on carriers. Ironically, the Navy ultimately backed out and decided to build its own dogfighting fighter-bomber. In fact, the Navy executed a perfect, fighter pilot backstab. First, it cancelled its joint effort on the F-111. Next, it declared that the proposed, lightweight FX fighter couldn't fly fast enough or climb high enough to deal with the MiG 25 and so pulled out of that joint effort as well. The MiG 25 had thrown a nasty scare into the Air Force brass; it was a massive, high-altitude, twin-engine jet with long-range radar and missiles. Instead, the Navy announced its own plans to develop a dogfighting jet—the swing-wing F-14 Tomcat, an unwieldy jet many pilots later referred to sneeringly as the "Tom Turkey." Loaded with bombs and external tanks, the Tomcat weighs in at 74,000 pounds. Stuck with all that weight and a modest engine, the underpowered, swing-wing Tomcat quickly loses energy in tight turns—just as Boyd's EM formulas predicted.

Afraid Congress would make the Air Force buy the F-14, the Air Force Blue Suits were forced to back Boyd's push for a fixed-wing dogfighting jet. That decision ultimately gave birth to the F-15 in the course of the 1970s. The design of the twin-engine F-15 Eagle drew heavily on Boyd's theories, but the Air Force soon piled on enough extras to drive up the cost and the weight—frustrating Boyd's yearning to build the perfect fighter jet.

He nearly resigned in disgust.

But two things forced the Air Force to design another fighter that would finally exemplify most of Boyd's theories.

First, the cost and weight of the F-15 and F-14 both continued to rise—making them prohibitively expensive.

Second, the Soviets upgraded the MiG 21 "Fishbed," their cheap, fast, mainstay fighter, and started cranking out massive numbers of stripped-down variants. Suddenly, Air Force war planners faced the prospect of seeing their gold-plated F-15s overwhelmed by the sheer weight of numbers in any direct conflict. Besides, most of the U.S. allies couldn't afford F-15s. Therefore the Air Force needed a cheap, high-performance, dogfighting fighter-bomber it could produce in large quantities to counter the Soviet threat and sell to allied air forces. The specifications required it to beat the performance of the MiG 21 "Fishbed" by at least 25 percent.

So now the Fighter Mafia designed a pure dogfighting jet optimized according to Boyd's EM theory, which by then he'd refined with hundreds of hours of essentially stolen Air Force computer time. The rapier-like jet would weigh 20,000 pounds—half as much as the F-15—at the cost of bomb racks and radar. The Fighter Mafia managed to finagle a budget for experimental designs for the YF-17 and the YF-16—using the prototype "Y" designation to keep the Blue Suits from realizing the jet would compete with their beloved F-15.

As news stories about the poor performance of the F-14 and the rising cost of the F-15 mounted, the Fighter Mafia once again found themselves inside the turn circle of their bureaucratic enemies. Desperate to impose reforms and stop the financial hemorrhage, the Nixon administration allocated $200 million to pay for competing prototypes before committing to multi-billion-dollar contracts. The Fighter Mafia arranged for the development of two, competing lightweight fighters. The wary Air Force generals relented, but only because they figured the limited range of such a lightweight fighter would doom it in the real world. They didn't realize that even though a lightweight fighter would carry far less fuel than an F-15, it also weighed so little it would burn less gas and end up with a longer range.

The Fighter Mafia, determined to produce the perfect fighter jet, exercised rigid control over every line in the design. After winning the crucial backing of incoming Secretary of Defense James Schlesinger, Boyd's Fighter Mafia finally got its chance to test a fighter jet designed to reflect Boyd's theories. In January 1975, the YF-16 prototype won the contest with the YF-17, based both on the figures and on the overwhelming consensus of the test pilots—who in an unusual move demanded by Boyd flew both planes. The YF-16 eventually morphed into the F-16 Fighting Falcon, while the Navy eventually turned the YF-17 into the carrier-based F-18 Hornet.

The Viper had arrived—at least in prototype.

Initially, the Air Force brass protested that it didn't need the lightweight fighter, fearful it would replace the F-15.

But when Schlesinger insisted, the generals started making changes in the design to make it more of a bomber than a fighter and prevent it from competing with the F-15. Designers added 3,000 pounds of electronics, hung weapons and bombs off the underside, added fuel to accommodate the increased drag, and fattened the nose to increase the size of the radar. That in turn required increasing the size of the wings to preserve its trademark maneuverability—adding more weight. Boyd fought a losing, rearguard action against every change. Finally he staged his last stand on the issue of the wing design. The original wing area measured 280 square feet. After the design changes added weight, Boyd pushed for a redesign to increase the area of the wing to 320 square feet. The Air Force settled on 300 square feet, in part to prevent the Viper from outmaneuvering the Eagle.

Boyd abandoned the struggle in disgust—convinced the Air Force would never build the perfect dogfighting jet.

Still, pilots consider the Viper a fighter pilot's dream, thanks to its revolutionary design and technology.

The F-16 was designed by General Dynamics to top out on Boyd's EM curve—right at the unstable edge of spinning out of control. By fusing the wing into the fuselage, connecting all the control surfaces to a computer, and outfitting the Viper with a single Pratt and Whitney F-100 turbofan engine, designers created one of the most maneuverable fighter jets in history. In fact, without the ceaseless manipulation of its control surfaces by the computer, the Viper would instantly spin out of control. However, that designed instability means the Viper can almost instantly change direction, turn, bank, roll, or dive. This was only possible because of breakthroughs in computer design that made the Viper a "fly-by-wire" design, in which the computer considers the pilot's use of the controls as advice rather than orders. That enables the jet to rise or descend or even slip sideways, without pointing its nose. In effect, pilots can maneuver while keeping the nose pointed at a target. It also means that predicting the Viper's movements from the cockpit of another jet in a dogfight poses a lethal puzzle.

Striving for a cheap, mass-produced jet, designers employed an innovative mix of conventional and high-tech materials and concepts. The single engine saved weight—holding the weight of the prototype to 17,000 pounds—but demanded high reliability. In addition, the single engine required an air intake for its turbines on the underside of the jet, giving the F-16 its low-slung, spear-like profile. However, this design also makes the F-16 vulnerable to sucking up debris off the ground during takeoffs and landings.

The airframe is a miracle of design: lightweight and composed mostly of conventional materials, but able to withstand sustained 9-g maneuvering. Such g-forces would cause most pilots to black out, so the designers hit on the brilliant innovation of reclining the seat by 30 degrees, dramatically decreasing the impact of those wrenching turns on the human body.

The Viper prototype outmaneuvered both the MiG 17 and MiG 25 in head-to-head tests, reaching speeds of up to Mach 2 at 60,000 feet. As an added benefit, the Viper proved difficult to see at a distance, in contrast to the bulky F-15 or the workhorse F-4, whose smoking engines make it visible for miles.

Since then, the F-16 has proven itself one of the most flexible, reliable jets ever built. Although the addition of bombs, targeting pods, electronics, radars, jamming systems, missiles, and even nuclear bombs quickly overwhelmed its role as the pure dogfighter the Fighter Mafia envisioned, the Viper has formed the aluminum alloy spine of the USAF for some twenty-five years. The Air Force eventually bought nearly 3,000 Vipers. Twenty other allies bought 1,000 more. That included the Israelis, who gave the Viper its baptism by fire in two wars with its neighbors. The slaughter of Syrian MiGs over the Bakka Valley demonstrated the dominance of both the F-15 and F-16 over any competing jets. The F-16's agility and electronic add-ons have also given it an unparalleled ability to outmaneuver SAMs. Currently, the Viper's air-to-air dogfighting score stands at 70 to 0.

The Viper immediately provided a crucial link in American alliances, since the U.S. quickly approved overseas sales. Anxious to win over European allies, the U.S. approved several European production lines, although that required juggling 3,000 different subcontractors. The contractors shipped 3 million components weighing 20 million pounds to Europe to set up the plant—slowing production and adding $1 million to the cost of each jet. But the use of the F-16 by most of America's key allies forged strong military and economic ties. The initial production cost rose slowly, from $4.5 million per jet to $6 million per jet. Eventually, add-ons and dispersed production tripled the original per-plane cost to $10 million—still a triumph of cost control by Air Force standards. (By contrast, the newest USAF fighter jet, the F-22 Raptor, costs an estimated $200 million per plane, a cost that has doubled and redoubled in the course of design and construction.)

The most recent F-16 variants, loaded with new weapons systems, radars, targeting pods, and a more powerful engine, cost closer to $30 million. The Air Force has been introducing upgrades to the F-16 for the past twenty-five years, giving each new version a new "block" number. The latest version is 48 feet long, weighs 18,600 pounds empty, and generates a thrust of 29,000 pounds that enables it to accelerate while pointed straight up and reach a speed of Mach 2 above 50,000 feet.

Continual upgrades have transformed its radar and added radar-guided air-to-air-missiles. The Air Force has developed an array of targeting "pods," generally built onto the underside of the jet with the optics, cameras, computers, GPS transmitters or other technology necessary to guide various kinds of "smart bombs," like the GPS targeted bombs that can strike targets with deadly precision night or day. The changes have dramatically expanded the Viper's abilities, so that it now can provide close air support for ground troops, take out enemy missiles and radar, destroy bunkers and hardened targets, and dogfight effectively.

Besides which, the Viper looks so cool it could make a young man— or woman—warp his or her whole life for a chance to climb in, lift off, jam on the afterburner, and spin it like a pinwheel.

The Viper stops the heart—just sitting there on the runway.

In the sky, it's intoxicating. The pilot sits high up, reclining beneath the exquisitely designed bubble canopy, seeing nothing but sky. The sleek, knife-edge jet is below and behind, even if the pilot turns to look to his six o'clock. He can barely see the wings, slung back to the rear, which explains why the jet trembles at the edge of aerodynamic instability. But the Viper doesn't feel unstable. It feels like thought. Like freedom. Like God. It is impossible not to fall in love with it—not to feel its yearning to transform you into something great and terrible. The smallest pressure on the stick will cause it to veer, dive, climb, slide, twirl. Sometimes it seems to respond to even a thought—and remakes the universe as it spins the world on its axis, turning earth to sky and back again, creating its own gravity. It is an addiction, to sit once at the controls—so that ever afterward all the ordinary world seems colorless, gravity a burden and earth a prison.

No wonder that the punks will now give up everything—risk anything—to climb carefully into that cockpit and strap on the jet.

They will bomb.

They will kill.

Risk death.

Abandon families.

Pass through the ever-finer mesh.

They will do anything to fly a Viper.

But first they must get past Doughboy and the other IPs, who are determined to prevent some stupid, ham-handed, slow-thinking, behind-the-jet punk from getting past them and out into the world where they'll do something stupid and get someone killed.

5

Basic Phase: Learning to Fly All Over

Captain Danny Lasica—"Ship"—glances down at his watch, letting the seconds tick off to the scheduled briefing time. He's the military crease in the trousers of the squadron—the honed blade that can gut you before you know you've been cut. He's all angles, cut from a block of marble by a samurai carver with sweeps of the blade too fast for the eye. He's Air Force Academy, precise as a machine. He's coiled, a steeled store of energy bent far back and snapped into place, motionless but bursting with potential violence. He's unflappable, like ice except not cold. He smiles, jokes—speaks easily, smoothly. But he seems hidden away, inaccessible. Or perhaps he's just so disciplined and focused that he seems inaccessible. He's among the most respected pilots in the squadron, although his fighter pilot ego remains coiled behind that same restraint. He treats the student pilots with dignified respect, just short of affection. He's uncompromising, brilliant, and instinctive in the air—but courteous, kind, and restrained. He has a knack for explaining things. Even better, he has an instinct for knowing when his students are confused and putting up a brave front. He's rawhide thin, with prominent ears, a narrow, incisive face, a pleasant manner, ink-stained fingertips, and close-cropped hair. He listens intently—sitting motionless, blinking with concentration. He never stammers and exudes intelligence.

Nine years married, he has five kids—all on a fighter pilot's salary, which isn't, in the end, very much. He doesn't look like the father of five. He looks like some shiny new Air Force Academy spawn—all spit shine, jargon, and ironed creases. But that's just the chrome of his facade. His grandfather yearned to be a pilot but had medical problems. His father wanted to be a pilot but hurt himself falling off a roof. The whole family was steeped in patriotism, discipline, and military virtues. His sister is a Marine Corps captain, fluent in Russian and based in Moscow. One brother is in the Air Force Academy. Another is a Latin teacher.

Today Ship is one of the top instructors at Luke and will be flying for the day with Perkins, assigned to his flight. Ship just wants to make sure Perkins can fly around without doing anything egregiously stupid—and land the plane without killing his damn fool self—although so far Perkins is doing great, flying "ahead of the jet," says Ship.

So in the tradition of a good IP, Ship has been piling on extra tasks.

Today, Ship is running through a briefing for one of the first solo missions, all in the dense, jargon-compacted style of an Air Force briefing.

They'll take off, fly down to the empty sprawl of the range, and then practice flying in formation—two planes, a flight lead, and a wingman, the basic combat formation. They spend a lot of time talking about the details of the ground operations, the flight checklist, and taking off.

"When you're ready to go, give the crew chief a thumbs-up," says Ship. "We're going to be all good in the chalks [before taking off] basically there. No spare jets down there—we'll take off when we can."

They'll take off, climb to 28,000 feet, and head south for the range. Ship speaks with casual deliberation, working off a checklist that includes detailed discussion about what to do if the engine fails and controls malfunction, including the diversionary airfields in case "you're pissing gas and on fire."

Perkins nods. Confident—or at least determined to appear confident.

Ship outlines the maneuvers they'll run through, all stipulated by the fifty-eight-mission syllabus.

"We'll pull up to 6 to 7 g's at 500 knots. Then take it back down. You want a nice pull to 4 g's and hold that 4 g's all the way round. No afterburners—just mil power—nice smooth 5, 6, 6.5 g's—then back down to 3 g's and hold that all the way around." The F-16 has a potent afterburner "overdrive," but that gulps gas and gives the students less time to react, so in the early going they don't use the afterburners much.

And don't hit any other planes, suggests Ship.

"Recognize, confirm, and cover—get away from other airplanes—I'll deconflict away from you—I will stay clear of you, that's my deconfliction hammer all day—until we get to the formation work. Every time you maneuver, you locate those other jets. Get your cranium back on swivel. If you're on chase, what is the chase formation? What are the issues you're thinking about?"

Bright, eager, smooth—the perfect student—Perkins replies, "Keep 1,000 feet back—no closer than 300 feet."

"What are some other things in terms of what he's doing with his airplane?" Ship presses.

"Altitude," says Perkins, faintly furrowed. "Not going below the floor," he adds, in reference to the simulated ground—set at 10,000 feet. Dipping below 10,000 feet will trigger an automatic bust—one of the four allowed in the demanding syllabus. "Don't get my nose up too high, or let my airspeed get too slow."

"Right," nods Ship. "Remember, I'd rather you talk to me out on the air—and I say, 'I'm good,' than not say anything."

Of course, that instruction will change. Right now, the instructors use radio chatter to keep track of the pilots. When a student gets overwhelmed and falls "behind the jet," they stop talking on the radio—or even responding to direct questions from the instructor. Later they'll learn that wingmen should keep their freaking mouths shut and the radios uncluttered unless they see a MiG on a sneak attack. But for now, those lengthening silences will provide a warning for the instructors.

"Now, you might wind up going blind and getting 'Helen Keller,' " and losing sight of the other jets in the formation, warns Ship. "Just call it. Call blind. And remain predictable. That's the main thing. That's the thing that's going to kill you—and me. So sing out," says Ship.

"Also—remember—if someone else bails out—you've got to keep clear. It takes 20 minutes for a chute to get down at 20,000 feet. So you've got to avoid the mothball effect," in which a helpful pilot flies toward the position of a pilot who has bailed out and winds up flying into the parachute. "I've seen it happen—where you get close and closer and slow and slower. You've got to keep a perimeter on the guy."

Ship talks about flying formation and identifying other planes. Jets maneuvering against a seamless backdrop of blue, or even piles of clouds, present tough challenges in perception. When an F-16 whips into a turn, it can generate up to nine times the force of gravity. A pilot could be flying on a curved path toward the ground, and the g-forces would make it feel like he's flying level. Two jets on a collision course at a combined speed of 1,600 miles an hour can rush into a collision in seconds. So just learning how to scan the sky remains a fundamental challenge. Staring out at a clear sky, the eyes reset to a natural focal point—usually just beyond the cockpit. Pilots say there are only two kinds of fighter pilots—those who have thrown the jet into a violent maneuver to escape the smudge of a bug on their cockpit and those who will soon do so. The speck of a jet on a collision course may seem like an undefined smudge until it's too late, so pilots learn to refocus their eyes constantly.

"So you have to cage your eyes for 6,000 or 7,000 feet," says Ship, of flying formation.

In addition, the pilots learn that certain visual details offer the best clue to range. "You want to hold formation at just about the distance that the fuel tank starts blending into the fuselage, so that you can't see the clear lines between the tank and the jet anymore," Ship notes. "We're going to do some maneuvering. We'll do some 90-degree turns—some 45s, some 180s. So if you go into a 90-degree turn and come out of it and acquire me—where are you going to go?"

"Line up in line of sight—at about the inlet," replies Igor. The inlet is the scoop under the F-16's fuselage where air is forced into the engine.

Stick also starts the long process of making sure they can fly formation without running into other jets, including the complexities of "stacking" at different altitudes when flying near other jets. "I'd like you to stack high—above my level—but if you stack low it's absolutely no problem. But don't get caught watching the paint dry," he adds. In the standard two-ship formation, the flight lead makes all the decisions and runs the mission. The wingman has only one job—to stay in formation and look ceaselessly over his shoulder to prevent an enemy fighter from sneaking up from behind.

"Clear behind your six [o'clock]. Clear beyond my six. Don't just focus on me. I should just be part of your cross-check, not your whole cross-check. So you look up, and say 'Hey, he's getting bigger.' Then you probably want to correct 15 degrees—maybe you're even going to end up on the opposite side if you're hooking into me. You want deconfliction all the way around."

They spend some time talking about maintaining formation and joining up if they've been separated. Flying formation poses a fundamental challenge. One of the primary goals of the training at Luke is to ensure that the students can maintain formation almost instinctively. Maintaining the proper spacing between two jets each hurtling along at 700 miles an hour in a featureless blue sky guided by the radar blips on the Heads Up Display (HUD) poses a fluctuating, deadly, split-second exercise in three-dimensional geometry. The HUD remains one of the brilliant innovations of the F-16, a clear screen in the pilot's natural line of vision that displays a bewilderment of information, connected to the onboard computer. The pilot constantly selects the mode of information for the HUD, depending on whether he's flying formation, patrolling for distant threats, dog fighting, or on a bomb run. The HUD continually displays the vital numbers, including speed, altitude, headings to selected navigation points, and radar blips for other planes detected by the radar. The different modes provide specialized information, including intersecting lines to determine when the computer has a missile lock, a piper for shooting the cannons, distances and headings to pre-programmed targets, an array of radar modes, and an onslaught of other information that veteran pilots learn to read with ease, but which overwhelms civilians and severely stresses punks. Eventually, they'll learn to line up on another jet's radar signal from 50 miles away and slide into perfect position, speeds precisely matched at the merge. They learn that skill by finding friendly ships in the aching blue sky, but the intercept is also the key to survival— the difference between sliding into the perfect kill position behind an enemy jet and bungling the approach and offering your enemy a free shot.

"If you come up behind me without enough energy, it just takes forever to join," says Ship. "You want about 150 knots of overtake until you're within about 6,000 feet," he notes, demonstrating the merge with his hands. "The thing a lot of guys do is they piss away the energy, then they jam the stick—they shoot past. Now that's dangerous. So if you do overshoot—for whatever reason you have too much smash—you've got to ease it back and not lose sight and not drop down right in front of my nose."

"If you're doing everything right," says Ship, "you're going to be high on energy," which means both high speed and high altitude—since altitude can be instantly translated into speed by turning the nose of the jet downhill. The B-course training is designed, in part, to instill an instinctive awareness of energy—speed and altitude. That's especially true when lining up for a landing, when the pilot uses the glowing lines in the HUD to touch down gracefully at the beginning of the runway—hopefully touching the ground in the first third of the runway. "What happens if we have too much energy? You roll out of your turn to the end of the runway at 7,000 feet and dude, we are way, way steep?" queries Ship.

"Float the turn instead of being aggressive?" says Perkins, a tentative note creeping into his voice.

"If you're high energy, you want to float the turn?" asks Ship.

"So you can high-g at the end," says Perkins, referring to a sharp, energy-dumping turn.

Ship nods, then gestures with his hands to indicate the jerky, back and forth "gnat's ass" landing of a pilot trying to dump excess energy before smacking into the runway. "Make a sharper turn, cut the corner, and put your speed brake out. I'll go around behind you," he adds, to avoid piling into the abruptly slowing leading jet. "Word of advice," adds Ship. "Make sure you line up on the right runway. Last time we had a punk try to land on the wrong runway, you know what he got for a name—'Pick a Runway Shithead.' Hard to get on the patch."

Perkins laughs, trying to sound like he can't believe the dumb stuff punks do. But the laugh has a nervous edge, because he knows that some days the bear eats you and you come out a steaming pile of bear shit.

It happened last week to Quattlebaum, the quiet, intense former cargo plane pilot struggling to make the transition to fighters. He's a captain, which means he's supposed to be leading the class—but he's remote, married, buttoned down. And falling behind the jet. Everyone busts rides. If you bust four rides out of the fifty-eight-ride syllabus, you can hear the ice cracking all around you—you can see the blue sharks turning tight circles down there just below your feet. If you bust five, they hold a gathering of instructors to decide whether you should return, disgraced, to the ranks of ground-pounders. Usually, they let you continue—then wash you out on the sixth bust. Or maybe they'll give you one more faint chance if there's a flicker of hope for your pathetic self. And Quattlebaum has already busted a ride—right in the beginning phase when they're just trying to take off and land without running into anything. These rides, you just try to keep at least 1,000 feet away from the flight lead and not fly through the goddamned simulated floor—generally set at 10,000 feet. Quattlebaum kept getting too close, his eyes trapped inside the jet as he struggled to monitor his altitude and speed and radar headings and radio setting. He'd look up and there was the flight lead, looming just 500 feet away. He kept floating up 300 or 400 feet in altitude. He kept slowing down—flying at 350 knots instead of 400 knots. All the little, niggling, irritating, perfectly natural stuff. But that small stuff will kill you. In truth, the main goal of the B-course is to make flying automatic—so you navigate, control speed and altitude, and fly formation without thinking about it and so wasting your precious brain bits on bullshit. They need to get as good with the control stick as a computer geek in a dungeon and save the situational awareness for the blips on the radar, the instant slash of fighter tactics, the fifteen alternatives for firing a missile, all available by toggling a button on the control stick. Flying formation, controlling speed, and sticking to the right altitude has to come automatically, like using silverware.

Quattlebaum—a steady, stolid pilot—got behind the jet. He busted the ride, but pulled himself back together on the repeat ride. Busting a ride on basic stuff so early in the program raises a warning flag. B-coursers like to save their busts for air-to-air combat or dropping bombs or meeting up with a flight of Vipers at 400 knots.

Meantime, Newlin has also busted a ride—which didn't really surprise anyone, since he came in on the extra supervision of CAP status. They all know Newlin eked by in basic pilot training. His entry reports were so marginal that the IPs at the Emerald Knights gave him extra supervision right off the bat. That means he would fly with only one or two different instructors, to ensure consistency and closer supervision. They hoped that he'd get the hang of it in a couple of rides and get off CAP—as Perkins had done. Instead, Newlin busted one of his early rides, flying through the simulated floor and falling behind on the checklist of tasks pilots perform on the ground before takeoff. Then he came in too slow and forgot to change his aim point. Normally, a little bubble attached to crosshairs appears in the HUD on a landing approach. You're supposed to put the crosshairs right on the end of the runway during the approach;

then as you level out close to the ground, you're supposed to shift the steerpoint further down the runway. But Newlin held the steerpoint right on the very end of the runway as he came waffling in. So he ended up bouncing down too soon and touching wheels nine feet into the overrun—not officially part of the runway. That's a bust.

On the other hand, Stihl has already distinguished himself.

Last week, Stihl took his first solo flight on the wing of "Opie," Major Tom Stewart, a tough, charming, deeply respected instructor with a knack for teaching without demeaning. Suddenly, en route to the bombing range, Stihl got an engine warning light. So they diverted to the back-up airfield, drawing on one of those routine chunks of the prebrief that most students never need in the whole course of training. He diverted to Gila Bend, landed perfectly, and then handled the complicated procedure of shutting down the jet without the help of a crew chief.

Stihl underplays the accomplishment with his typical aw-shucks self-deprecation, but the incident has changed his status. The instructors all know that such improvisation in the air distinguish the best pilots—when the bogeys pounce, the SAMs smoke upward from where they're not supposed to be, and the turkey vulture flies into the engine. They don't slap him on the back and buy him cigars, but you can see the difference in the way they joke with him. The other punks understand this. In some strange, inarticulate way, they hope something will happen to them too. They want to prove they have it. They want to earn the respect of the IPs. They yearn to outgrow their pukeness.

6

∞∞∞

RAGE AND THE FEMALE FIGHTER PILOT

CAPTAIN SHAWN ANGER—"RAGE"—sits patiently in the small briefing room with the whiteboard and the plain table that fills most of the room, counting down the seconds to the start of Lieutenant Julie Moore's briefing for her first solo flight.

Rage is a gifted flier, solid leader, brilliant teacher, and boisterous partier—although that's hard to believe when he's in the squadron, getting ready to fly, as serious as a declaration of war. The naming committee in his squadron in New Mexico dubbed him "Rage," partly to play off his last name but mostly to honor a particularly memorable binge. Unflappable, low-key, and easygoing, he gravitated easily into teaching—a crucial gift in the Air Force, which constantly retrains pilots to adopt new weapons and tactics. The Air Force devotes enormous resources to the initial training, with instructors outnumbering B-coursers two-to-one in many squadrons. But even after they finally head off to an operational squadron, Viper pilots undergo constant training and recertification, taking carefully structured courses on each new weapons system and strategy, learning certain formation roles, perfecting use of night-vision goggles. Unlike most Viper pilots, Rage meandered into his Air Force career. His parents were Canadian and he grew up in Michigan, outside the pervasive military influence that marked the early years of most of the other pilots. His father joined the Air Force and rose to the rank of staff sergeant, but would have had to give up his Canadian citizenship to rise any higher. So he mustered out. Rage applied to all three of the service academies, attracted to the idea of service and the discipline of a military life. He got into all three and selected the Air Force Academy, mostly for the skiing. From there, he gravitated toward flying. He excelled—as he always has—and had his choice of jets out of pilot training. He picked the F-16—for the challenge.

"I chose the F-16 because it did the most things. Even though the F-15 was the one you were supposed to want to fly, I wanted to do air-to-ground." Now, he's driven by that love of flying. "Part of it is the freedom, being airborne—leaving everybody else behind. The caliber of people I work with every day on the average is infinitely higher than the public at large. People who are always thinking, able to process things rapidly—just makes things enjoyable. Pretty high strung, work hard, play hard—you don't have very many lazy guys. Go out as a four-ship or an eight-ship, you want to be able to trust everybody else. Sometimes—if the mission's not too demanding—you look right, look left, and think, Here I am doing 500 knots doing one of the coolest things you can do. Those moments are rare—once every couple of weeks. You can see it sometimes in the students—when they go solo and things are not tasking them, they look around with that big smile—living the dream."

He works hard to make flying smooth, safe, predictable.

But sometimes, things get hairy.

He was flying Southern Watch, the long, mostly routine effort to keep the tatters of the Iraqi air force in their concrete hangars and away from the Shiite areas of southern Iraq. Mostly, those missions consisted of hours of flying in big circles and refueling three or four times on the air tankers. "I had just come off the tanker's wingtip, waiting for the number three man to get gas. Smelled a burnt oil type of smell. I was not going to take this jet into Iraq, but I can't pin down the problem. Turns out, one of my bearings in the jet was seizing up—dumping engine oil into the environmental control system—I was getting the smell through there. So I diverted to Saudi Arabia. The engine flamed out on the approach, so I pulled the engine to idle, punched off the tanks—which left me with a full internal fuel load, an ECM (Electronic Counter Measures) pod for jamming radar, and six missiles weighing a couple thousand pounds. So I was extremely heavy."

He brought it in with a dead engine and executed a perfect landing, grateful the bearing hadn't failed deep in Iraq instead of 60 miles from the Saudi border.

In fact, he says, he credits the F-16 ground crews—which also train at Luke—for the lack of losses over Iraq in the twelve years of Southern Watch. "You've got the one motor—lose that and things get real very fast."

But that wasn't the closest Rage came to dying in an F-16. He had a closer call in training. He was at Luke in a dogfight with another two-ship. They'd run the intercept—converging on the unidentified jets at just the right speed and elevation. Normally, a two-ship fight involves a precise and lethal ballet, with the flight lead taking the offense and the wingman providing support. That normally means the flight lead can concentrate on killing the enemy while the wingman concentrates on not smashing into him and keeping an eye open for a free shot or another enemy fighter. But a twisting, turning, fluid dogfight may force instant and repeated role changes—so that the wingman jumps in and takes the offensive if his partner begins to lose the struggle for position. That demands great instincts and instant reactions.

"We'd done the merge and fulfilled the training objectives—I'd seen everything I wanted to see out of my student, so I turned to kill the adversary. And I lost sight of my wingman for about five seconds, when he was still actively engaged with his adversary. I was supposed to get to a place to take a shot of opportunity. But I let my guard down for five seconds and went to take my shot. Out of the corner of my eye, I just barely saw him rolling down on me at about 200 feet. If I had not seen him in that split second, I guarantee he would have hit me. We had two of us in a gang fight against a single person—so my goal was to tie him up so that my buddy could come up behind him with the baseball bat. What should have happened is I should have waited longer, been further away—so I'm not a factor in his fight at all. Tactical error on my part."

Rage instantly rolled away from the student; narrowly averting a midair collision at 700 miles per hour combined speed.

Then he did the only thing a righteous fighter pilot can do when he completely screws up.

He went back to the squadron and told everyone—turned it into a training lesson and the perfect story for months of ridicule at the bar.

So he takes his briefings very seriously.

Dead is dead—even if it's just practice.

Moore walks into the briefing exactly on time, quiet, understated, and precise.

She operates like a stealth fighter, flying undetected through the tension swirling through the Air Force and the squadron over the nagging, dangerous, contentious issue of female fighter pilots. The shocking revelations of rape and sexual harassment at the Air Force Academy continue to spur ugly headlines. Senate hearings depict at the Academy an atmosphere rife with pressure, intimidation, and threats. Women cadets are suddenly testifying to dorm room rapes, demeaning comments, and outright threats. Some say that they reported the incidents, only to face a cover-up or pressure to retract. In some cases they persisted, but saw their complaints waved off; worse, many then faced disciplinary action—the rules forbid fraternizing and drinking, and the incidents usually involved both. Although over-the-top partying remain a prominent feature of military culture—especially among fighter pilots—it's all very officially against the rules. So some dismissable but routinely overlooked offense usually lies somewhere near the root of the reported incidents. All that has kept the growing number of women at the Air Force Academy quiet for years. They knew that if they report the hazing and sexual coercion they will have to admit to behavior that could get them kicked out. So many took it and said nothing. The Academy embraces harassment and humiliation as a cultural right of passage—usually inflicted on freshmen by upperclassmen. Sometimes, it is hard for women to define the line between the routine debasement of the Academy and sexual harassment.

Moore, a lean, long-distance runner with intense, dark eyes, close-cropped hair, a wicked but covert sense of humor, and a cool, calm distance, deals with the issue by pretending it doesn't exist. She has angular features, intelligent but guarded eyes, and faint tomboyish freckles, which invite you to underestimate her. She says she experienced no sexual harassment in the Air Force Academy—and doesn't know anyone else who did. Asked about the lurid revelations in the ongoing investigations and hearings, she shrugs and changes the topic. She does nothing to call attention to herself, but remains friendly and connected to the other punks. She's married to another pilot, who will soon start his own F-16 training at the base. She's friends with a couple of the B-coursers who were with her in IFF. She goes out drinking with them and often serves as the designated driver. She resolutely avoids any play to her gender. She doesn't swear or swagger, but she never bristles—and she laughs at all the raunchy jokes, off-color stories, and politically incorrect wisecracks that define fighter pilot culture. But she knows they're all watching. She knows that some of the IPs resent the enormous political shitstorm the sexual harassment and rape charges at the Academy have caused. Although they don't say it out loud, some of the old-line Air Force veterans are convinced that women pilots have been pushed through the system and imposed on the Air Force. They mutter darkly about political correctness. But they treat her with cool professionalism. They all know about the incident a couple of years ago when the first female fighter pilot in the Navy misjudged a carrier landing and died when she crashed into the sea. That's what happens when you pay more attention to gender than to skill, they figure. But they would never say that out loud—at least not to Moore. At least not sober in the daylight in the squadron. Those thoughts come out later, after hours—in the bar.

So Julie Moore walks the knife-edge, moving with a certain, quiet nonchalance along the honed blade. She's used to it. She knows that no matter how well she does, some will say she got a free pass. She gives no sign that she objects. So long as she flies an F-16. So long as they load the same bombs on the racks. So long as they give her a shot.

So far—she's on track.

She returns from her first solo ride for the debrief with Rage, her flight lead. Tall, buttoned-down, friendly but restrained, efficient and close-cropped, Rage is one of the few IPs who socialize with the punks—who stand on the wrong side of the pilot caste system. He never swaggers; he treats them with offhand respect. He's also one of the best pilots in the squadron, with the three-dimensional "situational awareness" that distinguishes the great pilots from the merely good.

They unbuckle their g-suits and turn in their helmets. The impression of the seal of her facemask around her nose and mouth is clear. Normally she moves with a restrained grace, thanks to her lean, taut, runner's body. Now she seems beat-up, drained by the pressure of the flight, which skirted the edge of a weather front.

Rage is typically low-key and supportive—without the slightest hint of patronizing. Like all the IPs, he's stingy with compliments, but his reputation with the punks doubles and triples the impact of even a sympathetic tease. So they run over the ground ops and he touches on some garbled communications with the crew chief that delayed takeoff.

She confesses that she was confused as to where she was supposed to line up for takeoff. She skipped an empty slot, heading for her originally designated slot. She should have taken the empty slot—procedure.

He seems to have perfect recall of the flight, tiny details that would have eluded anyone but an IP in the flurry of flying his own jet. "Your takeoff was good. Your climb out was good. Level at 6,000 feet. What heading?"

"290," she replies, referring to the compass heading.

"Any correction for wind needed?" he asks.

"I did later, but it was too late," she says, quietly acknowledging the small deviation in her course to the range that she was hoping he hadn't noticed.

"Right—so 287 would have been a good wind-corrected heading. Soon as you roll out, put a wind correction in there." They program headings into the computer during the permission planning, but have to change it in the air once the wind starts. He is teaching her now those automatic habits of flight that will save her life in combat. One of the most important things fighter pilots do is to form up with other jets, instinctively juggling the three-dimensional geometry of jets hurtling toward one another based on the blips on the radar screen on a 100-mile intersect. This ensures that you can hook up with friendly fighters—so you won't be caught alone and picked off like a sightseer in Baghdad. It also ensures that having flown the 20 or 50 or 100 miles toward an enemy fighter, you can slip up on his six o'clock for a kill.

"I'd really like to see you hit the navigational radial at about 20 [miles]. Certainly not 15 like the other day, or 18 like today. Climbing out of there was pretty good—it is nice to get to 18,000 [feet] sooner."

Now he moves to formation work—the basic skill of a fighter pilot. The F-16 was designed to shoot down other airplanes, and the fighter pilots who fly it still mostly dream about killing MiGs and becoming aces—even though they'll most likely spend any future combat stints dropping bombs. Fighter jets remain fatally vulnerable to backstabbing. In the history of dogfighting, 90 percent of fighters shot down probably never knew what hit them—blindsided from behind. So sneaking up on the enemy is the single most valuable skill for a fighter pilot. That lethal reality dominates the training of fighter pilots and the formations in which they fly. A fighter's radar works only to the front. So the two-plane formation remains the key to surviving in air-to-air battles. The flight lead devotes his attention to finding the target and searching the skies in front of the two jets for something to kill. The wingman devotes her attention to not colliding with the lead and to making sure no one sneaks up behind. Therefore, the wingman usually drops back and to the side and constantly cranks around in the seat to study the sky behind the formation for stalking enemies. That means the wingman must learn to keep formation with the flight lead automatically, so she can devote the bulk of her attention to scanning the skies for danger. It sounds simple, but keeping tight formation on another jet while flying at 500 miles per hour while looking back over your shoulder is a surprisingly difficult task—especially if your instructor sighs and shakes his head if your speed changes by 10 miles per hour or your altitude changes by 50 feet.

But Moore earns only a little head shaking today.

"The formation work was pretty good," says Rage. "Most guys have a tendency to be too wide, you had a tendency to be too close, but you were comfortable being in there, so that's good." In fact, the only thing worse than actually running into your flight lead is to hang back so far that you get lost when he starts maneuvering. Once the lead and the wingman have been split, they're both fatally vulnerable.

"Remember, if you can see the oval of the tailpipe, you're too far back. If you look back at your wingtip and my wingtip, you should be able to draw a line between them." Of course, in most combat situations, they would move much farther apart so they could cover a wider swath of sky. But here they're learning to fly tight. "A couple of times, you had a little bit of overlap. It didn't look like you were doing the throttle jockey thing," nervously speeding up and slowing down to maintain position. "You were where I expected you to be and I was where you expected me to be. So that's good. Keep that picture, it's working pretty good," he says, which passes for high praise from Rage.

They did some turns—pulled a couple of g's—all in formation.

"How did that feel?" he asks.

"I went way up high and wide outside your turn circle," she says. That's one of Moore's strengths: she's understated, calm—never defensive.

That's a prized quality in fighter pilots. The fighter pilot culture is built on ceaseless criticism—especially self-criticism. Fighter pilots screw up. Bound to happen. That's not a cardinal sin—unless it gets you killed or, worse, gets your wingman or flight lead killed. The real sin—the one that earns contempt and criticism in the bars—is not knowing when you fucked up, or—still worse—denying it when you're caught.

This flight included the first use of the acrobatic maneuvers that will eventually ensure they survive a dogfight. One is a formation barrel roll. She drifted away from him in the roll, setting her turn rate too slow. Most of the punks do that—since they last did barrel rolls in IFF in the T-38, a less-powerful training jet. Built for speed and maneuverability, the F-16 has thrust in excess of its weight, unless it's burdened by bombs. That means a pilot can turn the nose straight up and actually accelerate in a climb. "You were using the maneuver from the T-38," says Rage. "You can do a quicker maneuver now with the excess thrust."

Next they did a split—the mother's milk of jet fighters. It involves a barber pole-like weaving as the jets split apart, then rejoin, weaving back and forth. It's useful in positioning two jets in formation. It also represents the stalemate maneuver into which dogfights may degenerate, as opposing jets turn violently back and forth, each trying to outturn the other without overshooting so that they end up behind for a gun or missile shot. It's a crucial maneuver, but hell on the IP, who must violently maneuver his jet, avoid crashing into the student, and still have enough attention left over to grade the student's maneuvering. "Your starting parameters were good, but I had a little bit of a hard time grading that maneuver," says Rage. "I had too much airspeed and kind of got g'd off"—by the sharpness of the turns at a higher-than-ideal speed.

Then he suggests she give him more information about how she's doing, instead of lapsing into long radio silences—a sign that perhaps she's "fallen behind the jet."

"Don't be afraid to transmit your checks all day," says Rage. "'Doing a W-HOLD (to get weather information) that's all you've got to say. By the sheer fact you're saying you're going off the radio to check the weather, then I know what you're doing. Call a descent check over the radio, so I know you're doing a descent check. And do a gas check. I don't think that we did a descent check."

She nods, not sure whether this is a minor issue or a major one.

"Didn't we do it just before descent to 250?" he asks.

She nods. Moore will never excuse a mistake, but she's not going to supply the rope either.

"If you never say the speeds, I might not know you've completed the check," he says, which could cost her points in the grading of the flight. "You may have done it in the cockpit, but since you didn't call it out, then you get in a pissing match about whether you did it. Just leave nothing to the IP's imagination.

"Now, how about the approach?" he asks. In this case, they're practicing approaches to a dummy airfield in the desert well away from the base. They practice approaches on the dummy airfield to stay away from the busy airspace around the base and avoid flying over houses. When the base was established during World War II, it was surrounded by raw desert and scattered farms. Downtown Phoenix was 30 miles away. The Air Force could have bought land and development rights around the base for a pittance—but didn't. So now subdivisions have sprouted all around the base, although local politicians and city councils are belatedly scrambling to keep the subdivisions at bay, or at least outside of the area where the jet engines overwhelm any other sounds on the ground. But Luke now has only one narrow takeoff corridor for any jet loaded with live bombs, to be sure they don't accidentally bomb a backyard barbecue party. They also have to approach the base for landing along a few narrow corridors, designed to take them over the nearby mountains and avoid rattling the windows of the houses below. Fortunately, the looming threat of a national round of base closures has prompted belated, local efforts to buy up land around the base to protect the air space and the $1.5 billion a year Luke interjects into the local economy. Still, the houses already built have affected training and added a whole extra layer of considerations to the student's briefings.

"What was the maneuvering airspace request?" he asks, referring to the programmed approach to the airfield.

"I was really driving somewhere north."

"What was your heading?"

"I don't remember what it was," she says quietly. She's irritated at herself for not having the number instantly available. But she doesn't stammer or hesitate—just furrows her brow in concentration. "It was supposed to be . . . " She pauses again, trying to remember even that number.

"If you go in at 070," he says smoothly, noting the hesitation and then rescuing her from it without confrontation, "you just hit the steerpoint. You don't need maneuvering airspace," to correct her approach at the last minute. "How was your initial bank?" he asks, referring to her turn into the final approach.

"I went right to 30 degrees."

"That degree of turn was not in your initial brief, but not wrong. Long as you're in the parameters, you're OK. How were the winds?"

"Thirty-five knots."

"Undershooting or overshooting winds? Did it bite you?"

"Yeah," concedes Moore, with a small smile. Obviously, he noticed everything. Every damn thing. It's almost comforting. For one thing, she can just assume he noticed everything and not wonder what to confess. But it also means he's somewhere out in front of even her jet. So he's not going to let her fly into the ground or bomb the city hall. That's good— right?

"How can you fix that?" he asks patiently about the crosswinds on the approach. "Here's what you do: if you find yourself in 30 degrees of bank and you see that large track around the high school, just line up and fly the inside part of the track," he says, giving her the landmarks on the ground to hit to perfect her approach. "Now, how did the descent go? Anything different today?"

"I didn't know what to do about those clouds," she says, referring to a billow of clouds in the way of the approach. Officially, students aren't supposed to fly into clouds—too much chance the poor, addled, radar-challenged, stick-fisted dolts will slam into somebody when they go blind in the cloud. "So I leveled out at 9,500 feet."

"What I would recommend," says Rage, "is pull back the throttle for about five seconds, get the energy level back down—go 300 knots from the get-go and 7 degrees nose down, so everything starts to get a little rushed. If you go five seconds of throttle and 10 degrees nose low, that'll decrease some of my energy. I would just tell the tower you deviated for weather. Now we overshot the turn a little—probably because we were worried about the weather—so we ended up overshooting by about half a mile," when lining up on the runway, which puts them potentially over some of those backyard barbecues. "If it's a gross deviation and you're going to break off the approach, then I'd tell them that. But you were still within the protected airspace of the approach. If you have to violate an altitude restriction, tell them."

"And that's kosher?" says Moore, sounding relieved. The students live under the pressure of perfection, with every deviation noted and scribbled on some score sheet. After a while, they can barely remember which niggling details will kill them or bust a ride. "They'll say OK?"

"Just let them know. You looked pretty good from my jet. You got up to 170 knots a couple of times and you were making positive corrections to get back to 162. Is this the one you made a late change to 160?"

"Hmm," she says. She pauses. "Yes."

"Now you have to look at that airspeed and fly the airspeed, because that's what you said you were going to fly in the prebrief," he says. "You got up to 260, then down to 240, then pulled power back."

"I kind of overshot, corrected back, too big a correction, stabilized. Got there in the endgame, but I didn't like it."

"How was your pitch," he asks. "High or low?"

"Low?" she guesses, wondering whether it's even possible to land the damn jet without getting dissected into a pulpy mass of dumb mistakes she didn't even know she was making.

"High," he says. "Five degrees high. We were basically above the glide path and storming down to it—passing through it and leveling out. It just seemed more uneven than it needed to be. Did you see how much we got below the glide path?"

"No," she says, feeling flattened. She couldn't even get her mistakes right.

"About 5 degrees. Not sure how you do that. I like to use the bars a little bit. Get those things lined up and then look in the HUD. Set the precision glide path at what?"

"Two and a half degrees," she says from memory.

"Two and a half degrees," he repeats approvingly. That's something.

"I felt like I was fighting getting lined up on the runway," she says. "Was that because my turn was too soon?"

"It was a little early. Remember what I tell you to do when we get to here—roll out. Roll out. Flying this nice straight line depletes that energy. I'm looking at this aim point and I want this to be a 10 or 15 degrees nose low as I roll out. Take a good long time on final and make a nice smooth transition—pop the boards a little bit. I thought that was real nice. Roll out for a couple of potatoes [seconds], so you can roll right back out. I was a little bit shallower, [flying off her wing], a little more comfortable—it looked to me like you were a little steep—that's why I said, 'Hey, be careful.' Now, how was the actual landing?"

"I bounced."

"I could tell you bounced a little bit," he said, sounding friendly but glad she'd started more easily confessing her difficulties. "But you couldn't tell if it was a 10-foot bounce or a 1-foot bounce."

"The wind," offers Moore in explanation.

"Maybe it was a little squirrelly. Anything for the taxi back?" he asks, meaning the taxi to the hangar area.

She looks at him quizzically.

"You didn't wait for me—you don't have to wait for me."

"Did I miss them changing me over to tower?" This concerns which controller would tell her where to go once she got on the ground.

"Probably not. If there's traffic out there you're concerned with, they'll keep you on longer. If you're feeling like you need to switch over, ask them. I was just asking because I was switching frequency trying to talk to everyone."

"I thought you were giving me a hint, like I'd missed something."

"Anything else you noticed?" asks Rage, inviting her to confess additional sins.

"Coming back, the clouds were right at 6,500 feet. I wasn't really holding altitude—I was just dodging them"—changing altitude to avoid violating the training rule to stay out of clouds.

Rage nods. "I'd error low—there are airliners above 8,000 feet—so I don't want to be at 8,000 and look at this cloud and see it's 9,000—and you can't go over it. Just go down below the clouds."

"You can go below 6,000 and it won't be an issue?" she asks.

"Just tell the controller you're going low for weather," he says. The ceaseless communications, the plans, backup plans, and alternative backup plans seem tedious and obsessive. In fact, that discipline remains essential to combat and tactics. In combat, the F-16s will share the sky with hundreds of other planes. Battle planners juggle all the jets. Each battle unit flies at precise times and altitudes. That prevents them from smashing into one another—especially at night. It also means that the air controllers in the AWACS radar planes that control the battle, or the antiaircraft missile batteries on the ground, won't mistake a wandering flight on the wrong path for enemy fighters. It decreases the chance that a friendly fighter jet will lock you up and kill you. The complexity of a large-scale air battle is astonishing, bewildering, and potentially deadly. Gaps in communication and discipline frequently prove lethal. That's why F-15s shot down two helicopters full of U.S. soldiers in Iraq. So while Moore's debrief may seem a piling-on of innumerable, trivial details, it's really an attempt to instill the routine attention to detail that will determine whether she outlives her military career.

7

DRAGGED BEHIND THE JET

LIEUTENANT COLONEL TOM HOGAN—"AWOL"—looks out his cockpit at Greg Newlin's jet and ever so slightly shakes his head. Although they're close enough, Newlin doesn't see the gesture. He'd have to be looking slightly back over his shoulder, he'd have to be paying attention, he'd have to be ahead of the jet. In which case AWOL wouldn't have been shaking his head.

The jets fly in breathtaking formation. Newlin looks every inch the lethal fighter ace, helmeted and goggled, perched in the bubble canopy of the F-16, which sits in the very tip of the jet, nothing but blue sky all around. Up in the cockpit of an F-16, you can hardly tell there's a jet beneath you, because you're perched on the tip of the spear, just before the fuselage tapers to that single point. The desert sprawls all the way to the perfectly etched horizon 25,000 feet below, a masterpiece of design in browns and blues.

But AWOL notes that all of a sudden he's closer to Newlin, so he taps the throttle and slows down by 30 knots to maintain his distance. He does it effortlessly, with barely a glance at his airspeed indicator. A moment later, Newlin speeds up suddenly and overshoots, gaining 60 knots before settling back again to the original, briefed speed.

AWOL makes a mental note.

Newlin's definitely behind the jet—has been all day. He came to the briefing without all the right preflight checklist materials. He set his radio to the wrong frequency on the ground. He bolted into the air on takeoff and didn't slow down to wait for the rejoin. And now he can't get his airspeed right. Obviously, he is in that jet over there messing with the radio, switching the navigational displays in the HUD, trying to get the headings right to the preprogrammed navigation points. So obviously, he's used up all his brain bytes. He doesn't have anything left over to keep track of his airspeed.

AWOL sighs. This is shaping up as a busted ride.

It feels faintly like a personal failure. Tall, angular, genial, and soft-spoken, AWOL has more hours in the air than almost anyone else in the squadron, except maybe Doughboy. He has an interesting, expressive, thoughtful face, like the complicated and funny sidekick in an action flick. He's got a long, stretched-out face, tousled sandy blond hair, pale, intelligent, penetrating eyes. You'd never peg him for an Air Force colonel; he lacks that crisp sense of command—the ability to dominate any room he enters. But once you notice him, he holds your attention with his off-kilter good looks, easy charm, dark, quick intelligence. He had a full combat career in a variety of planes before retiring from active duty and taking a spot in the Reserves. Now he's an instructor at Luke, bringing his long career flying jets to bear on helping kids like Newlin chew gum and watch their airspeed at the same time. Newlin's still on CAP (Commander's Awareness Program, meaning he flies only with AWOL and a couple other IPs).

AWOL was sure he could settle Newlin down and make a fighter pilot of him—the kid is so eager, so conscientious. But he's freaking himself out. If Newlin can just settle down and stop trying to think his way through every single thing he's doing for fear of making a mistake, then maybe he'll quit making so damn many mistakes.

Besides, Hogan identifies with Newlin.

After all, Hogan, forty, doesn't really fit in with the hard-jamming, semi-swaggering fighter jocks among whom he has spent his career. He is the product of "white bread suburbia." His dad, a doctor, was drafted and sent to Vietnam for a year, where he spent his time trying desperately to keep frightened American boys alive. His uncle was a marine who saw combat in Vietnam. But his brother and three sisters all went into normal stuff, not the military. One brother is a commercial artist, the other a school psychologist. His mom's a nurse who quit to raise her passel of kids, but now does volunteer work.

So he can't really account for his lifelong obsession with flying. He remembers the day he decided to be a pilot—that day in 1968 as he watched the Apollo astronauts cavorting on the moon. After watching them on TV, AWOL went outside and stared up at the sky, lost in curiosity and wonder. He wanted to become an astronaut until the space program abandoned exploration in favor of aimless shuttle flights.

By then he'd seen his first F-16 take off—a big, gaudy red, white, and blue jet at an air show. He fell violently in love and spent the next ten years warping his life to get a chance to fly the Viper. His parents hoped he'd be a doctor and get a good Notre Dame education. Instead, he announced his intention to go to the Air Force Academy. "My mom never bought off on any of this flying stuff—she was like 'Oh God, what's he doing now?' "

But AWOL was determined to fly—even if it meant joining the Air Force and surviving the Academy. "I was real exited about going right up to the moment I showed up—and then I thought, 'Uh-oh, what was I thinking?' You get someone saying they really enjoyed the Air Force Academy, they're nuts. On the whole, everyone was miserable there."

He graduated and started pilot training. He ended up as a T-37 instructor for three years, racking up 1,500 hours in the air. "That was the best job I ever had," he says—in contrast with many T-37 instructors who see their assignment as a kind of purgatory. "They call it the Tweet—just a bare-bones airplane—the engine's old and noisy and chews up gas. The instrument cluster is a human-factors disaster area. There's no automation on the flight control. It's brutal in turns—I had two students g-lock (pass out in a high-g turn) on me. But it's the perfect plane for what it's supposed to do. And it's where I learned how to teach. Teaching is a hell of a lot harder than I ever thought it was going to be. You know how to fly the airplane, but you don't know how to teach it. I didn't know anything about people. Sometimes people don't learn things on the first try."

After three years, he was assigned to fly F-111 fighter-bombers, to his bitter disappointment. The first fighter with a turbofan and ground-following radar, it was rushed into service at the tail end of Vietnam with initially disastrous results. The last-minute design compromises soon started killing pilots. The swept-wing design seemed to offer both speed and maneuverability, with a change in wing configuration. But in practice the wings caused endless mechanical difficulties. It was a perfect example of the politicized, design incoherence that has plagued many aircraft designs. Designers tried to make the F-111 do everything, including land on aircraft carriers, but then the Navy refused to buy it and the Air Force got stuck with it. "It was a big mishmash," says AWOL. "We've never gotten out of that. We always end up saying, 'So let's make it do everything.' "

By the time AWOL started flying the EF-111 in 1989, twenty years of fiddling and a slew of pilot deaths had stomped out most of the bugs. It would fly over the treetops for long distances, drop its bombs, and make it home—although it couldn't dogfight worth a damn. It was useful for long-range bombing missions if you didn't have to worry about enemy fighters.

When the Gulf War broke out, AWOL was flying an EF-111 outfitted with radar-jamming equipment, which in conjunction with Doughboy's similarly aging F-4s could knock out the antiaircraft defenses ahead of the bombers. "Desert Storm, that was a good war," he recalls with satisfaction. He flew thirty-three combat missions.

On the first night, a squadron of combat-green pilots faced the first major air war since Vietnam. The Air Force had fought a couple of small-scale engagements—like the strike on Libya and the invasion of Panama. But Iraq had a fully developed, integrated air defense.

"The Intel officer comes out for the briefing on that first night and says 'We expect and accept one-in-five losses tonight from this wing to get this mission done,' " recalls AWOL. They were supposed to fly into Baghdad and hit the Republican National Guard armories where intelligence suggested they might have stored chemical munitions. "Back then, we didn't have maps—they were like 1950s and '60s maps with a copyright by the Iraqi army. We had all kinds of grids and all kinds of coordinates."

The EF-111s had the same kind of job as the Wild Weasels: they went in first to blind the radars of the SAM operators. When they picked up the tracking signal of the central warning radars, they could broadcast a jamming signal on the same frequency. But they'd be the first ones in, trying to hobble the Iraqi radars—which would presumably at least see them coming. That accounted for the high expected casualty rate. They worked with the Weasels, which had air-to-ground missiles. "We were supposed to go in there and blind the early warning radars, so the operator would say, 'I can't see what's going on,' So then the SAM operator turns on his tracking radar and the Weasel sees that and they know what to hit."

The EF-111 pilots all heard the prediction that one in five of them would not come back, but they mostly ignored it. "Who knows why Intel comes up with the numbers they do. I remember listening to this and going, I don't know about anyone else, but I'm coming back. We're aware we're going into Bad Guy Land—but one in five? Come on. Our wing commander—who was not a tremendously well-liked guy—gave us one of the best going-away speeches I ever heard. He had been to Vietnam. He said, 'Here's what's going to get you—you're going to run out of gas or you run into the ground—that's what's going to kill you tonight. The chance of you getting shot at by somebody is remote, so just don't screw up. If you don't screw up, you're coming home tonight.' "

Still, that "one in five" number stuck with them as they headed for the jets.

They hurtled in low—1,000 feet—roaring over the suburbs of East Baghdad. "I'm watching people under the streetlamps thinking, 'Wow, this is going to be pretty loud.' " Almost immediately, the sky lit up with antiaircraft fire. "Like a big orange water weenie," says AWOL. "So you just kind of ride it out and go 'OK.' "

The F-117s—the stealth fighter-bomber—went in just ahead of the EF-111s. Designed to absorb radar beams or deflect them away at an unreadable angle, the F-117 bombers went after the antiaircraft network of command centers and radars. Operating at night so they remain all but invisible, the F-117s represent the next generation of military technology—and the Air Force urge to buy the latest technology even at ruinous per-plane costs, the urge the F-16 so briefly countered. But in this case, the horrendously expensive technology helped derange the Iraqi air defenses.

"It was strange walking out to the jets. The war's not on yet, but we've got our sidearms on and the blood chits—little notes in Arabic that say 'I'm an American soldier—I know I'm in your country, but if you return me safely we'll take care of you.' And I'm thinking, 'God, we're really going into it tonight.' And all I want is for the plane to work, thinking 'Oh God, don't let me sit this out. Don't make me sit this one out and watch it on TV.' "

They flew into the heart of the Iraqi air defenses.

Jammed every signal that came on the air.

Watched the city explode into pillars of fire.

And didn't lose a single EF-111.

As near as he could tell, none of the SAM operators ever got a lock on him. "There were guys that came back every single night, saying 'Oh, I evaded this, oh, this happened.' Like fish stories. I'm either really lucky or I'm oblivious or they were just having really bad luck. There was a lot of triple-A [fire from antiaircraft guns], but they didn't know where I was. They were afraid to even turn on their radars. Sometimes I'd fly over an antiaircraft site and they'd be spraying all over the sky. They were definitely trying to get me. They could hear me up there. But it wasn't like they were tracking me through the sky. They were just throwing up everything they had, hoping to get lucky."

On that first night in 1991, the EF-111s loitered around the targets all night and came out after the last bomber had turned around. "We came off the low level back into Saudi Arabia—we were miles behind the rest of the formation. But the base was fogged in, so we went back to the tanker—waiting for the fog to clear off. It turned into a food fight trying to get down. We had jets landing all over the place. Everyone's screaming into their radios, which kind of freaks you out first time you hear it. Thing is, sometimes you have to scream if you're going to be heard over everything else. But most of it isn't about your flight, so you don't know what the hell's going on."

The chaos on the radio was so bewildering that initially on that first night, AWOL thought no one had hit his target. "So it's an hour's drive home back to the base, and I'm going, 'I think we got our ass kicked tonight.' We didn't realize until later it was just a complete walkover. Turns out, all those 'unsuccessful' calls were because the first guy in blew up the target. So your average guy watching CNN in his armchair in Cleveland knew more about the war than we did."

AWOL is among the last planes to land on the first night. "The ground crew comes out, and they've been watching it all on television, and they're all fired up."

AWOL climbs out of his jet and turns to the crew chief. "How's the war going?" he asks anxiously.

"It's a walkover," grins the chief.

"How many jets did we lose?" asks AWOL.

"None."

"None? What do you mean? How about the bombers?"

"Nope. Nobody."

"Everybody is back? We were supposed to lose one in five."

He walks across the desert runway, dawn coloring the sky. "Suddenly you realize that you've lived through it and it's the morning of the night you weren't supposed to survive, and now you can't stop talking. You're yakking at 100 miles an hour, because now you're a combat veteran. The day shifters are waking up and they're going 'Ooohhh,' and now you can't shut up so your commanders are saying, 'Hey, guys, out of here. Get breakfast.' I didn't sleep a wink the next night. We went in again at low altitude, and oh God, I was tired."

But soon, bombing Baghdad settles into a task-saturated routine. "The missions would get exciting every now and then. One time coming back in bad weather our squawk"—which broadcasts their identity to other friendly planes—"was broken so hard that the warning light saying it's broken is broken. This F-15 comes up behind us. I'm telling the AWACS, 'I've got an F-15 parked at my six, tell him to go away.' Meanwhile, I'm trying to look friendly—I'm sure as hell not going to try to evade this guy. But the AWACS can't find me, which means they can't tell the F-15 that it's me. At same time, the F-15 is talking to the same AWACS asking 'Who is this guy?' But the Eagle pilot is talking to some guy at the other end of the plane, and the AWACS guys aren't talking to each other. I look back over and this big black Eagle joins up on my wing and shines a light on my tail. I'm saying, I don't believe this; we're getting visually identified. So then he turns on all his lights, breaks away. So we go on the secure channel and just chew the AWACS a new one."

Four years later, another F-15 pilot didn't go to quite such lengths to identify his target when two Blackhawk helicopters on Iraqi Southern Watch, out of contact with the AWACS plane, failed to respond to his hail. The Eagle pilot shot down the two helicopters, killing ten—mostly Special Forces. "The only reason I didn't get shot down that night was that F-15 guy had enough discipline to hold his fire. Those Blackhawk guys weren't given the same treatment—and they ended up dead."

His squadron flew hundreds of sorties, but lost only one plane. "We never knew what happened. I knew him really well. He'd been just about ready to retire when the war broke out, so he stayed in. It was strange. He just disappeared. It's like when a guy gets moved from the night shift to the day schedule and you just don't see him anymore. Life just kind of went on. But the families, back in England and in the States, were very upset. The further you got away from the incident, the harder it was on the people involved. Now it seems like it's so long since I was that person, I don't even know why we did the things we did back then." The Air Force never did determine what happened to the missing jet.

But AWOL remembers their names—their faces. Doug Bradt. Paul Eichenlaub.

"Truth is, from the time we got into theater, all anyone wanted to do was get out of Saudi Arabia. I was glad I was there. But I was glad when I left too."

After the crushing victory, including the astonishing, nearly unopposed slaughter of the fleeing Iraqi army by the most accurate air strikes in history, the Air Force decided to phase out the aging F-111s. The targeting pods, smart bombs, vast tanker fleet, and increasingly sophisticated air-to-air missiles had made the F-16 as flexible as the F-111, without its ungainly trade-offs.

AWOL used every bureaucratic trick he could think of to get shifted to Vipers—the dream of his youth. "I'm volunteering for test pilot school, for Korea, for anything that would get me an F-16. And they're saying, 'You're an F-111 guy. You're nothing. You're scum.' So finally they're saying, 'You can get F-16s and go to Korea—but then after that it's a desk job.' And I jump at it."

Despite more than 2,000 hours in the air, the F-16 humbled him. "I come over here and got my ass handed to me. I didn't bust any rides, but why I didn't, I don't know. Thing about the Air Force, you keep getting recycled into cluelessness about every eighteen months."

That memory—that humility—makes him a great instructor pilot now, and gives him deep sympathy for Newlin. On the other hand, the memory of the chaos on the radio and the lifesaving discipline of the Eagle pilot reminds him of the consequences of sending an unprepared Viper pilot out into the world.

After retooling at Luke, AWOL headed to Korea—which mostly consisted of flying in bad weather. His life revolved around trying somehow to make flying a Viper as natural as flying an EF-111 had been. Then he rotated to Japan, where "everybody was miserable." Although the facilities were good, the people friendly, and the skies wide open, the wing commander ran them into the ground and punished any hint of typical fighter pilot rowdiness. Pilots will tell you, the attitude of the wing commander makes a huge difference. If they get a commander who understands you've got to "Let fighter pilots be fighter pilots," it's a gas. Get a tight ass and it's misery. "They'd had a drinking problem on the base, and the collateral damage hit the whole wing. The commander spread his minions all over the place, and it was like cancer invading the body. I was in Japan for four years, and you can still see the claw marks across the Pacific when I left."

He left the Air Force as a lieutenant colonel after seventeen years to take an airline job. But he couldn't give up the Viper, so he enlisted in the Reserves. Now attached to a Reserve squadron based at Luke, he's also a part-time instructor for the Emerald Knights.

He loves working with the young pilots, but insists he has never wallowed in the "glory" of being a fighter pilot. "I remember when we got home from Desert Storm we had a big parade in front of the President—and for three days I was cool. Never been cool in my life. Then they shipped me off to Turkey. I think that whole Hollywood fighter pilot thing works for some guys, but not for me. I wouldn't know if a woman was throwing herself at me unless she came up and held a sign in front of my face. Whatever I know about people I learned as a T-37 instructor. Mostly, I know machines. Put me in the cockpit and I'll program the whole damn thing. But send me off to schmooze and I'll say something sarcastic and stick my foot way up into my mouth with half a twist."

All the while—through the wars and the bureaucracy and the broken marriages and the blunted hopes—the flying has sustained him. "I remember this night—alone in a Viper, taking off from Japan. I watch the sun set over on this side and then the moonrise on the other side, coming up out of the Sea of Japan—all red. And so I'm flying into the dark, with the last light on the volcanoes in Japan with their snowcaps, and this enormous comet comes into view—like a quarter of the sky. And nobody else on earth has this view. You couldn't even take a picture of it—you just had to experience it."

On 9/11, he was flying an East Coast route in an airliner that put him in the air at the same time as the three hijacked airliners. Three weeks later, on his first flight since the attack, he could hear the silence on the airwaves—the absence of that routine check-in from United 173.

"Every time you crash an airplane," he says, "its number gets retired. So all these ghosts were around me. We took off and got up to 18,000 feet and didn't say a thing to each other for the next hour and a half."

So all of that—the columns of smoke from the World Trade Center, the silence on the radio, the war, the Eagle pilot that didn't kill him—all that means he's probably going to have to bust Newlin on this ride, much as he wants to make the kid into a no-kidding Viper pilot.

Then on the approach to the runway, Newlin clinches it.

At Luke you have to fly a carefully selected path to the runway that brings you in around a range of mountains to avoid the encroaching subdivisions below. AWOL and Newlin come around in a big, wide turn to line up with the runway. Newlin lines up all right, but he's tunnel-visioned on the end of that runway. He doesn't notice that Doughboy and Perkins have come in from another direction and they're also lining up on the runway. Except they're making a straight-in approach as Newlin comes off the turn. AWOL's watching them carefully—he's had them on his radar for ten minutes and heard them talking to the tower. A veteran pilot tracks every goddamned mockingbird on the runway approach, just as a motorcycle rider keeps track of semis and minivans. But Newlin seems oblivious. Doughboy has settled in for his approach, when Newlin comes off the perch and turns right in front of him. Doughboy can't believe it. Fucking punks. But he was also watching Newlin, like you watch a lady on a cell phone in the fast lane, so Doughboy pulls up out of the pattern to go around again, trailing the faintly confused Igor on his wing.

AWOL shakes his head.

Now that's definitely a busted ride.

8

⸙

MISSING THEIR WAR

LIEUTENANT COLONEL JOHN SIEVERLING, "OLD MAN," the squadron commander, glances up at the television set as he passes through the squadron's bar and poolroom. President Bush's deadline has expired and FOX News is fulminating about the onset of the second Iraq war. Everyone figures the U.S. will start bombing the hell out of Iraq tonight—maybe tomorrow. Old Man forces himself to look away.

That's his war. HIS war.

He's going to miss it.

Best not to think about it.

He continues through the room to get ready for the upcoming pilots meeting. He doesn't look like a fighter pilot. He looks like an accountant—a geek. He's tall, balding, thin-featured, with pale blue eyes and glasses. Glasses, for Christ's sake. He doesn't act like a fighter pilot either. He's mild, subtle, polite. He's like a computer nerd mistakenly picked for the football team—so he sits around making coded messages from jersey numbers of the big bone-crunchers sitting on the bench. But then, if you go by appearances you're going to get killed. That's one of the lessons fighter pilots learn. Stealth. Deception. The joys of a backstab. So Old Man doesn't mind at all if you underestimate him. He doesn't have to preen. He's got the patch and the solid respect of every fighter jock in the

squadron. He's a Weapons School graduate, with the situational awareness of a psychic on hallucinogens.

His dad, a civilian flight instructor, taught him to fly. His dad
would pile up phone books so his boy could reach the stick. He got his
pilot's license on his sixteenth birthday and discovered he had a three-
dimensional brain perfect for flying—like Einstein must have felt
when he discovered math. His family didn't have much money, so he
knew he needed scholarships to go to college. He applied to the Air Force
Academy—which, after all, is free. He sailed through, aced pilot training,
chose the F-16—and spent the next nineteen years helplessly in love with it.

He started his career in the throes of the Cold War and trained to fight
the Russians, while helping out the fledgling air forces of allies like Iraq.
It's a strange world out there, especially from the cockpit.

He missed the first Gulf War while working a tour as an IP at Luke.
"That was a little bit hard to take," he recalls. He'd sit in the squadron
bar and stare up at the TV watching Desert Storm, where the F-16
squadron he had just left was obliterating the fleeing Iraqi army on the
"highway of death," absolutely eating his liver—like Prometheus waiting
for the vultures of morning chained to the goddamned rock.

Now here he is—Gulf War II—commanding a bunch of liver-eating
IPs, watching the tube.

"You can cut the frustration with a knife—the guys just want to be
there. It's like you've been a fireman for years and years, and you leave to
get some advanced training, and the morning you leave they have a four-
alarm fire. It's not that you want to kill people. I don't think you'll find a
fighter pilot who enjoys the lethal aspects of his job. But if it has to be
done, we want to be the ones to do it—it's like any career field. The cop
who checks parking meters won't get an audience at the bar. The one who
was in the shootout with the robber will. So you want to be there."

His flawless instincts in the air and his intense but low-key perfec-
tionism earned him a slot at Weapons School—reserved for the top 5
percent of pilots. He did so well at that, they asked him to become a
Weapons School instructor. Him. The geek accountant. Doesn't image
count for anything anymore? Is it all sheer ability? Strange.

He says great instructors mostly need to listen—and communicate. "I
know guys who are great aviators—but because of their demeanor, they
just turn people off—or they aren't able to capture how that student

learns. You have to teach at the student's level. I'll ask a student, What did you major in? He says, outdoor recreation. So I'm going to try to think about pictures, not numbers."

Anybody can fly the F-16. The computer keeps you from doing anything grossly stupid, like stalling. That's fortunate, because the designers built in so much maneuverability that the jet always flies on the edge of spinning out of control. Only the computer's unceasing adjustment of the flaps keeps it stable. "We can solo you in six flights. But we're not training F-16 pilots; we're training single-seat, single-engine fighter pilots who fly F-16s. That's an attitude. A single-engine fighter pilot's got three things. One, he's a perfectionist, because there's only one engine. When the engine starts to cough, you can't say, excuse me, can you get out the checklist for me. Second, he's aggressive—but not to the point of obnoxious. If there's a task to be done, a fighter pilot wants to do that task. They want to be the first on the flying schedule if you're going into Bad Guy Land—and they're frustrated if they're here and their buddies are deployed. Not dangerous. Not out of control. But they're going to make things happen. The last thing, after being a perfectionist and being aggressive, is mutual support—from the time they wake up in the morning to the time they go to bed. If Lieutenant Newlin starts struggling, another student's going to help him out with his mission planning. If they're in the officers club and one of them has had too much to drink and he's about to make a fool out of himself in front of the wing commander—his buddy is going to grab him and throw him in the trunk and take him home."

He tells himself this, reminding himself of the importance of turning pups into attack dogs, so that he won't think about the vultures coming for his liver once the bombs start falling in Iraq—without him.

He stops to talk to Lieutenant Colonel Bob Egan—"Festus"—his second in command for the squadron. Nicknamed for the sidekick in *Gunsmoke*, Egan's a disciplined, mild-featured, buttoned-down, tempered-steel tough man. He doesn't preen or boast, but he exudes command. He's the guy who gets everyone to lean forward and stop talking by lowering his voice.

About two years ago, he lost an engine over Luke's sprawling desert gunnery range. One minute he was flying along happily at 500 feet and 500 knots, in his 3,600th hour in the air—which had to that point cost the taxpayers about $18 million. The plane was loaded with bombs and packed with 11,000 pounds of explosive fuel.

Then something went violently wrong with his F-16. "It was like cruising along on the freeway and then turning off on a dirt road at 70 miles an hour," says Egan, whose seventeen-year Air Force career has included dodging SAMs over Belgrade. Suddenly, the 29,000 pounds of thrust blasting out the back of his jet seemed devoted to shaking apart the arrow-sleek jet.

With the cockpit shaking so violently he can't read the displays and the ground a fraction of one wrong move away, Festus reacts instantly. He pulls back smoothly on the control stick, signaling the jet's computer to tilt the spear-point nose up 30 degrees, just as the ravenous engine dies in a great gout of flame.

But Festus doesn't know he's on fire. "I thought the engine compressor had stalled—sucked in a bird maybe, or a non-uniform airflow. I thought it was a problem I could solve."

Besides, he can't bail out yet—since blasting out of the cockpit at 650 miles per hour in the thick air at 500 feet would break most of his bones.

The dying F-16 turns its rapier tip to the heavens and on sheer momentum rises to 6,800 feet in ten seconds and slows to 230 miles per hour. By now the emergency electrical power has kicked in and Egan can hear the excited warnings of his wingman, a Japanese exchange instructor pilot.

As soon as Egan hears that 50-foot-long jets of flame are blasting out his back end, he pulls the big, rubber-coated, yellow-handled ejection seat lever. "I pulled the handle, and I remember thinking, 'Why am I not getting out of this airplane?' I looked back down at the handle and suddenly I'm out," says Festus, a calm, crisp, understated pilot whose affability conceals iron discipline and drive. His thinning hair, mild eyes, and contained manner belie his lethal reflexes and consuming passion for flying.

Blasting outward in the ejection seat an instant after explosive bolts blow away the canopy, Festus is immediately seized by howling winds. Three seconds later the parachute pops open, the seat falls away, and a rubber raft that doubles as a survival shelter tumbles out of the survival pack and inflates beneath his feet.

"There's this violent rush of wind—like a hurricane—until you're in the chute—then you're coming down and it's completely quiet. I never did see what happened to the plane," says Egan.

The seven-minute drift to the ground is the worst.

"It seemed like an eternity. I'm afraid of heights," says Festus, one of the most experienced F-16 pilots in the world and the operations officer for the Emerald Knights training squadron.

That was one of twenty-two crashes at Luke in the past decade. Six were due to pilot error—including the death of a veteran colonel who became disoriented in a high-speed, low-altitude maneuver and flew into the ground. One was the result of a turkey vulture flying into the air intake. The rest stemmed from mechanical failures in the aging jets, including a recent rash triggered by microscopic cracks in the superheated afterburner section. Most crashes took place in the 2.7-million-acre Barry M. Goldwater Gunnery Range some 60 miles south of Luke, which provides a precious empty space for both bombing runs and the demanding and dangerous maneuvers needed to train a Viper pilot.

Festus drifts to earth, spreads out his chute as a marker and waits ninety minutes for the arrival of a U.S. Custom's Service helicopter, second-guessing himself and looking over his substantial new collection of bruises. "It was ninety minutes of quiet time in 115 degrees,'" says Festus ruefully. "The only thing pleasant about it was being alive. Coming back without your airplane is kind of embarrassing."

He is back at the job the next morning, although "I can no longer say that I've had as many landings as takeoffs," says Festus, one of those off-hand fighter jock jokes that define this tight, disciplined, headlong, gung-ho brotherhood. Like most of the pilots in the squadron, he can't remember when he didn't yearn to fly. His dad spent twenty years as a enlisted communication specialist on EC135s, waiting for the order to launch doomsday. His father met his mother in the ashes of Berlin after World War II. Festus was born on an airbase in Spain and grew up on an airbase in Nebraska. His family was steeped in the military values of service and discipline. Moreover, his German mothers' experience during the war in Germany made their impression, underscoring both the need to control the military and the devastating consequences of defeat and conquest. His sister and brother each spent six years in the Navy, and another brother spent four years in the Air Force. Festus graduated from college with a degree in civil engineering and designed a couple of bridges and overpasses before yielding to the dream that had gnawed on him all his life.

He promised his future to the Air Force, excelled in his classes, and lusted for a fighter pilot slot. On his first training flight in a two-seater

T-37, they were flying straight and level on the way back to the airfield when Festus abruptly got airsick. "I remember feeling extremely bad about doing that," recalls Festus. "I could have washed out. But the thing was when we got on the ground, the IP said 'Bob, you don't have any worries.' The next day I was flying the airplane."

He's been addicted to flying and the F-16 ever since. "It's the freedom," Festus muses. "When I'm flying in an airplane, the world comes into focus. It's easy to shed the toils behind here on earth. I'm in control of something. I've yet to fly a perfect mission, but I'm trying every day. It's addictive. It's the Porsche you strap on for that long, winding road on a Saturday afternoon. You can't live without it. Love is not too strong a word. It's my mistress—its looks, its capability. It's like sitting on the tip of an arrow."

He has rotated from base to base, like all F-16 pilots, including stints in South Carolina, Germany, and Korea, a frontline posting that afflicts almost all F-16 pilots and crews and requires a year away from their families. When the Gulf War struck, Egan was stuck training pilots in the states. "I had the lowest feeling in my gut, because I wanted to be there. I remember my mother-in-law asked, 'Why are you upset?' And I basically ripped her head off. I said 'I should be there.' It's not that we're warmongers, but it's what we're trained to do."

He joined up for the joy of flying, but understands that he's in the death business. "You don't want to die for your country—but you do want to make sure the other guy dies for his country. Our business is harsh. When the President says you have to go to war—you're going to make people die. We're victims of our own success, so the public thinks we can fight a clean war. War is not clean—there's no chivalry, no glamour. The use of the military should be the absolute last resort, but when you decide to use it, don't limit it."

So when a friend up the chain of command offers to help get Festus a slot in the Air Force deployment to cover the efforts of American and UN troops to halt Bosnia's slide into genocide, he instantly accepts. "I didn't call my wife—I just said yes. She saw what it did to me to miss the last one."

Soon Egan was flying combat missions from a base in Italy, assigned to draw the fire of SAM missile sites on the ground and knock them out.

On his first mission of a 100-day stint, the Serbian missiles nearly get him.

Hal, his computer, spots the launch immediately, and Betty's soft, insistent, computer-generated voice whispers to him in his tight-fitted helmet. Immediately, Festus flings his jet into a series of maneuvers to break the missile's target lock, and blasts radar-confusing chaff out the back of the Viper. Fortunately, the Serbs had only older versions of the Soviet SAMs and the first missile lost its lock. But he has now shed speed and altitude, which makes him an easier target for the second missile. Calling on the now-instinctual, exhaustively rehearsed skills of his 3,600 air hours and seventeen years, Egan twists and dodges and rolls. Finally, the missile explodes nearby—an offset flare of death.

"I got back, kissed the ground, shook the hand of the crew chief and spent about half an hour walking around the plane looking for holes. When you get down after getting shot at, it's a sensation you never forget. It changes you. It changed how I viewed certain things, changed the way I fly, the way I teach. And you try to impart that to the students. So now I will put them under as much stress as required to make them do their best," he says quietly.

So you wouldn't think that he would be suffering as much as Old Man in missing this war. He's had his war. He's nearing retirement—or a graceful ascent to a big-brass desk job. He's even bailed out. He doesn't need to prove anything. Still, he makes a conscious effort not to stop and watch the TV, not to go out there in his mind like a radar contact at the edge of your range—where he yearns to be.

Besides, he has to get ready for the pilots meeting.

And figure out how to get these kids on track.

Already the busted rides are piling up—and they're still in the basic transition stage. The program lists busts in each stage and overall. Quattlebaum busted a ride—mostly little stuff, like failing to keep track of his speed and altitude when flying formation, or making bad radio calls. Newlin's already got two busts, including turning in front of another jet—a more serious matter. One guy busted for coming in to fly an hour early, breaking the mandatory twelve-hour "crew rest" between flights. That's a lot of busts for the basic phase, before they even start in on the Basic Fighter Maneuver (BFM) phase, doing the slightly more complicated stuff they'll need to start dogfighting.

Worse yet, different punks have been late to classes or briefings three or four times. Inexcusable—the kind of inattention to detail that gets people killed. There's something wrong with this bunch already—they're not gelling. No one's moving into a leadership role—least of all the captains, who should be out front. Nope. He's got to get in front of this—figure it out. No time to be eating himself up because he's missing the war, because the guys he's come up with and flown with all these years are out there getting shot at while he's sitting here nursemaiding punks who can't show up to a class on time. Best not to even think about that.

Everybody's feeling that, of course—with the TV flickering in the background. On the surface, life goes on in the squadron. The TV plays continuously in the bar, and pilots between flights and awaiting briefings inevitably collect, staring up in fascination at the images—especially the surreal light show over Baghdad.

But even though all the morning flights take place precisely on schedule, the war completely changes the atmosphere of the squadron. The pilots are like thoroughbreds in the stables on the morning of the Kentucky Derby—or like fighting dogs waiting in wire boxes with the smell of blood in the air. They stare. They joke. They spin off into war stories. But they secretly curse their timing. They could be over there, picking off Iraqis and watching their laser-guided bombs heading through the preselected window of Saddam's freaking palace. Maybe they'd even get a shot at a MiG—although they remember the combat stories from the first Gulf War, in which the Iraqi pilots were completely overwhelmed. Eventually they just ran for Iran, and the F-16s and F-15s harried them all the way there, shifting patrol routes to catch them as they ran. All that crap about chivalry in the air—the Red Baron saluting his doomed enemies with his silk scarf screaming out behind—a bunch of bull. NEVER settle for a fair fight if you can sneak up and stab the slow-jinking fool in the back. So the American pilots all loved that moment when the radar blip of the dumbass MiG way out in front suddenly shifted, indicating that the MiG pilot was turning to run—offering an easy tailpipe shot.

On the screen in the lounge, the TV shows a picture taken from the weapons pod of an F-16, with a bomb in flight. A truck, speeding down the road, takes a sharp turn to the right, its path clearly visible on the grainy black-and-white image. The nameless F-16 pilot shifts the aiming point to track the truck. A moment later the truck vanishes in the explosion.

A soft exclamation shimmers through the room.

"Hey," calls out Gilligan as the pilots gather for a scheduled pilots meeting. "Did you know the penalty for a right-hand turn in Iraq is death?"

That gets a laugh.

Everyone likes Major Chris Robert—"Gilligan"—a quick, stocky, wisecracking veteran with big eyes, thinning hair, a boyish manner, and a sardonic worldview. He's trying to be a good sport about being stuck here as an IP, but you can tell it's eating at him. Sometimes he's tempted to just slaughter the damned punks on a training sortie, but he knows he can't let the punks know how bad they are—at least, not all at once. They'd be completely demoralized if they realized how easy they'd be to kill if the IPs ever went full up. So the instructors hold back. They see the kill shot developing and they ease up on the turn. They see the student contemplating a mistake and they nudge him away from it. They see their own deaths coming and they let it happen.

"You can't go 100 percent with these guys," says Gilligan. That takes its toll on a bunch of fighter pilots who live to kill—and prove that they're the baddest asses in the sky. "We hardly ever get opportunities to show them how much we hold back," says Gilligan. "But this business is all about making sure they see something over and over and over again—so you have to set up the picture. Because if they've only seen it five times in training, they won't recognize it happening in the world—and that's the end of them."

Great pilots don't necessarily make great teachers, notes Gilligan. "I came into Luke with the impression that because I was a better pilot, I could create better students. It's not necessarily true. I started out thinking I could teach them all the tricks. But the bar's been lowered so that now I figure as long as I can teach the guy the basic concepts and he can execute a training mission safely, I've done my job."

Besides, he understands how badly they want to get better—to be fighter pilots. He fell in love with flying at the age of six. His parents were immigrants—his father French, his mother German. His dad worked in the knitting industry—his mother was a homemaker. Now his brother works in manufacturing and his sister trains horses. They don't know what to make of the fighter pilot in the family. He's not sure he does either. "I had no fricking clue what I was getting into."

Must have been the thrill. "Initially, it's like a lot of adrenaline sports—maybe skydiving, or racing motorcycles—it's just a real adrenaline hit.

It wears off after a while though, you get a little numb to it—after 400 to 1,000 hours, there's not much more you're going to see."

He always had an inordinate need for excitement. That's why he also took up rock climbing and skydiving. He had done five hundred jumps when he broke his jaw on a four-person formation jump. He got kicked in the face as they pinwheeled to get into position. He passed out for a while as he plummeted toward the ground before waking up and pulling the ripcord. He passed out a couple of times after, which nearly ended his career as a single-seat fighter pilot. But the fainting spells passed and he gave up skydiving.

He still climbs cliffs though. "Rock climbing is only as high risk as you make it. The fun part about skydiving is the freefall. The canopy ride down is boring as hell—you're in a little glider going 25 miles an hour. As you get more experience, you can make the canopy ride down just as fun as the freefall portion. Most skydiving injuries and fatalities are going to be very experienced skydivers. People that I see dying are not the young ones. They're supervised, with an instructor. But once throwing yourself out of a perfectly good airplane seems natural, you start doing things like hook turns at low altitude. Then you hit a dust devil and your canopy collapses. Now on rock climbing—sure, my rope could get cut. But it's one of those sports you can really control. I'm a fatso now—don't have time to go out and climb with a wife and two kids—she'd kill me if I went climbing every weekend, which is what you have to do to stay in shape."

So it makes sense Gilligan wanted to be an honest-to-God, death-defying fighter pilot. When the Air Force recruiter told him he could apply to the Academy and get a free education and a fighter jet, "I took it hook, line, and sinker."

At the Academy, "I had absolutely no idea what I was getting into—like about 20 percent of the rest of the people there." The Academy plunges students into the military culture, like semi-molten horseshoes on the anvil. Suddenly, they're lost in a world defined by absolute deference to authority, intense competition, the embrace of humiliation, isolation from the outside world, idealization of tradition, bonding misbehavior, and mindless discipline. The system seeks to melt down and re-forge loyalties, goals, and ideals. Most of the kids who end up in the Academy come from military families and so were raised in a Great Santini world. Ordinary, thrill-seeking kids like Gilligan who just want to fly suffer a disorienting culture shock.

"Academically, it was not terribly difficult. But the impositions on your free time were probably the worst for me—there was no free time. Overall, it turned me into a flaming asshole. I'd like to think that it didn't change me too much. But I know it did. I was always a perfectionist. But after the Academy I was much more likely to yell at someone for not being a perfectionist. I'm less of a nice guy than I was when I went there. It definitely changes a person."

He's been shuttling about the world for the last eleven years. But his timing sucks. He always seems to miss the war.

And here he is again. Missing the freaking war. For a bunch of punks. He shakes his head and looks away from the muted TV as the room begins to fill up with pilots—and with the tension.

The B-coursers watch the war news with a faint air of anxiety. Every one of them longs to fly in combat—to drop bombs and break stuff. But they know they're not ready. They can barely fly formation and still approach each landing nervously. They haven't even started to absorb the complexities of the weapons systems.

Moore seems especially somber. Yesterday she busted her first ride—an air-to-air combat with Rage, the first ride of her Basic Fighter Maneuver (BFM) stage. The rules of the engagement substantially favor the punks, since they can go all out but the instructors can't punch in the afterburner. In one set, the fight starts with the instructor behind the student, who must twist and turn sharply enough to prevent the instructor from centering the targeting piper (sight) for the cannon on them long enough for the computer to consider it a kill. A very good student might even force the IP to fly past him and then reverse positions. In another set of simulated dogfights, the student starts out behind and tries to lock up the IP.

But on nearly every setup yesterday, Moore ended up dead. She started her turns too soon, or didn't pull enough g's in the turn to frustrate Rage's shot. She made big, wide, easy turns. Rage gunned her every time. Then he told her what she had done wrong. Then they did it again. And he gunned her again. Shot her into bitter little bits and pieces.

She busted the ride. So she watches the flash of the bombs on the TV screen with the hidden knowledge that she'd be so much fresh meat—even for an Iraqi MiG pilot.

The outbreak of the war has a different impact on the IPs. Fighter pilots spend their whole lives preparing for war, like Babe Ruth in batting practice. Some of the IPs, like Gilligan and Old Man, have been in the Air Force for fifteen or twenty years and missed every single war—even the little UN police actions. Somehow they always ended up in the wrong place at the wrong time. Never dropped a bomb in anger. Never blew up a single thing. Never so much as saw a MiG. Of course, they wouldn't openly bitch and moan. That might make it sound like they were warmongers—who wanted to kill people, obliterate truck drivers and bunkers full of women and children. Besides, it would violate the code. Fighter pilots don't have emotions—save for the purposes of mocking themselves. They sure as hell don't whine and complain.

So they converge on the briefing room at precisely the appointed hour for the weekly Friday pilots meeting. Never mind the war—this is a big day. Now, nearly two months into training, it's time to name the punks.

Doughboy, the squadron safety officer, leads off with a discussion of accidents, crashes, and stupid stuff pilots have done lately. Up at Nellis, two F-15 instructors just ran into each other in midair. Both planes crashed, both pilots ejected—and $60 million in tax dollars ended up in smoldering craters.

"We just had a whole lot of big discussions on flight discipline—flight leads and wingman deconfliction," says Doughboy shaking his head. "Who knows what changes this is going to produce," he adds, thinking of the training restrictions under which they already labor. This is bad. Who knows what new safety rules this will generate? Used to be—back in the Phantom days, back in the prop days—training accidents were routine. Commanders figured if they weren't pushing training just past the edge of safety, they weren't simulating combat. Best to let the weak swimmers drown in training, instead of sending them out into the world where they would get their flight lead killed. Commanders used to figure they had to pull g's along that edge of realism all through training, or they'd be sending the punks out to get bounced by MiGs and drop their bombs on friendlies. But it's different now. More rules. More restrictions—simulating ground levels, detouring clouds, dropping dummy bombs, imposing bigger deconfliction bubbles, stopping a dogfight the moment you lose sight of another plane. Partly, this is because rules build up over time—like a coral reef. It's also because the cost of the planes have escalated—$30 million for an F-16, $100 million for the new Joint Strike Fighter—so you can't afford to crash them for that extra 10 percent of training edge. Even the pilot costs these days, since it takes at least $4 million to fully train a fighter pilot.

"This is gonna trigger all kinds of knee-jerk reactions from above," says Doughboy. "So get ready for more directions."

It's a delicate point. The F-16 is perhaps the most nimble, maneuverable, and effective close-in dogfighting airplane ever built. In the hands of an American pilot, the F-16 has never lost a dogfight. Viper pilots know in their bones they can fly circles around the big, twin-engine, turd-heavy F-15. But the Eagle owns the air-to-air mission in the Air Force because of its big-ass radar, which means an F-15 can lock up an approaching F-16 with its missiles at longer range. So even though Viper pilots all sleep, eat, and dream air-to-air combat, the Air Force brass—dominated by bomber and Eagle pilots—periodically questions whether the upstart F-16 pilots even need to know what to do in the neighborhood of an enemy fighter. That would be just perfect: two Eagle pilots crash into each other and the brass cuts air-to-air training for the F-16s.

Leastwise, that's the way some Viper pilots think.

"You guys got to get your craniums on swivel on this one," says Festus, addressing the punks—noting the covert exchange of glances in the back row. He knows they're thinking about those two pilots, the small margin of error and the design of the ejection seat. He knows that they must find that line between caution and confidence. Fighter pilots have to fly brave—but not reckless. Hesitation is fatal up there, at 9 g's, beyond the sound barrier. But so is that moment of inattention, closing at a combined speed of 1,200 miles per hour. "All I can say," says Festus, in his unflappable, low-key way, "is you're heading into your BFM stage and the air-to-air phase. And that's the most dangerous phase we do at Luke."

He knows that everyone will gather later for some partying and drinking at a send-off for one of the IPs. Fighter pilots love parties. They gather every time someone comes, every time someone goes—and they're coming and going constantly. The single pilots—and the recurrently divorced—generally hang out together, shutting down bars and swapping lies. The married pilots gravitate toward one another—holding backyard parties on the weekends. Their wives all know each other and get together frequently. The birth of a baby to anyone in the squadron provokes prolonged celebrations.

Festus remains the official father figure—a colonel past his hard-partying glory days, affectionately tolerant of the off-duty high jinks and hard liquor. He's one of those commanders fighter pilots love—all business in the air, a brilliant pilot himself, and obsessive about flying airplanes and operations. But he doesn't expect fighter pilots to act like a bunch of recruitment posters—like the showboat Thunderbirds on a PR mission, creased sharper than their pants. He understands you've got to "let fighter pilots be fighter pilots," which means partying and inflicting a certain amount of property damage—so long as they show up precisely on time Monday for the briefing, razor wire sober and ready to work.

"Now in the festivities this evening," says Festus, "make sure that if we have a few crevasses, that we have someone to drive. Gilligan," he adds, fixing the boyish wisecracking Gilligan with a hard look, "I don't want your keys in my pocket."

"I'm hearing that you might not go," says Gilligan, smirking. "You know, don't you, if you don't go, you're a pantywaist."

"I can't hear anything back there," retorts Festus. "Just crickets."

"I said, if you don't go, you're a pantywaist."

Everyone guffaws.

Fighter pilot humor. Very sophisticated.

The tone deteriorates further as they adjourn the pilots meeting and move to the squadron bar and poolroom for the "Crusades," a theoretically weekly gathering intended to bond the pilots together as the IPs tease each other and humiliate the punks. A fighter squadron remains a saturated male environment, where cohesion and morale are built on teasing, humiliation, and political incorrectness.

The Crusades revolve around telling a lot of embarrassing stories about the week's screwups, with ample toasting to the same.

Major Jeff Lovelace—"Bongoo"—is the ringmaster of these morale-building circuses. Everyone loves Bongoo—punks and IPs alike. He's the pulsing, fluttering, skip-a-beat heart of the squadron.

Tall, lean, jar-headed, he's got a touch of Jim Carrey in him—a handsome man who loves to make himself ridiculous. He's the class clown—irrepressible, quick, wickedly funny, crude, kind, loyal, and fearless. He's also one of the best pilots at Luke—no small claim. He wears the Weapons School patch—the sign of the alpha male in a world of rutting egos. But he wears it lightly, as though it represents a private joke—a fast one pulled on huffing, puffing, humorless generals.

He's proud of his nickname, which he acquired while serving with the "Fabulous Flying Fiends" of Osan Air Base in South Korea. He says it means "divine wind" or "fart" in Korean. He says he earned the name—and strives to remain worthy of it.

He also has the uncanny ability to hold in his mind a three-dimensional picture of the action in any given chunk of sky—like one of those computers that can reconstruct the path of every jet in an engagement after the tapes have been fed in. Except Bongoo can do it in the air. It's like he's psychic, sensing the panicky brain waves of the poor, dumb schleps he's about to kill.

Moreover, he can put his jet through astonishing maneuvers with offhand grace, like he's some freaking kung-fu fighter from *The Matrix*, whipping around with effortless speed as the bullets toil toward him in exquisite slow motion. He can fly, instruct, and kill you while he's making wisecracks—like a guy in a tuxedo juggling knives on a unicycle while drinking a glassful of water and throwing his voice to a ventriloquist's dummy on his damned lap. He's that good. And yet he's constitutionally incapable of taking anything seriously—especially himself. He's like Bill Murray in *Stripes*—a smirking, good-natured, sardonic misfit who invariably triumphs. He embodies the fighter pilot ideal—a deadly, disciplined, individualist who is unafraid of either MiGs or generals.

What's more, he's a brilliant instructor, among the most popular with the B-coursers. Partly that's because they respect his skills. Partly that's because he manages to tease them without demeaning them—or at least he never ridicules them more than he ridicules himself. And finally, it's because he always maneuvers them into precisely the right position, thanks to his "global situational awareness." The B-coursers say it's easy to be Bongoo's wingman. The punks have to cling to the backwash of the jets of some instructors, trying desperately to position themselves—or struggling to understand what's expected without asking an overtly stupid question. But Bongoo always seems to know when to drop a hint or a reminder. Flying on his wing seems easy. Somehow, without fully realizing that Bongoo was orchestrating everything, the students end up sliding effortlessly into the right position. So they love him. And it doesn't hurt that his nickname is "Fart."

Of course, Bongoo laughs at any praise. The punks like him because he buys liquor easily, he confides.

"I try to keep it fun—there are times for harassment—typically when you're getting ready for a mission—but generally I'm not a big believer in tough love. Everyone here wants to do well. So when you see guys who aren't, you just want to find them early and help them get the picture."

In the beginning, Bongoo wanted to be an astronaut. His father spent two years in the Army, but both his parents ultimately spent their lives working for the phone company. Bongoo discovered an early aptitude for math. "The only advice my dad ever gave me was: take math and join the Air Force," he says.

So he joined ROTC in college. "I just always wanted to fly—I don't know why. I thought airplanes were the coolest things going, until I discovered women. Now I'm not saying that flying is better than sex, but if you're talking about a particular mission and you're making a comparison, then you have to ask, Who am I going to be fucking and what does she look like?"

He was a statistics major at the University of Memphis—and a band geek, playing the trumpet. "That's what actually paid for my education—plus I married the band director's daughter." Growing up in Memphis, he got hooked on the blues right along with airplanes. He still plays gigs with local blues bands.

He blew through pilot training, got a Viper, and headed off to Korea.

But in truth, Bongoo has one defect as a pilot—bad timing. He keeps missing the wars.

He was in training during the first Gulf War—and missed the big show.

He did pull two tours in Southern Watch, but not a damned thing happened. "We were just playing traffic cop. First time we were there, we couldn't even drop live weapons—just boring holes in the sky, mostly at night."

His squadron deployed to a later tour of Southern Watch, where they did bomb SAM sites—but Bongoo was relegated to doing most of the mission planning and so missed all the fun—the actual dropping of bombs. "That's a sore spot—it was a real cowboys and Indians thing. You get kind of antsy when you don't get to do your job. But like I said, always a bridesmaid, never a bride."

Then damned if he didn't miss Bosnia too.

He was based in Korea when the Supreme Leader of North Korea died—and things looked dicey for a while. "We thought that was it. We thought the fight was on. That's the thing about Korea—everything you do there is getting ready for war."

No such luck.

Still, Korea was cool. At one point, a North Korean MiG 19 defected and Bongoo listened to the intercept over the radio. The South Koreans got to merge and order the defecting North Korean pilot to land. Bongoo did get to scramble on a couple of North Korean mini subs trying to put spies ashore. That fizzled too. Would have been cool to blow up a sub. Still, Korea remains the best place in the world to be an F-16 Viper pilot, short of an actual combat zone. They didn't even have to worry about the damned Eagle drivers, since the nearest F-15 squadron is based in Japan. That means that the F-16s got to do it all—bombing, air-to-air, bomber escorting—one long, intense combat training mission, interspersed with nightly parties, binge drinking, and seedy nightlife.

"You're the tip of the spear, ready at a moment's notice," says Bongoo.

Of course, it requires a certain dexterity of leadership to combine the intense, precision flying with the partying. "People in Korea work very, very hard and for that reason they play very, very hard. People walk right up to that line all the time. And a lot of people cross it. So the question is how does the squadron commander deal with that? Is he in your face, or is he OK? You want a guy who knows guys are going to be idiots—but knows where the line is. He's got to care about the important issues like combat capability, not the damned paperwork. He's got to let fighter pilots be fighter pilots—there's a lot of heritage there. It gets back to the old joke, 'Mom, when I grow up, I want to be a fighter pilot.' And mom says, 'Son, you can grow up. Or you can be a fighter pilot. But you can't do both.' There's a lot of raucous and rambunctious behavior—it's who we feel we need to be to develop that esprit de corps. It's a lot more difficult in this day and age than it once was. But being in a squadron and singing and acting like an idiot with your brothers is important to finding out who the guy is next to you."

He shrugs at the honor of his selection for Weapons School, a six-month ordeal of hard flying and harsh criticism. The counterpart to the Navy's Top Gun school, the Weapons School is where the Air Force sends its best pilots to memorize every wire and bolt of their jets and weapons systems. Then they're supposed to return to their operational squadrons and teach everyone else what they've learned. But it's six months of anal-retentive hell, flying against tyrannical instructors in a blur of eighteen-hour days. Not only do the instructors demand dazzling flying, they relentlessly deconstruct every syllable of your briefings. "Lots of very, very, very long days. I wouldn't say it's hazing—but expectations are well beyond what most people have the capability to project. It was horrible. Absolutely humbling. You get into these large-force deploy-ments—like sixty or eighty airplanes—and you're scrutinized to the nth degree for every little move you make in the air. It makes you think so much further ahead."

He did come pretty close to dying on one mission at Nellis.

He was in a four-ship with a buddy, doing a high-g defensive maneu-ver at low altitude. He was straining against the g-force in a sharp turn, when suddenly something exploded in the cockpit. Something slammed the stick to the side, forcing the jet into a rolling dive toward the ground. He looked down to discover that the zipper over his inflated g-suit had ruptured and the pressurized lining of the suit had burst out and was pushing against the stick. With the plane in a wrenching turn, the com-puter kept pumping air into the g-suit. "The airplane is doing this barrel roll into the ground at 3,000 feet." So Bongoo released his grip on the stick, lifted his leg away from the stick and barely recovered control before slamming into the ground. Then he dug out his pocketknife, slashed open the g-suit to deflate it. "That was the closest I ever came to dying in a jet," he says.

Ironically, his wingman and good friend on that fated day flew into the ground and died a few months later. "He was too low over shallow water with a lot of reflection—the water was still and flat and calm—and he just didn't know how low he was because he didn't have a good visual reference. He was doing a defensive maneuver much like the one I'd been doing at Nellis and just flew into the water. He was a veteran pilot. Father of two. Loving husband. A legend in the Viper. It happens. I got the call about his death the day after my father died. That was a tough week. You can't mit-igate all risk. But it's like the Great Santini says: it beats dying of piles."

Of course, once the Weapons School graduate gets back to the squadron, he's like a gunslinger with a reputation whom all the hot young pilots want to take down. "All of a sudden, you're expected to know everything about F-16s. That's very difficult, because there are a lot of smart guys out there who haven't been to Weapons School. If anything, it makes you a very accomplished bullshitter—which will hold you in good stead in your Air Force career."

He loves teaching pilots. "You hear some IPs saying they can't wait to get back to a go-to-war squadron, and I do miss that. Being in that combat-ready posture is a great thing—knowing you can deploy anywhere in the world and kick somebody's ass. But there's a lot of satisfaction in working with these guys. In six months, they go from having no clue to almost being capable in the airplane."

The IPs have to bring them along gradually—adding one task at a time. "It's wholly deliberate. We could humiliate them anytime we wanted—ed. But you only give them what they're ready to learn."

He knows he's training a lot of dedicated young people to drop bombs and kill people on a moment's notice. But that doesn't bother him. "Tell you the truth, I don't think we use our true wrath as much as we should. The whole term 'limited war' is nonsense. The military is not about limited war. We ought to be about overwhelming power to get the job done and get out as unscathed as possible, as opposed to twelve years of boring holes in the sky over Iraq. We're not meant to be policemen. You don't want to put marines on the ground to enforce laws—marines are bred to kill people. That's what they're supposed to do. I like to picture this sign put up in front of the Air Force: Break glass in case of war. That said, you have to trust the machine—you can't second-guess intelligence. You can't second-guess your leaders. You have to trust that they did the research for you."

He knows that when the call comes, he'll kill lots of people as efficiently as possible. "I know a guy from my first squadron who flew in Desert Storm I—a pretty religious guy—and he was hitting troops in the open with cluster munitions—which do nasty things to people. On this one raid, he must have killed four hundred troops. When he came back, and his flight lead said, 'Hey Charlie, you OK?' He said, 'Hey man. They were on the wrong side. They'd have done the same thing to me.' "

But Bongoo doesn't spend much time on such serious subjects.

He'd rather get off a quip.

So as they start the Crusades, he takes charge. He plays the clown—a gifted storyteller with a quick and wicked wit.

"Hey," says Bongoo, "remember, if you're unfit to function following this function, give your keys to your wingman—and he'll take care of you. Now, remember the rules: a poor story told well is better than a fantastic story told poorly. Also, the 10 percent rule is in effect here. Only 10 percent of any story has to be true—so lie, lie, lie. After every story, you will loudly and proudly toast the Knights. The response to that is 'Hear, hear,' or 'Strength and honor.' I'm your sheriff, I'll be writing your story in the book—so if you're fucking up, expect to have a bad story taken down. If you win this fine piece of hardware," he says, holding aloft a medal that will be awarded to the person who made the most bone-headed maneuver of the week, "you are compelled to wear it proudly until the next Crusade."

Everyone cheers.

Now Bongoo glances at the TV set in the corner, sound off, showing the war in Iraq.

"First off," he says, raising his glass for a toast. "Fuck the French."

This draws a tremendous cheer and much laughter.

"Hear! Hear!" shouts the room, as everyone downs a shot.

"Do we have any actual stories?" asks Gilligan. "Surely we got something."

Long pause.

"No stories?" asks Festus. "You've got to be kidding me."

Another pause.

"I know Bongoo missed his parking space [on the runway] at least once," says Festus, trying to get the embarrassment started.

"OK, I got one," says Bongoo. "I got Spears, on a BFM," he says, referring to a training run from the Basic Fighter Maneuvers course. Matt Spears is a buttoned-down, rock-star handsome lieutenant who went all the way through West Point before realizing all he really wanted to do was fly fighter jets. He's one of those rare transfers from the Army to the Air Force. Now he looks like an Air Force recruiting poster, with a crisp, aw-gosh military manner, but he takes a lot of guff for being West Point.

"So we talk about pictures and line-of-sight cues—what you look for," continues Bongoo, "looking over your shoulder. Break turns. Everything. And I think he's absorbing everything. I speak for like an hour and thirty fucking minutes. And then there we are—a perfect setup. He's sitting right on my six. And I am like this freaking mil power (no afterburners) kind of guy—at 1.4 freaking miles. So he over-rotates, pull, pull, pull—and he's coming in with 500 knots of closure. And good God damn it, he goes swwwwoshing past, zooms out front, and then does this big slow turn right in front of me."

"That's called a Syrian lead turn," says Festus, referring to the slaughter of the Syrian air force by the Israelis over Lebanon. The intensively trained Israelis flying F-16s devastated the poorly trained Syrian MiG pilots, who were all flying in inflexible formations under tight control from the ground.

Everyone turns to Spears, who is blushing faintly under his crew cut. It's a test of character, really—responding to ridicule. Bongoo just told everyone Spears is a dumbass—a West Point punk who can't absorb a briefing or maneuver his jet.

Spears grins, holds up his glass, and declares, "I learned from the best."

Big laugh—at Bongoo's expense. The right stuff.

"To the Knights," says Spears.

Everyone takes a slug.

The silence settles. Festus adds, "There's got to be something else."

Gilligan steps forward. "To the Knights."

Everyone drinks.

For the past two weeks, the punks have been in trouble because people keep showing up late for briefings or classes. Mind you, IPs start most briefings by counting down on their watches to the second. They synchronize their watches about twice a day. All of that is intended to instill in the punks a reverence for plans and timing, so that when a swarm of fighters and bombers dive on a target at twenty-second intervals, no one smashes into another plane because he's running a little late. So the smattering of late-shows has irritated the IPs. "One of the things we try to teach is tactical deception," says Gilligan. "By the end of the week, sure enough—we got the punks lined up, checking in. So for learning tactics—having decided to deceive us by actually showing up on time—I nominate the whole class."

"Hear! Hear!" say the IPs, but it has a sarcastic edge. The punks sip their beers sheepishly.

Now Doughboy tells a story on a pilot from Japan who is undergoing training in the squadron. He's an F-15 pilot who finally came to his senses and got an F-16. Viper pilots love to ridicule Eagle pilots—although there's a certain bitter undertone. Viper pilots say Eagle pilots spend all their time flying in circles above the bombers waiting for enemy fighters that never show up. Meantime, the F-16s are down there doing all the real work. And God forbid an Eagle ever gets close enough to a Viper for a real dogfight—instead of shooting missiles from a couple dozen miles away.

"So we're doing air-to-air, and I'm thinking, 'This rocks'—because I'm absolutely gunning his brains out," says Doughboy of his dogfight with the re-treaded Eagle driver. "So we come back to the debrief, and I say, 'You didn't jink. You're at like 13,200 feet, I'm gunning you, and you're just sitting there.' So then he says, 'Oh, I am used to the Eagle. I thought you were way farther away.' "

Everyone laughs. They just love insulting Eagle pilots.

Now Chris Lehto, the surfer-dude punk, stands up. He's an odd one. He has none of that fighter pilot swagger. His eyes don't glint. Most of the other punks say they have wanted to be fighter pilots since before they can remember. He says that in high school he decided it might be kind of cool. He's like, way out of place, dude. But he's irresistible—laconic, witty. He's got a sly, charming, lopsided, Harrison Ford grin. No one takes him seriously, since he has obviously wandered into the wrong career, but you still can't help liking him.

"So this is my BFM 3 ride, with Festus. I'm looking for, like, a kill—because that's what I was born to do."

"The jury's still out on that," interjects Festus.

Lehto grins, freaking charming—unflappable, impossible to offend—like he's on something. "So I get my ass kicked—handed to me. I don't think I got a shot off. So I come back. I look at my gas. I am just about out of gas," he says—a significant detail, since jets nearly out of gas get priority for landing so as to avoid crashing into some subdivision on the go-around. Point being, Festus is the flight lead and he should be getting his gas-fumed punk on the ground, pronto. "But there's lightning off the far end of the runway. OK. Drag two—we go around. OK. I just try to maintain sight of the runway and stay out of the clouds. But Festus, he goes right into the thunderstorm, and I lose him. So I'm turning and I'm just flying instruments on the final turn. And like, I saw a lightning strike go by me. I didn't have any other options. So I guessed where the runway was. And somehow the plane landed itself," he says, getting a big laugh.

"It does that all the time," he adds. "And so to our faithful leader . . ." he concludes, lifting his glass.

"Hear! Hear!" shouts the room, laughing.

It's brilliant: Lehto manages to tell an aw-shucks story on himself that boomerangs around and hits Festus—who should have been stuck to Lehto like a heat-seeking missile, making sure the punk landed safely before running out of gas. It's a nugget of fighter pilot guerrilla warfare, since the purpose of the Crusades is to inflict some instructive humiliation on the punks. Instead, Lehto guns the colonel, for Christ's sake, all the while grinning and letting the damned airplane land itself. A sneaky, deadly, improvised upside-down maneuver—a fighter pilot trick. Might be more to the surfer dude than meets the eye.

Festus laughs with everyone else, knowing he just got gunned.

"I will have one rebuttal," says Festus. "No quibbling," he adds, so it won't sound like whining, although he wants to get off a shot on his way down. "It's always interesting when you go out on the BFM sortie. They've got a [single seat] C model, so they've got 500 more pounds of gas. But when you land, they're out of gas, and you're just a little low."

"That's quibbling," declares Bongoo, savoring the moment.

Doughboy gets up again. He tells stories with a more cynical, acidic wit than the slapstick Bongoo. Apart from Rage, he's the only IP who regularly socializes with the punks. Maybe it's because he's hanging loose—single now that the demands of an Air Force career have shredded his marriage. But mostly it's because he loves teaching and bringing the young guys along and being a fighter pilot. The punks love him—he's one of their favorites—although this may be because he always shows up with booze or buys the first round.

Now he recounts a flight with Moore. "We're out there and I'm just plodding along out front, trying to give her a shot. OK kid. Gun me. Gun me. Boring as shit. Flying in circles. So we're sitting in debrief, watching the tape. I call out, 'Fight's on.' And she's calling out, 'Fox one, Fox two' "—the call marking the launch of an air-to-air missile. "And it's, like, nothing. We go through three fucking sets of this. Nothing. Turns out, she's not uncaged. She's got an AIM-9 [heat-seeking missile] called up on her weapons control console and she's trying to shoot the AIM-120 [radar-guided]. I'm looking, saying, what? Don't you know a *BBBBBBJBJBBJBJJBB* from an *EEEEECCCCCHHHHH?*" he says, offering a credible, squealing imitation of the contrasting sounds of the different missiles.

A big laugh at Moore's expense.

She grins sheepishly—endlessly good-sported. Then she stands. "So we're in academics," she says. "We don't study that much, but we'll finally show up," she adds, getting a laugh and perhaps slightly defusing the irritation with their tardiness. "We fully studied all the workbooks beforehand. So we're focused on that—and on showing up on time— and we're not at all worried about our check rides. And they're saying, 'You're going to get the WAD, you're going to put in channel 20 and put in the WAD and channel 1154, and you're going to put this in and that in, and they say you've put in the load and channel 15 and BEEEEEP BEEEEEP,' " she says, describing the complicated process of programming the cockpit computer for each mission.

She gets a laugh. She's getting it. Don't get pissed. Don't defend yourself. Make fun of yourself—and learn, of course. Got to learn.

"We're trying to take notes and all this shit. We're writing like, BEEEEP, BEEEEP. So finally the instructor stops and I'm staring at him, glazed. And I say, 'I got a real serious question.' " She pauses for effect. "'What happens if you blow your wad?' "

That gets a BIG laugh.

They've all been a little leery about Moore. She's sharp, low-key— not grinding axes or burning bras or making an issue. But everyone's following the pillorying of the Air Force Academy. Women fighter pilots are still a novelty. No one's sure what to do with them, exactly. Fighter pilots are crude, macho, and testosteroned. They ridicule everybody—especially each other. They curse, drink, smoke, chase tail, brag on their bomb scores. Interjecting women into the squadron changes things. The commandant of the Air Force Academy got busted—forced into retirement—because he didn't react to reports of rapes and sexual abuse. This whole sexual harassment thing is like flying through airspace bristling with SAMs. Scary. But Moore seems like a good stick. I mean, that was a fighter pilot joke—delivered with her big eyes and a sly smile. "Shot her wad." Pretty good. Yeah. She's OK. Maybe.

So now Bongoo recaps, reminding them that they'll hand out the reward for the screwup of the week based on the volume of the cheers.

"To recap," he says, "we got Spears—a Ph.D. graduate of the Syrian School of Left-Hand Turns."

Modest cheers.

"We got Festus—'Where's my punk?' "

Big cheer.

"Plus quibbling," adds Bongoo.

Bigger cheer.

"We got, the Eagle jockey—'Oh, my, oh my, these jets are so clooooose.' "

Enthusiastic cheer.

"We got Moore—'Oh my, they never told me Fox 3s make noise.' "

Modest cheers.

"We got the B-course—'I've been late for class so much that the whole class is in a world of shit—let's see if I can make it worse.' "

Big cheer.

Seeing doom approaching, Festus interjects. "Maybe we should give it to all the protestors in San Francisco—especially the one who fell off the bridge and died."

Big cheer.

For a minute, it looks like maybe Festus will win the Screw Up award. But that would defeat the whole purpose—which is to rub the punks' faces in their astonishing incompetence.

So Bongoo puts it to a revote.

He points first to Festus. All the punks cheer lustily.

Then he points to Spears, the practitioner of the Syrian lead turn.

All the IPs cheer raucously. Since the IPs outnumber the punks two-to-one, Spears wins in a raspberry.

9

What's in a Name

The IPs gather for that most sacred of ritual humiliations—the naming of names.

Fighter pilots have secret identities.

Well, not so secret.

Rather, an alter ego—Superman, Spiderman—a nickname. They refer to one another almost entirely by nickname. They have patches displaying their nicknames, which they wear on Friday in place of their normal patch.

Apache warriors did the same thing—it's a warrior tradition with tangled roots. Among the Apache, warriors earned their names by some deed or characteristic. They often changed their names after a big battle—or after death.

So do Viper pilots.

But you can't just make up your own name. Most bases have a naming committee, charged with christening the newcomers. The most influential naming committees in the F-16 world operate at Kunsan, a base in South Korea close by the bristling demilitarized zone. All F-16 pilots rotate through Korea, a "remote" assignment, which means a one- or two-year separation from families. As a result, Kunsan remains the last refuge of the true "fighter pilot," with everything that implies: legendary parties, pranks, jokes and general—loud, over-the-top, raunchy behavior. And great flying—every day—live-weapon sorties along the edge of war and destruction, with MiGs on the radar and a sense of imminent, trip-wire, kick-ass obliteration. Pilots form bonds in Korea that they sustain throughout their careers. They also push training and tactics right up to the edge of war here, learning the formation work, communications, and two, four, and eight-ship tactics that will keep them alive in actual combat.

Most pilots end up using the nicknames they get in Kunsan for the rest of their careers, unless they arrive with a name that everyone concedes is already perfect.

Mercifully, although the Luke IPs take naming duties seriously, the Luke names probably won't stick once the punks head off to their first operational assignment. They'll probably get a new name there—and another one when they get to Korea. Eventually, one of those names will stick.

But the naming ceremony for the Emerald Knights remains a rite of passage, mostly dreaded by the punks and treasured by the IPs. The committee privately sorts through all the possibilities—most demeaning— before adopting the publicly awarded nickname. Naturally, every punk yearns for a cool name—Maverick or Mad Dog or Ace or Red Baron. Fat chance. Mostly, the names fall into one of two categories: a pun on their names or a permanent reminder of a major screwup. Punks never get cool names. Partly that's because the half-derisive, dirty joke of the name captures the fighter culture in a sly, raunchy, self-mocking quip. It's like the slave who ran alongside Caesar's chariot as he rode in triumph through Rome, whispering, "Even this shall pass away." They may be hotshot fighter pilots who can twirl a $30 million jet on its axis at 500 knots and kill a MiG at 30 miles, but they've still got to wear that awful name—and like it. Like the Boy Named Sue. Builds character. But the gleeful mockery of the naming ceremony also offers the IPs a small, socially acceptable way to express their head-shaking disdain for these poor, innocent baby-seal pilots who only dimly realize how clueless and pathetic and clubbable they really are. Of course, the IPs would never say this; the IPs try not to even think it. But fighter pilots run on ego and testosterone and a deep, irrational faith in their own skills and indestructibility. The halting, struggling, vulnerable punks are a dim reminder to the IPs of their own mortality. Besides. They're missing the war. THEIR WAR. So they stick the punks with their awful names.

They file into the big briefing room, joking, laughing, playing grab-ass. Naturally enough, Bongoo serves as master of ceremonies. Songs like "Bad to the Bone" and "Highway to Hell" blare on the speaker system.

Festus leads off. This will be his last naming ceremony as the squadron's operations officer. He's been tapped to head up the academics division—a step up the administrative ladder in a distinguished Air Force career. "All right, gentlemen," he says to the slouching, grinning IPs, "you know the ROE [Rules of Engagement]. Seeing as how this is my last naming ceremony . . . "

Bongoo interrupts. "We have to name one 'Festus.' "

"Negatori," retorts Festus, pained at the idea of one of the punks making off with his name. "There will be no Festus in this squadron."

"Moore," retorts Bongoo. "She deserves that name."

Festus shakes him off. "Moreover—there will be no, 'Oh, I want to give this guy a good name.' Screw it. If we have a good name in terms of what they've done—or haven't done—or how they earned it—then we're going to go with it. But I'm not going to go with this, 'Oh, my God, we can't call him that.' "

Cheers.

Now Bongoo takes the stage: "You are privy to one of the age-oldest fighter pilot traditions. This is serious shit."

Now comes the expected knock at the door. It's Spears and Moore, with two cases of beer and a couple of bottles of scotch—a group bribe from the punks intended to soften the ridicule of the names they're about to receive. The bribe comes at the end of a long process of calculation. The naming subcommittee has already met a couple of times to come up with a list of possibilities for each candidate. Individual punks could try to influence individual IPs—maybe even offer bribes. But that's a risky strategy. Most likely, the IP would drink the bribe and then report it to the committee, which would cheer the initiative of the scheming punk and then punish him with a truly terrible name. The safest strategy is to chip in as a group, and make some sacrifice to calm the gods. It rarely works. But then, an inadequate bribe would no doubt inspire the IPs to a creative fury of humiliating names.

Moore and Spears deliver the bribe and stand a moment, uncertain and a little shamefaced—like they've been caught at something. Bongoo scowls at them and they scurry out of the room.

The IPs pass around the beer.

"All for one, and I'm definitely number one," toasts Festus.

"You're not that drunk," retorts Bongoo. "Shut the fuck up."

Now he turns to the serious business at hand.

On the screen in the front flashes a picture of Captain Kenn Cook, one of the two captains in the class, senior by reason of his previous incarnation as a navigator on a C-130 cargo plane. He's a quiet, reserved, likable, earnest man, without the slightest hint of fighter pilot swagger. He seems miscast in the aggressive, fast-talking fighter brotherhood. His hairline is already in full retreat, his eyes mild, his manner modest.

The names proposed by the naming committee flash on the screen: Khu-khu-khu Kenney, Radar, Chief, Old Man, Gramps, Squid, Forward, and Sewer Pickle—which is a sodomy reference. Some such outlandish insult almost always makes it into the first cut.

None of the names draws consensus enthusiasm. Then Gilligan notes that Cook has been blowing the doors off academically, applying a precise, scientific mentality to the complex material that most of the fighter pilots view as an irritating obstacle to pulling g's and uncaging missiles. "Swear to God," says Gilligan. "He's in a class and the instructor is talking about landing in the desert and Kenn goes, 'Sir, is the reason your landing roll is longer at higher temperature because the air molecules are spaced higher apart?' And the whole class goes—kachung. I go to any one of them and say, 'What is the deal with that guy?' And they say he says that kind of shit all the time."

Bongoo then explains the logic of the naming committee. Cook shortened Kenneth to Kenn, keeping the two ns. That somehow reminded the naming committee of the movie *A Fish Called Wanda*, with the stuttering loser named Ken—hence, KKK Ken.

"That's too hard to say," says Rage.

"Sewer Pickle?" suggests Bongoo.

Everyone laughs, but they know you'd have to really—REALLY—screw up to get that name.

"How about 'Beaker?' " suggests Gilligan, on account of Cook's studious and scientific disposition.

The door opens, everyone pauses, and Doughboy enters. He just got done flying. "The news says the Turks just invaded northern Iraq," he says. The TV has reported a Turkish invasion, a scary widening of the

Iraq War—although it proves a false report. But for a moment, the possibility of an unraveling fur ball involving Turkey and maybe even Iran flashes through the room. And here they are. Naming punks.

"Shit," says someone.

They then agree on "Beaker" for Cook.

Next up—Captain Quattlebaum, an intent, sparse-haired, reserved, redheaded pilot who does his job, keeps his mouth shut, and doesn't mingle much with the other B-coursers. He exudes a certain ruthless, remote efficiency—and flies with restraint and attention to detail, but without flair. The naming committee mostly grappled with his peculiar name, since neither his personality nor his flying had yet distinguished him—for better or worse. So they came up with Que Ball, QB, Quatto, Yoda, Q Bomb, Data, Dead Meat, and Atari.

"Not too many fighter pilots named 'Quattlebaum,' " observes Doughboy dubiously.

"We don't know if he's a fighter pilot yet," observes Gilligan.

"Cyborg?" suggests someone.

"Shaved Dog's Ass," someone yells, another enduringly popular choice.

"What's with the scars on his cranium? Anyone know about that shit?" asks Bongoo.

"How about Lobo—short for lobotomy. He's got the scars to prove it. We're onto something here," says Gilligan.

"How about Plate, for the metal plate in his head?"

Discussion shifts to his prominent ears.

"Yoda—check out the ears on this boy," says someone.

"Wing Nuts?" suggests Gilligan.

"Gremlin?" suggests Ship.

"Yeah, we're getting there, we're the group," says Bongoo.

"Gizmo?" suggests Doughboy.

"So when they say, 'Why do they call you Gizmo,' " laughs Bongoo, "he can say, 'Cause I got these huge, fucking, stupid ears.' "

"Dumbo?"

"Bert?"—of Sesame Street fame.

Everyone starts chanting, "Bert, Bert, Bert," but in the end they settle on Pong—a play on the name.

Chris Gough—wide-eyed, charming, and earnest, the son of a son of a pilot with a lopsided grin—faces two problems: the weight of family tradition and a last name that rhymes with "off" and "golf" and combines easily with other words to make bad puns—Goofy, as in goofy golf, or Putt-Putt (golf).

Someone suggests "Bogey"—clever since it's both a pun (Bogey Golf) and slang for an unidentified, possibly hostile aircraft.

Someone else calls out "Scratch," as in scratch golf, but Gilligan countermands it, "Wait, that's flattery—we can't have that."

Finally, inevitably they settle on "Jack"—which means that for the rest of the B-course, any time anyone uses his nickname, they'll silently complete it—Jack *Off.* This should amuse his Air Force brass family.

Lehto, the surfer dude, poses a problem.

The IPs, to their surprise, like him. No one took him very seriously at first. He didn't distinguish himself in IFF. He didn't screw up exactly, but he drifted along in the middle of the pack. He's good-looking—handsome even—with a killer, understated charm that springs from his easy, crooked smile and kind but mischievous eyes. But he's such a dude, man. He never breaks a sweat, loitering along, looking like he just dropped in for the briefing or the test or the dogfight on some kind of a dare. He doesn't take himself seriously. In fact, he doesn't seem to take anything seriously. It's like Pauly Shore joining the Marines, for Christ's sake. All the other punks have wanted to be fighter pilots for so long that it's like bone cancer; they're feverish and twisted into rawhide knots. But Lehto acts like he's just killing time waiting for a Grateful Dead concert in Phoenix. Only thing is, he picks up stuff like a fucking sponge. And he never gets rattled. Every time an IP piles on another brick, he flashes that shit-eating grin and stashes the brick in his pocket without leaving a bulge. He's got hands. He doesn't make serious mistakes—and he loves to mock himself for the little ones he does make. He's popular with the other B-coursers, drinks heavy without getting stupid, jokes with the IPs without being an asshole. So most of the names sound almost affectionate. These include some puns, like Eggo, Stihl (makes "stiletto"), Leggo, and Shorty. Someone recalls that he had some trouble on his first BFM flights, when he kept getting into position and then not firing his guns.

"He didn't use the gun once," snorts Festus.

They work on that. Gunner. Door Gunner. Shooter. Killer. Shithead. Deadeye.

All too cool—even sarcastically.

Besides, Doughboy notes, "I flew BFM4 with him—he had the best piper [gunsight] control of any B-courser."

"Dumbass?" suggests Bongoo.

In the end, they settle on "Stihl"—which combines with his last name to make Stiletto—way too cool a name for a punk.

Now they face the politically delicate matter of naming Moore. What do you name a woman fighter pilot with a name like "Moore?"

"This is gonna take maximum creative energy," observes Bongoo. They're all tempted by crude sexual innuendos—but they've got to consider the context, what with the Air Force Academy sex scandals. But God damn it. This is the naming ceremony—the last refuge of the fighter pilots—an affront to the whole concept of political correctness. And she's named "Moore" for Christ's sake. It's like some kind of complicated, reverse crisis of conscience.

The naming committee didn't flinch—and mostly built on her name, with Gimmie, Less, Head, Dinty, Getsome, Skid, Alittle, Gil, and Rush. They even threw in one name based on her hard landings—Slammer. Rage grouses, "she had the worst braking technique of anyone I ever met in my life. It was binary—full-on or full-off. I don't know who taught her how to use a flight path marker—it's like she never even knew it existed."

"She's a gun-only kind of girl," notes Doughboy.

"How about Dome—as in 'Do Me Moore,' " suggests someone.

"Her husband's name is Mickey," notes someone. "We could call her Minnie."

"OK," says Bongoo. "Top Three: Slammer, Getsome, Gimmie."

"What happened to Festus?" says Gilligan.

Festus scowls.

In the end, they settle on Gimmie—not terrible, but proof that Viper pilots won't be intimidated into overt political correctness.

Lieutenant Newlin gets the worst of it. He's already busted three rides—not stupid stuff like breaking crew rest, but honest to God, behind-the-jet busts. He works hard, absorbs criticism endlessly, wordlessly, pours effort into flying and studying and tests. He never complains and always puts out. But he's not getting it. He's like a boxer, beaten bloody, eyes swollen shut, staying on his feet out of some dim, reptilian brain instinct. Newlin's an Air National Guard pilot. And he's married, with kids—and devoted to his family—so he doesn't drink and party and bond with the other B-coursers. But mostly, he doesn't seem to have the instinct for flying, so he's hanging on by dint of his huge effort and his checklist. In the end, you can't get through on a checklist. You have to absorb all the basics, so that flying the jet seeps down into the reflexes. You've got to control your speed and altitude and position in the formation easily, by instinct, so you can concentrate on the weapons and the glowing flurry on the radar and the flicker in your peripheral vision that might be a MiG—or just a bug on the canopy. You have to be out there, way ahead of the jet—like a chess player thinking six moves down the road. Once you fall behind the jet, you're not only dead—you're a danger to your flight lead. Newlin's been on CAP from day one and every time he seems ready to get off the extra supervision, he fucks up again. None of the IPs expects him to make it—so they have no mercy in the matter of naming. They figure he should know that he's wandering around like a zombie from *The Night of the Living Dead,* already smelling faintly of decay. Maybe if they give him a final wake-up call in the matter of his name, he'll pull his poor, pathetic, earnest self together. Maybe he'll give up and go home, before he flies up someone's tailpipe trying to set his radio frequency.

So the naming committee proposes all sorts of terrible names—mostly relating to flying skills. Slammer, Brick, Darkstar, Class A, Deadbeat, Triple X, Meat Whistle, Psycho, Porno, Shoe Clerk, Spinner, Postal.

"With his landing technique, he came down so hard he lowered the elevation of Gila Bend by about two feet," grouses Bongoo.

In the end, they settle on a terrible name.

Rex.

That might sound cool to outsiders—like Tyrannosaurus rex.

But it's slang for a missile decoy.

Now everyone who glances at Newlin's patch will know.

He's behind the jet. Way behind the jet.

After Newlin, the rest of the naming goes smoothly—as though the IPs had exhausted some store of frustration.

Perkins—the stolid, amiable, gifted Alaskan bush pilot—ends up with Igor—because on one cold morning he wore a turtleneck under his flight suit, which made him look like a hunchback.

Lieutenant Spears, the popular, square-jawed West Pointer, avoided the obvious—Brittany, He Went to Fucking West Point (HWTFWP),

Throwing (Spear), and Asparagus (Spear). He nearly gets "Smiley," because he grins a lot but doesn't say much around the IPs. Or "He Never Talks—Thank God He Knows How to Land." So they settle on Pap—as in "Pap Smear."

So they chatter and hoot to a conclusion, having done their duty.

Rex is a marked man.

Gimmie didn't intimidate them.

And only Stihl got a cool name.

10

✦

The Sacred Naming of Names

Before they can actually hold the sacred naming ceremony, everything changes.

Festus gets promoted. He will be in charge of academics for all the training squadrons. Old Man still commands the squadron, but the operations officer provides day-to-day leadership. The loss of Festus snaps a connecting link between the IPs and the punks. Lieutenant Colonel Jay Paulis—"Ozone"—has filled in, but that's just temporary, pending the assignment of another operations officer. The shift has worked a subtle change in the squadron already. In the limbo of the interim, the squadron has lost cohesion.

Ozone leads the crucial Friday pilots meeting that will lead into the half-serious, half-satirical ceremony in which the punks will get the names they've been half-dreading for the last month.

But first, the week's comments, plaudits, and complaints.

First, Ozone compliments one of the B-coursers who ratted himself out. After a week of dogfighting, Kenn Cook's arm had developed a painful swelling as a result of the rupture of veins under the pressure of 9-g turns, which increase the apparent weight of a 180-pound pilot to nearly 2,000 pounds. Training rules require pilots to report even minor physical problems, although it is fighter pilot code to sneer at death, injury, and hardship. No one wants to sound like a wimp. Still, Cook ratted himself out halfway through a dogfight, quietly reporting that he was having trouble using his arm. He said it was nothing, but he knew he should report it. Rage broke off the fight and they headed home.

"How's your arm?" Ozone asks Cook.

"Still sore," he says, with a wry smile.

"You guys did the right thing. We had another B-course student who had gallstones for the last two months of the course—we had no idea. He could have had an attack at any time. Don't do that. Tell us. If you're getting sued for palimony or something—we don't want you to go down there and crash the jet." He pauses, considers how that sounds, and adds, "And we don't want to lose you guys, number one."

Now he gets stern. Two punks showed up late to class this week—a couple of minutes. He's pissed. "This late stuff—how many times do we have to say it's got to stop? We just can't stand it anymore. We were this close yesterday to saying, no naming until they grow up. When you're grown up, you can have a fighter pilot name. Instead of this FNG thing," he says in disgust, referring to the practice of calling them FNG 1, FNG 2, and so on until they have proper nicknames. "That's how close you are. You are letting the fighter pilot brethren down. We shouldn't be at that point. We shouldn't be having two or three talks every two or three weeks about being on time, being where you're supposed to be. We're kind of out of the group-think solution to the problem, we're going to put the laser beam on it. You're going to face a letter of reprimand if it happens again. You guys have got to work together. Don't come here thirty seconds before the pilots meeting—you guys all be in here first."

The punks exchange hangdog looks. They haven't yet pulled together as a group. Instead, they've formed subgroups. The young, single, academy graduates form the core, partying on the weekends, taking trips, grousing, drinking, and pulling each other through. The married guys keep largely to themselves, hurrying home to their families. Most of them are still trying to get their wives used to the idea that they're going to be fighter pilots.

But the biggest breech in the ranks has opened up between the lieutenants and the captains, the ranking officers who are supposed to provide leadership and promote group cohesion. Partly it's because the captains are married and so don't socialize very much with the other B-coursers. But mostly it stems from the issue of where the pilots will be assigned once they finish the B-course, a question that is decided by the time they're barely halfway through the course. Normally the commanders give the group a list of available assignments and leave it to the B-coursers to decide who goes where. Some of the assignments are great—an idyllic base on the coast of Italy. Some suck—stuck in the desert somewhere. Usually B-coursers draw lots to establish the order in which they choose. But this time two of the captains—Cook and Quattlebaum—insisted on making the choice by rank. They both have families and want assignments near home. Despite the bitter indignation of all the lieutenants, Cook and Quattlebaum insist on pulling rank. The rest of the B-coursers could have balked and kicked the decision back to Old Man. But that would constitute an admission of failure—and a breech of cohesion and teamwork even worse than the original offense. So Cook and Quattlebaum got their first choices and everyone else drew lots.

Needless to say, the B-coursers haven't coalesced, which could account for the chronic lateness—surprising in a group of obsessive overachievers.

This week they've been doing mostly formation work: learning how to cling to the right position as a wingman. Almost all fighter tactics rely on the offensive and defensive power of the wingman formation. This two-ship formation remains the basic unit, but it can be snapped together into four, eight, and twelve-ship formations. The lead jet remains in control, directing the wingman to his targets. The wingman's primary responsibility is to scan the skies constantly for enemy fighters and protect the formation from a lethal surprise from behind. Well, actually, that's not true. The wingman's main responsibility is not to collide with the flight lead, no matter how violently the lead jinks, rolls, and breaks.

"What's the most important thing you do as a wingman?" asks Ozone. "Deconfliction," he says, answering his own question. "You've got to deconflict the entire time you're the wingman. When you're in formation, don't bump into the other guy. That's your job as the wingman. Can you deconflict if you're not visual?"

"Only on radar," volunteers Spears.

"Negative," says Ozone, demonstrating why most punks don't volunteer answers in such a large-group setting. "You can still altitude deconflict," he says, reminding them of the reason for the elaborate pre-mission planning. Every plane in a formation, and every separate formation in the airspace, has its own assigned altitude. That's one reason flying the jet— maintaining a consistent speed and altitude—must become second nature. In training, it's mostly just an anxiety-provoking rule, since climbing too high or diving too low in the mostly empty sky will bust the ride. But it's training with deadly importance. In combat, hundreds of planes all have programmed flight paths, with altitudes that will keep them from running into each other. Equally critical, the AWACS controllers, who run hundreds of square miles of airspace full of planes loaded with bombs and air-to-air missiles, can easily lose track of planes flying at the wrong altitude. Worse, those circling F-15 pilots and the Patriot missile batteries down on the ground might track and lock up a plane flying around at the wrong altitude.

"Deconfliction is number one," says Ozone.

He promises to continue the pilots meetings, although the schedule needs some deconfliction. Scheduling the airspace over the vast, empty stretches of the Goldwater Range requires complex geometry. But a rash of mechanical problems with Luke's fleet of aging, second-string F-16s has compressed scheduling. Normally they try to avoid scheduling missions for Friday afternoon, so pilots can gather for the weekly meetings. But lately, they've been forced to schedule more and more flights on Friday to make up for flights canceled due to mechanical problems earlier in the week.

"I would like to meet with all of you over the next two weeks, just us," says Ozone, hoping he can maintain the cohesion, pride, competitiveness, and humor that Festus seemed to inspire so effortlessly. He knows that a wobble has already crept into the squadron, but he's not sure as to the source—since the B-coursers have mostly kept the anger at the captains among themselves. "As far as I'm concerned, the gloves will come off if we need to wrestle over something. I don't want to talk about the late thing anymore. If you have questions, comments, things you see that could be done better—just talk to me and tell me what you think you need. Or kudos. If some of the IPs are helping you out. I'd like to do that every couple of weeks."

He shifts then to the topic that preoccupies them—the naming ceremony about to take place. "The naming thing is supposed to be fun. If you're a little bit nervous—that's OK. It might be a little bit humiliating, but we've all had to go through it. I want you to enjoy it. Unfortunately," he adds, "no alcohol until after the naming." Until recently, the naming ceremony included a lot of toasting and booze. But one B-courser—with a lamentably elevated blood alcohol level—was so excited about his new name that he head-butted another B-courser, causing a considerable flow of blood and a change in the regulations for subsequent B-coursers. "In the last B-course, we were cleaning up blood."

He's just looking out for them, he says, so long as they don't abuse his kindly interest. "You guys are my little brothers," he says, and then remembering Moore adds, "and my little sisters. And I'm going to be watching out for you until you cross me. And then you can't be my little brothers and my little sisters anymore."

"So how do you think we're doing, minus the lateness thing?" asks Spears.

"In total, I'd say you're about average. Attitude is good."

Now Old Man takes the podium. Everyone listens intently. The students remain in awe of his flying skill. He has a knack for positioning himself and his wingman in the sky, with a minimum of fuss, effort, and nudging. In the three-dimensional geometry of the air, he's like a martial arts black belt, who turns the energy of his enemies against them, sending them flying across the room with small shifts in his position. He's also unflappable and has his ego under tight control, so he feels no need to put the students in their place. He treats them as peers, although they both know that if it ever came to a real dogfight he could kill them twelve times before breakfast without breaking a sweat.

"I understand that Spears here had an event in the air—and handled it effectively. You want to tell us what happened?"

"I was getting engine out-of-limit fluctuations," says Spears.

"And a good job by Major Robert"—Gilligan—"bringing him back in," says Old Man. "And then what happened today?"

"Same thing," says Gilligan, only this time it was Perkins. "He was in a defensive set. Initially, the surges were within limits. Then they rapidly got out of limits with the nozzle fluctuation plus or minus six—so the engine was going from mid-range to mil power. Some of the leads on the nozzle were opening and closing—and some were not."

Everyone's listening intently now. They know that the F-16 hurtles along in routine violation of physics—unstable by design. That gives the jet its uncanny ability to turn and chase its own tail, but if something goes wrong with the jet or the computer that really flies the jet, the F-16 will spin out of control instantly. So all the while a Viper pilot's flying, he knows he's just a malfunction away from a violent and unrecoverable spin to the ground.

In this case, the fluctuations were so serious the pilots broke off the mission and landed immediately at the backup airfield at Gila Bend, where mechanics went to work on the balky jet.

"Landing out of pattern at Gila Bend—anything?" asks Old Man.

"Had a third engine anomaly. Throttle at 85 percent—fluctuating, plus or minus 15. Push the throttle up and it drops down to 20, 25, 22."

"Didn't you tell it to stop doing that?" says Ozone.

Everyone laughs.

Captain Trimmel, the squadron's maintenance supervisor, moves to the front to report on the malfunction. "That one turned out to have an oil sensor issue," he says. "Turns out the jet hadn't flown in five or six days. We had a new crew chief. You're supposed to run it dry when it's been sitting. He was a young fellow and didn't do the proper warm-up— it was under maintenance. But, you gotta figure—Luke is also training the crew chiefs."

Luke does train most of the crew chiefs for F-16s in the Air Force. For every hour an F-16 spends in the air, it takes a three- or five-person crew one or two full shifts to perform adequate maintenance. That's especially true now, with many of the jets more than twenty years old. The pilots get the glory and the thrills; the crews work all through the summer on the simmering runways in 115-degree heat. They make a fraction of the money and hold the pilots' lives in their hands every day. In a well-maintained squadron, 5 or 10 percent of the jets can't fly on any given day. In a squadron with maintenance problems, that rises to 20 or 30 percent. In the Iraq wars, poor maintenance posed a much bigger threat to the Air Force than the Iraqi MiGs.

"Our ramp sucks, you can see all the goo coming out of the seams," adds Trimmel, referring to the upkeep of the runway. The F-16 fairly leaps into the air, but it demands a clean runway. A piece of gravel sucked into the low-slung air intake under the jet can wreck the spinning turbine blade—perhaps even crashing the jet on takeoff. "We had to shut four or five of you down a week ago. Apologize for that. We had just done our walk [across the runway to look for debris] and some of our supervision came out and found five or six chunks"—of asphalt worked loose from the deteriorating runway. "We did another FOD [foreign object damage] walk, and found a bagful on our second FOD walk of the day. We'll do five FOD walks a day if that's what it takes. And if you guys are out there walking around and see something, pick it up—or tell the crew chief."

Rage chimes in. "What are the chances of getting the crew chiefs to clean the canopies? We're getting a lot of bugs. I've run into a couple of crew chiefs who look like they've never done it. Or they say, we already did it once today. Almost seems like it should be standard before every go."

The maintenance captain nods and makes a note.

"Another incident note," adds Doughboy. "Tucson [airbase] had an incident when all twenty-eight [antimissile] flares came off the back with the power off. They're tracking that down, but be aware. I was flying with Rage and I did a flare check"—to be sure the flares were enabled, but not fire them off. "About a minute later, Rage is flying line abreast and he sees flares coming off my plane. No warning light. No chaff light."

"Bottom line," interjects Bongoo, "it's still a complete anomaly."

"Copy," says Ozone. "No good news. Now, one more thing," he says. "We got a new guy." He gestures to the new guy, a Marine F-18 Hornet pilot learning the F-16 as part of an ongoing cross-training program.

"Hello asshole," everyone shouts in unison.

"Stand up, tell us about yourself," says Ozone. "Stand up."

The marine captain stands up.

In unison, everyone yells "SIT DOWN!"

Confused, the captain sits abruptly.

"God. That never gets old," laughs Ozone.

Old Man retakes the lead. He notes that several jets from the squadron will do a formation flyby over the Diamondbacks Stadium for the first game of the season. And no—no free tickets.

"Unless they have a really bad season," grouses Gilligan. "Then we'll have plenty of free tickets."

Old Man notes that they've fallen behind schedule, and have lost some IP slots, not to mention Festus. "I'm a little concerned we're going to be doing a little more flying with no more people."

Bongoo jumps on that. He's a weapons and tactics officer for the base—which means he works with all the squadrons on tactics, weapons restrictions and capabilities, and updating manuals and procedures. As a Weapons School graduate, he's supposed to download that expertise. But that means he doesn't get to do as much flying—which he loves to the point of addiction. He's "attached" to the Emerald Knights, so he grabs IP flights every chance he gets. "So you're saying the attached guys should fly more," he says eagerly.

Old Man laughs. "Nooooo. I'm not saying that." It is one of the wrenching dilemmas of a fighter pilot's career path. All they really want to do is fly—preferably killing MiGs and bombing downtown Baghdad in the process, but nursemaiding punks if they must. Except the higher they rise and the better they get, the harder it is to hang onto a job that lets them fly a lot. Eventually—if they're brilliant and successful and politically adroit and peerless in the air—they'll get some terrible, well-paid, two or three or four-star job in which they don't ever get to fly at all—like getting buried in a coffin with just a penlight and an air hose.

"Keep in mind," resumes Old Man, "the days ahead are going to be good. We have some adversaries coming up. We've got some F-15s to fly against. We'll get some Smurfs [T-38s]. They're fun to fly with," he says of the light, slow, highly maneuverable training jets. "You go shooting past them and you're looking around and they're so small they're just gone— seriously—'Where is that guy?' No joy. It's a case of 'Near rocks, far rocks,' " he says, referring to the habitual cross-check a pilot makes as he flies, focusing his attention first on the mountain ridges close up, then deliberately shifting his attention to the more distant mountains—dealing with the immediate stuff first, but planning ahead to make sure he's at the right altitude and speed by the time the "far rocks" turn into "near rocks."

"We've got the ORI team inspection in two months. So we want to get everything in order before the inspection teams arrive—but we don't want to peak too early. From a safety standpoint, we had three great examples today of being a single-seat, single-engine fighter pilot—and taking care of those things in the air. Remember, no need to rush and make a bad landing when you've still got good, usable thrust—so good work there."

He pauses, checks his notes and realizes it's time for the naming ceremony. He looks toward the back, where the punks wait nervously. "Remember, if you break your helmet, Sergeant Bell will beat you. If you get anything on your life support equipment, you clean it." Then he laughs. "There are just eight white faces there in the back."

"But they're sober, sir," quips Gilligan.

With that, the punks are banished to get their helmets and a strobe light for the theatrics of the naming ceremony.

The IPs hustle about to convert the auditorium-like briefing room into a setting for the naming ceremony. They spread plastic on the floor under an armchair. They arrange strobes and black lights all around the room. They set a six-foot-long model of an F-16 on the stage. They crank up a smoke generator. They unearth a Viking helmet with horns and a full, frazzled wig. They set up the projector.

Finally they settle back into their seats, chattering, joking, making rude, clever, and caustic comments. A fighter squadron between briefings, when there are no official duties, resembles a victorious baseball team in the locker room—drenched in testosterone, brimming with ego, and suffused with off-color humor, competition, and affection.

The lights dim and the screen lights up with the opening battle scene from the movie *The Gladiator,* to set the proper warrior tone. Most of the IPs are sipping beer, which remains forbidden to the punks. On the screen, someone comments, "People should know when they're conquered." Someone yells "Fuck the French!" and everyone laughs.

Rage takes the stage, absurdly outfitted with the bewigged Viking helmet and brandishing a long sword. After some preliminary posturing, he calls out, "Let them enter and assume the position."

Gilligan opens the door and shouts, "Bring in the slugs. Each shall pass and pay homage to the king."

The B-coursers file in, fully flight-suited and helmeted, with their visors pulled down so that they're nearly blind in the dimly lit room. The IPs all pull out their flashlights and strobes and wave them wildly.

"Take your position against the wall," commands Rage. "No smiling. No talking."

The punks shuffle into a lineup along the wall, looking like Star Wars storm troopers.

"Hear ye, hear ye," intones Rage. "Welcome to the Emerald Knights super-secret naming ceremony. The feast of the best of the terrestrial orb. Welcome to the proletariat, mud-movers, sovereigns of the sky, elopers, pounders of the dirt, daubers, and in general, just badasses. Again I say. Welcome."

Everyone yells furiously, inspired by the pagan rite.

"We gather here to be-knight these plebs into the ranks of Viperdom, so that all posterity may marvel on the superhuman feats of the Emerald Knights and stand in awe. Warriors, a toast to the Vipers—that embodies all that is a knight, delivering sure and certain death to their foes. When I say hail to the Viper . . . "

He's interrupted by a roar from the IPs: "Hail to the Viper!"

Rage nods.

"Behold the lamp of learning," he says. This prompts a gout of flame from a blowtorch sitting on the stage alongside the smoke generator, which pours out vapors at a redoubled rate.

"Only through baptism of fire can true knowledge be procured," adds Rage.

The flame flares. The pilots cheer.

"The wings of the most superb fighter of all time summon those with a proclivity for cheap death—for trials to be surmounted—a testament to courage, perseverance, and sheer lethality. To commence the knighting and naming—behold the egg," he says, holding aloft a single raw egg.

"The egg, the egg, the egg," chant the hosts of darkness.

"The ovum. The beginning and essence of life. So these plebs may be reborn, they must devour unto themselves its substance, pith, and vitality," intones Rage. "Take the egg as you would the flesh of thine paramour, yet as gently as thou would gird thy loins. I want swift, decisive motion—ingest the gamete whole. Upon successful consummation, stand eagerly by—awaiting the nectar of life. Then you may wash it down," he says, holding aloft a glass of water, or maybe it's vodka. "Behold your tippling indulgence—flowing directly from Bosnian chicken farms—is the mix of Abraham and water—embodying the soul of the feast. However, take care—the first drink may bring heaving and sickness. By the third, thou wilt surely be addicted for life—forever under the spell of water."

"Hail the Viper!" shouts the room, before taking a deep drink.

"You plebs shall be ignited and anointed with call signs chosen by this august body. Stand, face the knights of the round table—and partake of the Viper Venom."

Captain Kenneth Cook comes forth first.

"Stand tall," says Rage.

Cook straightens up, bug-like in his helmet and tubes.

"Behold the orb," says Rage, handing Cook the raw egg. Cook takes it, flips up his visor and considers it for a moment. He is a small man, with fine features. The egg is larger than his mouth. He studies it dubiously.

Now Rage reads the list of possible names—Elvis, Pepsi, Crank, KKK Ken, Lost, Lefty, Zoolander, Shut the Fuck Up, Rainman. Each draws cheers, until he comes to the preselected name—Beaker. Now the room erupts.

"Beaker," says Rage, satisfied. "Ingest the orb."

Beaker holds the egg a moment, then his mouth gapes open. He forces the egg into his mouth. He closes his mouth, which fills to bursting with raw egg. He half gags and struggles to swallow.

"He's looking red," someone calls out.

"Pressure stall," hoots someone.

"Don't get that egg in your mask," shouts someone.

"Get the spare."

"Sucking wind."

Finally, he swallows and reaches for the water, or whatever it is.

And so it goes, as the B-coursers trade in their numbers for nicknames by which they'll be known for the remaining four months of the course. Each hears the list of names considered—rife with crude insults—and then winds up with a new name.

Quattlebaum is Pong.

Gough is Jack.

Lehto is Stihl.

Perkins is Igor.

Spears is Pap.

They all swallow their eggs without too much difficulty.

Then comes Moore's turn at the pillory. They read off the possibilities—Slammer, Pounder, Dirt, Dinty—before settling on Gimmie. Could have been worse.

But when she takes the egg into her mouth, she can't get it down. She bends over and spits it out, just short of vomiting.

Everyone groans.

"Must have a redo," cries Rage.

"Redo. Redo," chants the room.

"It's either a redo, or we rename her," says Rage.

God knows what they'd change it to. She holds her hand out for another egg. She stuffs it into her mouth without preliminaries; this time she bites into the front so the contents spill into her mouth, followed by the emptying eggshell. She chews a moment before swallowing. She knows it doesn't matter what it takes—it's getting the wings, earning the degree, finishing the course—swallowing. You do what you have to do. Keep your head down. Keep moving. Near rocks. Don't run the whole race from the beginning, just the mile you're in.

"Who says she can't be trained?" shouts someone.

She seizes the water and downs it with a snap of her head.

The only one who ends up with a truly terrible name is Newlin. He gags on his egg, nearly spits it out—keeps his mouth clamped shut and swallows by sheer force of will. Then grins good-naturedly, although there's a wound behind his grin. Rex. A target. Chaff.

He understands what they're telling him.

Worse than that, all the other B-coursers understand what they're telling him.

He grins and says nothing.

"Stand up," calls out Rage when they have all received their names. "Congratulations and felicitations. Look on this moment and savor it. You are one under the stars. Remember it so you can say, I was once a Knight. Always a knight. We hail your entrance into Viperdom—the baddest badasses in the Valley. Always enter battle without fear and always die while upholding our motto—strength and honor."

"To the bar," calls out Doughboy. "Let's party."

II

⬧

Buster Takes Charge

Lieutenant Colonel Gerald Lanagan—"Buster"—enters the squadron with a show of quiet confidence, knowing he'll have to earn his place now that he's arrived to replace Festus.

That won't be easy. Festus ran the squadron for several years and had it down cold. He managed that perfect blend of distance and familiarity—both stern and friendly. He was a gifted flier who had handpicked his flight commanders—with whom he played golf regularly. He knew the base and how to get things done.

Buster, who has never run a training squadron, takes over halfway through the B-course. He has reviewed the files—the long, detailed evaluations of every single mission. The students are nearly through BFM, the second major phase of the program. Soon they'll start all-out dogfighting, the most dangerous phase of the program.

Rex has four busts—with all the hard stuff still ahead. In his most recent bust, he bungled simulated emergency procedures for an engine flameout. Another time, while flying into a merge and trying to get to an offensive position, he overreacted as soon as the IP jinked, ending up out of position and vulnerable. He has always managed to pull himself together and pass the ride when he re-did it, but he can't get off CAP.

Pong has two busts—one for repeatedly going through the simulated floor, demonstrating a worrisome lack of awareness in the air. He missed the right altitude by a good 300 feet, enough to spur a midair collision. He kept speeding up and slowing down by as much as 50 knots, which screwed up his formation flying and his merges. He kept missing his turns, ending up wide of the flight lead and forced to speed up and slow down to slide, sloppily, into position.

Gimmie has two busts—one for screwing up her radar settings, one for poor maneuvering and going through the floor in a disastrous flight with Rage. She wasn't aggressive enough in her turns, pulling 7 g's when she should have whipped into 9 g's. She had trouble working the targeting system in the HUD, trouble picking the right missiles for air-to-air. On a couple of nose-to-nose merges, she seemed indecisive—so the IPs had to jink to avoid a head-on. She flew formations too erratically.

Pap, who all the IPs initially figured would blow through the course and get the Top Gun prize, has suddenly faltered. He busted one ride for a variety of problems—including screwing up his air-to-air radar settings and flying through the floor. On several nose-to-nose merges, he failed to offset—going right at the IP and forcing him to roll to avoid a collision. He mismanaged the targeting in the HUD.

Beaker has busted one ride, for flying through the floor while maneuvering. He would set up the run at his enemy properly, but then overreact or point his nose too low in the merge, throwing himself out of position.

Even Jack has developed problems, although everyone figured that with all that family fighter history he'd breeze through. He's a puzzle. Most of the time, he flies perfectly. He's eager. Bright. Hardworking. Great attitude. But then, unpredictably, his flying goes to hell. It's like he's thinking about something else. On the bust, he ran low on fuel without realizing it. He couldn't remember stuff he'd previously had down cold. He set himself up for a shot, and then forgot to shoot. He made sloppy radio calls. He had trouble merging smoothly with the IP.

It's all typical punk stuff—but it seems like it's piling on. It's hard to see how Rex is going to get through. And now Gimmie and Pong are both in trouble. Students that seemed strong and confident—like Pap and Jack—suddenly look shaky. Meantime, the two guys who looked marginal coming in—Igor and Stihl—have clicked into the grove. It's a puzzlement.

Buster sighs.

This could be tougher than bombing Serbs.

But then—that's the Air Force way. The minute someone gets confident, rotate the hell out of him. That especially holds true for the commanders. It's cross-training run amok—like an obsessive-compulsive trying to scrub the Sears Tower with a toothbrush. All right. That's overstated. But base, wing, and squadron commanders change ceaselessly—without a clear rationale. As a result, the top officers shuffle from base to base, forcing their itinerant families to continually adjust to new cities and new schools. It prompts many of the best pilots and most valuable officers to reluctantly resign their commissions after fifteen or twenty years, each one taking $10 million worth of flight training and priceless experience away with him.

But Buster figures it's like having to take over a football team in the fourth quarter—it's part of the game. A 1987 Air Force Academy graduate, Buster has amassed 2,500 hours in the air—at a cost to taxpayers of about $15,000 per hour. For a fighter pilot, he came to his obsession late—in high school, after taking one of those career aptitude tests. "I looked at the list and the only thing on it that sounded fun was 'pilot.' Rock star and professional football player weren't on the list."

His dad was the high school football coach, his mom was the school nurse, and he was the star quarterback, the fifth of seven kids in a conscientious, supportive, Catholic family. His dad was his hero, who went overboard to avoid giving him any hint of special treatment on the football team.

But when Buster didn't get a college football scholarship, he decided to take the free education offered by the Air Force Academy. He didn't know much about jets, but the family doctor took him for a flight in a Cessna during high school and he'd had a blast. His dad was all for it; his mother dubious. Now these thousands of hours in the air later, she doesn't worry so much anymore. But he lives all over the world—and they miss him. He's the only child who strayed more than 10 miles from home.

Now Buster figures he's really doing the same thing his dad did as a football coach—molding young men, instilling a sense of discipline. "My dad would have made an excellent squadron commander," he says, "because of his leadership—that sense of, This is right, this is wrong."

And he figures that the Academy was like football camp—where you puke your guts out in the summer heat. "It's the price of admission," he says of the harassment and the toughening. He says only one of the upperclassmen really harassed him—running him ragged on personal tasks and demanding endless push-ups for minor or imagined infractions. Ironically, that upperclassman became a Viper pilot—and died in a training accident. He g-locked in a turn and flew into the ocean. "He was just a really strict military guy. His dad was a general and he was going to be a general too."

He doesn't remember seeing any sexual harassment at the Academy, but doesn't deny that it happened. "My dad asked me at one point whether Lizzy, my sister, should go to the Academy. I said Lizzy could handle it, but at the same time there are nine or ten guys for every girl, so the girls get more attention, which can become an unhealthy thing. There were certain women who could not handle the extra attention. Others can. When they first said they were going to let female fighter pilots in, I said, 'Shit hot.' I know there are women who can pull more g's than me—do everything I can do better than I can. Like my little sister. Or I've got two daughters—and Molly has fighter pilot attitude in everything she does—tenacious, she won't be denied. That's the point—putting your bombs on target, surviving the enemy and killing the enemy. Sure, the squadron is a male environment—making fun of each other and giving each other funny names—but that's a bonus. Being successful at the mission does not necessarily require all of that.

"Like Julie Moore. Her personality—her tenaciousness—her attitude—man, she's got her shit together. And she's the first woman that's ever been in a squadron I've ever flown with. And maybe she has to do that extra amount to win her space—because she stands out and everyone's watching. But that can be a good thing too. If you're a shit-hot fighter pilot and everyone's eyes are on you, then you'll have the opportunity to progress faster. But if she's borderline, she'll probably get cut before the guy who's equal."

Once he got to pilot training, Buster found himself unnervingly stuck in the middle of the pack—solidly "average." He busted some early rides—stupid stuff, just trying to find the pattern for a landing. But in IFF he started to pick it up. "Some people's brains work fine at 200 miles an hour in the T-37, but not so well at 400 miles an hour in the T-38, or at 600 miles an hour in an F-16. Like a quarterback—you have to make a decision and stick with it. Good quarterbacks are just right more often than they're wrong."

He did all right at IFF, despite the hazing of the IPs—which he attributes to their frustration at being stuck teaching trainer jets. He pulled some stupid stunts. He got into a drag race with another student leaving the airfield and forgot to raise his landing gear—a potentially fatal mistake. He busted that ride, but passed the course.

And moved onto the F-16, training at Luke.

That was before a whole new generation of weapons, bombs, and tactics dramatically expanded the role of the F-16. "When I was in the B-course," he says, "all we had to know was the basics of how to get the weapons off the plane. We didn't have the laser-guided bombs and the HARMs shot off the block 50s and everything else the F-16 is doing now out in the world. So the IPs didn't have all this experience and knowledge base. It was a different world."

To his everlasting regret, he missed the first Gulf War. But he proved a gifted pilot and a squadron workhorse. He threw himself at every new task, like a million termites in a soggy foundation—relentless, patient, thorough. He had great hands; he was a smart, quick, dependable flier. He devoured tactics and weapons. He also proved one of those pillars of teamwork and morale. He wasn't flashy. He didn't need to be the center of attention; he usually hung back during the bar bullshit sessions. But he always volunteered, never complained, and never criticized. He always showed up early, stayed late, and did his homework. He was a deft wingman and then a natural leader. He made other pilots feel confident and lucky. He didn't pick fights and he never backed down.

Like many veteran pilots, he got his nickname in Korea. He was enjoying a party in one of the tough little bars on the edge of the base, where the "Mama San" often screamed at the raucous aviators. He was involved in some sort of a grab-ass struggle with a guy from another squadron for possession of a strange hat adorned with blinking lights when they somehow broke the overhead lightbulb. Everyone hooted, yelling that he was "busted," and that the "Mama San" was going to kick his ass. She came into the room screaming that she was going to call the MPs because that was an antique light worth $200. So then the whole crowd starts chanting, "Busted, busted, busted."

After Korea he was selected for Weapons School—officially certifying him as a fast-tracked member of the fighter pilot elite.

He missed Bosnia in Weapons School, but got out in time for his war—Kosovo.

He flew thirty-five combat missions there, providing cover for the NATO peacekeepers straining to keep the Serbs from slaughtering the Muslims in their effort to pull together and ethnically cleanse the disintegrating remains of Yugoslavia. Most of the pilots were a little confused as to the details. Buster got a book and read it, puzzling over the complexities of the politics in the chaotic nest of old hatreds that had spawned World War I. The mission seemed righteous to him, as near as he could make out.

So he went off to do his duty, which involved killing a lot of Serbs.

"We flew seven strike missions into Yugoslavia, mostly dropping laser-guided 2,000-pounders—but sometimes we dropped cluster bombs on tanks and ground forces." Once they went in and killed a slew of construction workers trying to repair a military runway hit in a previous raid. The memory of all those guys running across the runway in the last few moments of their lives still bothers him a little.

Most of his missions he was flying forward air control, wandering around ahead of the bombers looking for something to hit—since the Serbs quickly learned to hide their troops and armor in the thick forests. "That was extremely challenging. You'd have to find the target, fix the target and then identify it," mindful that the Albanians and other factions were also gathering in the area. "We had guys waiting to come bomb whatever we found."

The conflict represented an almost unique attempt to achieve a victory using air power alone, since neither the U.S. nor NATO wanted to risk sending in ground troops. The USAF had often promised to achieve a decisive tactical or strategic victory with unsupported airpower, but had never actually delivered. But the Balkans conflict represented the first such effort since the widespread introduction of smart bombs, which dramatically increased the effectiveness of airpower. Fairly soon the Serbs yielded and pulled their troops out of Kosovo—one of the few times in

The F-16, the most agile, flexible, and valuable fighter jet ever built.

Luke Air Force Base, Glendale, Arizona.

Lt. Chris "Stihl" Lehto

Lt. Julie "Gimme" Moore

Lt. Greg "Rex" Newlin

Day or night, an instrument of deadly precision.

Lt. Chris "Jack" Gough

Captain Kenn "Beaker" Cook

Lt. Chris "Igor" Perkins

Lt. Matt "Pap" Spears

Captain Kevin "Pong" Quattelbaum

Loaded with new weapons systems, radars, targeting pods, and a more powerful engine, the most recent F-16 costs close to $30 million.

Pilots sit high, reclining beneath the exquisitely designed bubble canopy.

Forty-eight-feet long and weighing in at 18,600 pounds, the F-16 can generate a thrust of 29,000 pounds.

the history of warfare that airpower proved decisive without the support of troops on the ground.

"It was tough, because we had no spotters on the ground," says Buster. Instead, they had to rely on Viper pilots, flying low enough to spot hidden troop concentrations, while also keeping an eye on the radar for SAM locks and ground fire. "It wasn't like there were huge tank battles. You'd see people running around in villages, you'd see vans parked outside of houses that were being burned down. But it was hard to tell what was going on from the air. And mistakes were made."

For instance, one squadron mistakenly bombed a civilian convoy loaded with refugees.

"My squadron commander said some of the most important bombs were the bombs we didn't drop. Fortunately, we didn't make a lot of mistakes."

Most of their missions were spent flying around looking for something to kill. "Kosovo is the size of the state of Connecticut, so there are plenty of places to hide a tank. They would drive a tank right through the side of a house and hide it under the roof. We got so we looked for that—tank treads that led up to a house and then didn't come out the other side.

"You'd go in, gas up, fly around for an hour, gas up again, and fly around for an hour. It got so you'd almost hope someone would shoot at you, because then you could go after it."

They also worked with unmanned Predator drones, which flew about relaying a TV image to their ground controllers. If the Predators spotted tanks, F-16s were called in.

On one mission, a Predator detected activity around one of the endless fields of earthen bunkers that dotted the landscape. "So I'm looking around there for tanks and all of a sudden I see this stand of trees shaped like a dog bone about 200 yards long. I wheel in there and they actually shoot at my wingman from in the trees—triple-A. I could just see a ton of guns in there, but if they hadn't shot, I'd have never seen them. So I call, 'Jewels, jink, evade, you're being shot at—climb to safety.' So we got up a bit, and Jewels has general-purpose bombs—Mark 82s with airburst fuses that go off 15 feet above the ground, which pretty dramatically increases the blast effect. So I talk him onto the target and he makes a perfect pass on the guys who were just trying to kill us—made it a pretty damn bad day for them. I was using an infrared targeting pod and I could see the hot spots from the engines of the tanks down in under the trees. We just destroyed everything. Then we went for gas and came back and there was no movement at all—no one even came for those guys."

On another mission he bagged a MiG 21—on the ground, unfortunately. "Normally, they tried to hide their fighters in tunnels and whatnot. So we were flying around out there outside their concrete revetments. I bombed one MiG with a laser-guided bomb—saw it blow up. That was very satisfying."

Usually they faced only sporadic air defenses—mostly non-radar-guided antiaircraft artillery (triple-A). The earlier clash in Bosnia had destroyed most of the SAM sites in the Serb arsenal.

Still, his squadron commander got shot down by a lucky triple-A gunner, which means he never got a radar lockup warning to trigger evasive maneuvers. Buster won't use the pilot's name because the commander deliberately kept his name out of the press. He figured that the real heroes of the incident were the Special Forces guys who came in by helicopter to rescue him.

"And he was right. I was just choked up watching these young Special Forces Operations guys going in there. They don't even think twice about going in there in harm's way to pick up a guy who has been shot down. I mean, an F-16 is very maneuverable and very survivable—but they're going in there with these lumbering helicopters to pick up a guy they don't even know. Those guys are the heroes."

The commander was over Belgrade in a four-ship assigned to take out air defenses ahead of the bombers. "You'd be ahead of the bombers and when you'd see the SAMs light up, you'd roll in there and attack the site. We were equipped for it, but that wasn't something we normally did—which was close air support or forward air controlling."

The commander, wearing night-vision goggles, never did see what hit him. They'd picked up fleeting signals from ground radar on the way in—but the wary SAM operators would risk only a quick flick of their radars. The commander saw the launch of a missile, but it seemed headed for someone else. He went into a defensive jink anyway. As soon as he came out of that maneuver, the jet shuddered—probably hit by a stray scrap of triple-A.

The engine cut out almost immediately, leaving the crippled F-16 gliding silently through the dark over Belgrade, above the swarming, frustrated Serb army. He glided for as long as he could, hoping to clear the populated area, then ejected.

None of the other planes in the formation had even seen the hit in the darkness. Suddenly they heard the codeword for an emergency. "Hammer 34 has been hit," he called out. "Hammer 34 has taken a hit. Hammer 34 engine is damaged. Egressing 270," he said, giving a heading based on a classified navigation point, which would therefore be useless to the Serbs listening on the ground.

Fortunately, the pre-mission briefing included a complete plan for just such a crash into enemy territory. He had an escape and evasion kit and had memorized a whole sequence of places near the target area to head for at once if he needed rescuing—plus a GPS locator that would give him the headings to those pickup points. He also had a complete set of codes for talking to potential rescuers on the radio—all elements of the briefings for the B-coursers as well.

"For the most part," says Buster, "as fighter pilots we're not going to go too far. We're not going to try to navigate 50 miles through Bad Guy Land. We're going to get to the pickup point and wait for rescue."

The commander hit the ground and hid about twelve miles out of Belgrade, hoping the Special Forces would reach him before the Serbs.

He made contact immediately, giving his coded coordinates. The Special Forces helicopters were already in the air. The Serbs peppered the helicopters with small arms fire repeatedly as they hurtled past. The Special Forces guys plucked the pilot from a ridge, threw him into the back of the helicopter, and headed out through renewed fire from the ground. When the bullets started pinging against the helicopter, several of the Special Forces guys threw themselves on top of the pilot—who was sitting on the floor, still not strapped in. Initially, he felt flattered. Later it occurred to him that he was on the bottom of the pile, and all the bullets were coming from below.

They had him back at his base in Italy within six hours—arriving only four hours after the enormously relieved and jubilant members of his flight. They swarmed around him, popping the corks on chilled bottles of champagne. But he wouldn't drink, insisting that he was slated to fly that night.

"He had no fear issues—and I think he wanted to show his guys that everything was OK." He ended up not flying that night, however. His wife was too upset.

Every year since, that rescued pilot travels to the base of the Special Forces team that rescued him and throws them a party. It's impossible for any member of that crew to buy a drink in the same bar as that pilot.

Buster says bombing Kosovo was strange—since they were based in Italy, with their wives and children. They would suit up every morning, go to war, then come back to their families as though returning from a day in the office—with the television brimming with images of the war. "It's infinitely more demanding on the wife and kids than on the pilot. The pilot is confident in his machine and tactics and training—we don't train our wives on how to sit at home patiently for the next twelve hours waiting for me to call as soon as I land. I'd try to tell my wife when we'd actually be over the target—so that she could concentrate her worrying on that particular time." She had the worst time during the night missions—lying awake watching the clock, waiting for her peak worry time to pass. "But the wives were just awesome—which they are in a fighter squadron anyway. Every single baby shower is attended by like 75 percent of the wives in the squadron. We celebrate every high point and gather at every low point."

He says that pilots have it easy compared to the grunts on the ground. "You don't see the bodies. You don't smell the gunpowder. It's clean. Antiseptic. We see it from a mile up and five miles away. That's not fair for the guys dying on the ground. But, lo and behold, if I ever send these guys out into a fair fight, then I've screwed up. Of course it's not fair—we don't want it fair. That's why we want the F-22, so we can kill them before they ever even see us on their radar. We kill 100 to 1? That's good. But I want 100 to nothing. Then I'll be satisfied. We're equipped and we train and we hope our leaders put us into a completely unfair fight so we can go and kick ass. Still, even if intelligence says you're facing 50 percent losses—you're still going to go in."

So Buster walks into Festus's office and sits down like he belongs there. Like it's always been his office.

The B-courser grade books are sitting on his desk—each one already thick with evaluations.

He remembers his wingman, flying over that copse of trees bristling with guns, depending on his quick warning and instincts.

He remembers the doomed Serb construction workers, running uselessly from the cluster bombs.

He remembers the Special Forces helicopter flying through the flak, down low, looking for the pilot.

And he knows he can't afford to doubt himself now. He's got to crank out a fresh batch of wingmen who can go out there and do their jobs without getting their flight leads killed.

They'll just have to forget about Festus. Buster's in charge now.

And he's got to figure out what's wrong with these punks.

12

⊸⊸⊷⊶

BUSTED RIDES AND BASIC MANEUVERS

DOUGHBOY SITS IN THE CRAMPED BRIEFING ROOM trying to figure out what he should tell Jack so he won't bust this damned ride again.

Doughboy tries to remember when he switched to F-16s—once the Air Force finally retired the muscular Phantoms that he so loved—that Chips so loved. He remembered how tough it was switching planes, being a punk again.

"It was like starting all over as a pilot," he says. "They'd made such a humongous technological jump," over the F-4. "I was lost. Everything happens a lot further away—like three times as far away as with the F-4. Now, if you haven't done something by the time you're within 20 miles of a bogey, you're in big trouble. And he's doing the same thing in the other cockpit—so everything's much faster."

That's why the next generation of fighter jets—with stealth technology that makes them harder to see on a radar screen—promises to change fighter tactics dramatically. The stealth pilot can spot the conventional aircraft 10 or 20 or 30 miles before the other guy sees him—which gives him a lethal advantage. But if the stealth fighter costs ten times as much, sheer numbers of the older fighters can prove overwhelming. Usually, the Air Force opts for the complicated, expensive weapons system, even if it means flying a billion-dollar B-1 bomber halfway around the world to bomb a target worth less than the gas it took to get there. The F-16 is a rare counterexample to that deeply ingrained Air Force tendency—cheap, flexible, and adaptable with a minimum of exotic technologies.

Even after he switched to the F-16, Doughboy's luck held.

He got another war. Kind of. When Saddam Hussein kicked the UN weapons inspectors out of Iraq, the Clinton administration staged a brief show of force, and the Air Force sent him to fly around and intimidate Iraqis. "That was about the time when Monica showed up in the news and we were dropping bombs for, like, five days total. It was extremely benign. We went into Iraq and all the lights were on in Baghdad. It's like we were a nuisance, they didn't take us seriously."

The Iraqis did take a couple of missile shots, which made the exercise marginally more interesting. "From that time on, we could start dropping bombs on SAM sites—the great desert gunnery range. 'Oh, boys, the range is open.' "

But the pilots felt a faint echo of the frustration many pilots felt in Vietnam, when the politicians picked the targets and the pilots were straining at a tight leash. "It was a huge drain on us—Southern Watch—just flying around in circles. Guys would go out there and come back after ninety days in the desert not current in anything," he noted, since the Air Force decrees a never-ending training schedule, encompassing every element of the mission, from instrument landings to bombing techniques. But at least Doughboy got to drop the latest smart bombs and watch them plunge toward the grainy black-and-white image of the target through the camera in the nose of the bomb. Very cool.

As soon as he finished his futile tour over Iraq, the Air Force sent him to Korea.

By then his marriage was over. "We'd been married eleven years—with two kids. You can't blame her—I was a workaholic, and she didn't like that. She was a lot younger. Her dad had been in the Air Force—she ended up marrying her dad, I guess. She just got fed up with it. Became a nurse—married a doctor. We actually get along better now than when we were married. We might have worked it out, but I was too much of a workaholic. Even when I wasn't on remote and back home, I was spending fifteen-hour days in the squadron."

Now his kids live on the East Coast, and he sees them when he can. His daughter, Nicole, is fourteen—a "super genius"—who only reluctantly gave up her ambition to be a whale trainer to shoot for a career as a Disney illustrator. His son, James, is twelve—a computer game wizard who wants to program computers. Doughboy softens and glows when he talks about them.

As his marriage was disintegrating, he was stationed at the forward USAF base in Korea, half a world away from family and friends. He threw himself into the flying, which was intense due to the proximity of thousands of MiGs and the whole North Korean army a few miles away, and the party scene, which was equally intense as a way of blowing off steam. "It's changing now, I think," he says. "But when I joined, alcohol was king and partying was the name of the game. We hold on to some of those traditions—especially in Korea—but we're a lot more careful now. Society has changed. It's just not acceptable anymore to do those things. Some of those changes are for the good, but it has also taken away some of the warrior spirit."

He rotated back to the States and became an instructor pilot, taking on completely new challenges. "You've got to be able to look at them and see that they're not understanding—and you have to be able to make a judgment that they're just not going to get it. It's not the flying—with enough sorties, you can teach a monkey to fly. It's the situational awareness—that ability to fly the airplane while you're doing four other things."

So now he studies Jack's grade sheets, trying to decipher the odd pattern of brilliance and inattention. Jack's like a radio with a loose wire on a dirt road—blaring, then turning to static, then blaring again.

Jack enters, professional, grinning, faintly hesitant.

Doughboy counts down to the start of the briefing, wondering how basic to get. Several days ago Jack busted his BFM ride. Doughboy likes Jack—everyone likes Jack, with his gung-ho attitude and faintly goofy charm. But he's inconsistent, and Doughboy wonders how to pinpoint the anomaly. Doughboy jokes, drinks, teases, gabs, and clowns—so it's easy to underestimate him. He has a comic's face, quick, expressive—with a too-wide mouth, pale blue, sparkling eyes, and mobile features. He's completely irreverent—he cannot resist a pun or a sharp remark—and cynical about the ponderous, often-senseless Air Force bureaucracy. But he's also a natural teacher. His criticisms are detailed and serious, but he softens them with humor; he talks to the students at their level. As a result, he's among the most popular instructors at Luke.

After finishing the checklist of preliminary details, Doughboy focuses on the lack of initiative that led to Jack's busted ride. "Don't just hang out and watch me fly around in circles. Come in and kill me. The biggest threat is the Old Ugly out front—that would be me—going blind when we're maneuvering."

Doughboy talks about the landing, warning that he may call out for Jack to simulate having lost a motor—which means cutting his engine and approaching the runway in a glide.

They cover the procedures for a crash—a routine but intensely drilled part of every briefing. He also covers disorientation—the most dangerous problem facing even veteran pilots. An F-16 that's turning, climbing, or diving creates an inaccurate sensation of motion, so pilots can easily lose any sense of depth and distance, staring into a featureless blue sky or out into a night-shrouded sky. The mind plays tricks. You think you're climbing when you're actually diving; you think you're moving away from another airplane when you're actually moving toward it. "If you think you're getting disoriented, look between your legs, not at your HUD: get your eyes recaged."

Now Doughboy moves to the dogfight setups.

"We'll talk about things—what I see, what you're doing. I may be asking you questions in the middle of a fight—airspeed, altitude. Just answer. What is your game plan? Let's say we're 20 miles apart, beak to beak—what do you do?"

"Offset," says Jack, knowing he's not supposed to aim for a midair collision.

"How much?"

"I'm going to continue to get my offset to see if the aspect changes at all. Throughout the whole thing, I'm going to be checking my vertical offset," to avoid a collision.

"How much?"

"About 5,000 feet."

"OK. But no more than that."

He questions Jack closely to make sure he understands what the other jet should look like from the cockpit as they converge. "You're going to see the guy going from really not moving in the canopy, to all of a sudden starting to shift," says Doughboy. Fighter pilots get a great deal of information about the speed and heading of an enemy by noting how the tiny plane grows and shrinks and moves against the canopy. If the other jet gets bigger without changing relative position, it means the two jets are heading straight at each other. If the jet gets bigger and drifts from one area of the canopy to another, they're in a turn. It's all based on instantly grasping the "picture" of the other jet and then reacting.

"If he's moving fast in the canopy, you're starting to pass each other and you're going to miss—and you need to do something, right now. So ideally, you're going to get as much of this turn out of the way as you can. We know this guy is a power-limited kind of guy," says Doughboy, referring to the rules of the fight that prevent the IP from using his afterburner. "You're going to get a good lead turn out of this. You're coming uphill—you get about 45 degrees—he's a heater-only kind of guy—and he tries to turn across your tail."

"It's a two-circle fight," says Jack quickly, the classic fight in which the jets turn away from each other, each making a circle in the sky, each pilot hoping to outturn the enemy jet and end up behind him. Equally matched planes and pilots will end up flying in tightening circles, neither able to get to a shooting position. But usually the most maneuverable jet—the jet with the most power and the tightest turn—will win the deadly struggle for position.

"So what's this hand doing?" says Doughboy, waving his left hand.

"Hitting the afterburner"—giving the student that precious advantage in power.

"Right. Afterburner. Don't forget it," says Doughboy. "Now, where's your nose?"

"Going low," says Jack. Making that vital turn going downhill adds power, since gravity adds to your energy.

"How fast you going?"

Jack looks up. But doesn't answer.

"Aim for 350 knots, that's the Viper's best turn rate."

Doughboy continues. "OK, now let's say instead of a two-circle fight, he turns into a one-circle fight." In a one-circle fight, the "offensive" pilot turns toward the jet he's trying to kill. It's a risky maneuver. The offensive pilot wants to get inside the other guy's turn circle so he can get off a quick shot from behind. But he's taking a chance. If he overshoots, he'll end up in front. If he slows too quickly, he'll have only a fleeting shot and then wind up on the defensive. Most fighter maneuvers offer this kind of deadly trade-off between a quick shot and a patient turning battle.

"So he doesn't want a rate [two-circle] fight. He wants to scare you. Get you to overshoot," says Doughboy, illustrating the positions of the contending jets with two pointers—each one tipped with the cutout of an F-16, one red (bad guy), one blue (good guy). He puts his whole body into the demonstration, leaning to the side, whipping the pointers through the air. He grimaces, he squints at the planes. It's quite a performance—natural, absorbing, and effective. He huffs and puffs; the planes slide, zoom, slip through the air, and crash together. "Uh oh," he says, as one jet loses the offense. The blue jet turns tighter, regains position. "Whew, that's better—things are much better now," exclaims Doughboy, completely absorbed by the deadly puppet show. "I'm going to kill him when I get inside 3,000 feet or end up on that 3,000-foot perch above him. He's got to pull the power and turn more—do the dance—and dump energy. Then you've got him. So you keep threatening and he keeps losing energy, until he gets to where he can't move anymore. He's going to put out flares and pull his power back and turn, turn—and I'm going to let him do it and stay at a higher energy rate until he's pissed away all his energy—and then I'm going to kill him," he concludes, illustrating the instant, flaming death with his blue and red puppets—happy as a kid at a carnival.

He pauses, worked up from the simulated combat. "OK, now, you're on a two-and-a-half mile perch and this guy has a fully performing airplane—how are you going to fight?"

"Roll out, get the burner cooking, go for turn circle energy."

"What speed?"

"400 knots."

"Don't get beyond 500 knots. So how's this guy going to defend himself? Where's he going to be when you get to his turn circle?" asks Doughboy. The key to any fight lies in driving toward the other jet in such a way that when you reach the arc of his curve in the air, you can turn inside his circle. If you drive straight for the other jet, you can't maneuver into the lethal six-o'clock position in the rear. Therefore, the offensive pilot has to work out the merge in three dimensions, so he's at the right speed and altitude when he reaches that perfect point in the sky behind the already turning opponent.

"He's starting his turn."

"He may get all the way around," says Doughboy. "He's trying to keep you in sight. So you're back looking for that lead turn opportunity cue. And you're thinking back now to that original two-circle game plan. Now the issue is how many g's can you pull as you're going downhill, hoping he's gonna make a mistake. So you're under sustained g in this pull, and he does something bizarre. Usually, it's going to take three seconds to recognize this guy has done Stupid Pet Trick Three."

The fight usually comes down to this circling spin toward the ground, with each trying to take advantage of a split-second mistake. The guy in front wants his enemy to overshoot; the guy in back wants to line up a shot. At some point in each of the descending spirals, there's a possible shot.

"Look at the radar—see what his airspeed is. If he's incredibly slow, you may see him trying to turn this into a single-circle flight to make you overshoot. But if you've been good—you can use your extra energy and get back to that 3,000-foot perch and reorient on his nose. Fine. Fine. Now go back to following him around. Use your energy advantage."

Jack nods, concentrating furiously on the movement of the red and blue jets.

"Now, what did you do last time?" asks Doughboy.

"Last time I had a weak pull. I didn't sustain it."

"You were going really fast," prompts Doughboy.

"I started fast—510—then pulled down to 450. I kept it in burner the whole time, and I was way fast and didn't turn sharp enough to bleed the energy," says Jack of his busted ride.

So he overshot, flashed in front of the tight-turning Doughboy, and wound up dead.

Doughboy nods. Satisfied. Jack has the picture.

And sure enough, once they get out there in the deep blue sky in a deadly spiral, Jack "demonstrates proficiency."

He even kills Doughboy.

Sometimes you got to give the kids one.

Half of being a hotshot fighter pilot is practice—skill.

The other half is confidence.

Well. All right. Maybe not half.

But something like it.

13

MAKING OF A WINGMAN

THE WAY BOB CHURCHILL—"PUNCH"—figures, they're in the business of hand-tooling wingmen.

And they'd better not cut corners—since the lives of their buddies depend on the details.

A pilot straight out of an Air Force recruiting poster, Punch first trained as a paratrooper. The thirty-four-year-old Punch figures the B-course sets the pattern for a career. But then, maybe that's just because he's one of the few IPs still carrying around his nickname from his punk days. And he earned it the hard way—bailing out of a dying jet.

Punch had just dropped his simulated bombs and was hurtling away from the target over the cactus and the unforgiving, jagged volcanic ridges at 1,000 feet when his engine came apart, swallowing its own turbine fan blade. "That was the biggest adrenaline shock ever," he recalls. He compares it to jumping out of airplanes during his paratrooper training—"except triple that."

He was doing 530 knots at 730 feet when the blade popped off and he immediately lost all power. Almost instantly, the engine caught fire. "It was so violent, it felt like I'd hit a tree trunk with the wing." The remaining fan blades were still spinning at 3,000 revolutions per minute, but now wildly out of balance—which threatened to shake the plane apart. "The vibration was so violent I couldn't read the engine gauges."

Somehow, he turned the crippled plane around and set a course for the emergency backup field at Gila Bend, remembering even to jettison everything attached to the underside. Fortunately, his IP had covered the emergency airfield headings with his typical precision—those lifesaving habits.

"All I could think was that I'd ingested a bird—sucked a turkey vulture down the intake. So I called, 'Orca two has had a bird strike, going to Gila Bend.' "

The instant the jet started shaking itself to death, Punch thought, "Holy shit, what did I do wrong?" Then, "Holy Shit, what am I going to do to fix this?" Then as the engine is exploding and everything is shallying around it's, "Holy Shit, what caused this?"

Fortunately, the emergency procedures drilled so relentlessly in the flight simulator by irritable old fighter pilots kicked in: aviate, navigate, communicate. Fly the jet, find the airfield, talk to the flight lead and the air controller.

Later, it turned out Punch hadn't done a thing wrong. The brilliantly efficient, expensively maintained Pratt and Whitney engine was already past its original design life. The B-coursers fly the oldest F-16s in the Air Force, and Punch's crash was one in a flurry later traced to metal fatigue in the turbine blades. For a while it seemed like another F-16 was crashing every month or so in the twisted desert reaches of the range.

Punch finally had to punch out 3 miles from the end of the runway, saying a small prayer of gratitude to the guys who designed the rocket-propelled F-16 ejection seat. Only two F-16 pilots have ever been killed in the process of ejecting, both because they were an instant too late pulling the handle. Earlier seats often subjected the pilots to such violent accelerations that they often came down with broken arms and legs and spinal fractures. But the F-16 seat is a marvel of engineering that has saved hundreds of pilots' lives.

The cool, correct handling of his crippled jet won Punch the respect of his IPs. Once he got to Korea and told the story in the bars a couple of times, it earned him the nickname that has stuck with him ever since. That proved fortunate. Before that, the all-powerful Kunsan naming committee had dubbed him Briefs, which Punch explains, "had to do with a mysterious set of underwear stolen by an ex-girlfriend."

It's easy to credit a complicated story involving out-of-control female behavior in Punch's case. He's square-jawed and clear-eyed, ruggedly handsome, with light, twinkling, penetrating eyes. He exudes charisma and the right stuff. He's like Dudley Do Right, with a wink. He's so freaking perfect that at first you figure he must be putting you on, acting the part. But no. He's a charming, funny, patriotic, idealistic, bomb-dropping Good Guy—irresistible to women. He's even aw-shucks, self-mocking about that—just a guy who likes to fly, Ma'am, and defend his country and bring his wingman home alive. And if that's not bad enough, he also plays the freaking viola—chamber music for Christ's sake.

Punch was six when he decided on a career as a pilot. His father bought him a model of an F-16 and they built it together and painted it red, white, and blue. That pretty much settled the course of Punch's life. His dad was a helicopter crew chief in Vietnam. He did his combat tour, then decided he couldn't raise a family on a military salary and got out to manage a grocery store. His grandfather had been a supply sergeant.

Punch took to science and dreamed of flying. "I was always fascinated by anything that went boom—model rockets, whatever." He dimly remembers his first air show, at the age of four, which included the Thunderbirds. He applied to the Air Force Academy but was "too stupid to make it," partly because the movie *Top Gun* had just come out and everyone in the goddamned universe wanted to be a fighter pilot. So he joined the ROTC program at Worcester Polytechnic Institute and took up playing the violin and the viola while he got himself ready to fly. He insists that playing chamber music improves hand-eye coordination. The other guys in the squadron don't know he plays chamber music, though. The ribbing would be merciless.

Of course, just to balance things out, he also was a competitive marksman when he was a teenager.

He earned a mechanical engineering degree with an aerospace minor, but by the time he graduated the government was cutting back the post-Cold War military and he couldn't land a pilot spot. The best he could do was an assignment to the space command, flying satellites from the ground. "I was hugely disappointed. Everything I'd done had been designed to get a pilot slot—so here I was with $20,000 in student loans and a commitment to serve flying satellites in the reserves."

As his day job, he went to work for Pratt and Whitney, working on the engine for the F-22, a stealth-technology fighter intended one day to replace the F-15—at a horrendously higher cost. But all that paid so poorly that he also took up waiting tables at a women's bridge club—partly to pay for his very expensive private flying lessons. Who knows how many hearts he broke in a women's bridge club—although that was before he had the whole fighter pilot thing down cold.

He spent nearly three years in space command controlling $4 billion worth of satellites—keeping tabs on the aftermath of the Gulf War, an attempted coup in Russia and an actual coup in Haiti. In fact, the unprecedented air supremacy the U.S. has enjoyed since Vietnam depends critically on the nation's network of satellites. U.S. strategy now almost assumes an unlimited supply of photographs with 1-foot resolution of any target anywhere in the world. Even more important are the global positioning system (GPS) satellites, which can guide GPS bombs to within 1 or 2 feet of any place on earth, without forcing the plane that drops them to hang around, keeping the targeting pod laser beam on the target. These precision munitions have transformed air-power, finally fulfilling the wild strategic promises of World War II and Vietnam. The devastating first-day bomb runs of both Gulf Wars depended on exhaustive satellite coverage of every possible target, followed by hours of mission planning and briefings. In modern warfare, any nation with a comprehensive satellite network has a lethal advantage.

But Punch hated flying satellites.

"It was tedious. We did some important things, but I came in going, 'I want to break things and kill people. I'll use a rifle if necessary, but I'd like to use an airplane.' "

He figured he would give up his Air Force Reserve commission and join the Army. He'd tried everything else, including applications to every Air Force National Guard and Reserve unit in the country. "I just wanted to fly something." He also kept applying for active duty in the Air Force, hoping for a pilot slot. Hell, he'd even fly helicopters.

Then one day—for no reason he could later figure out—he got lucky and landed a 1 in 100 shot at an active duty slot. Maybe it was his obsessive athletics. Maybe it was winning the military pentathlon, which involves shooting, running, swimming, navigation, and grenade throwing on a marathon of an obstacle course. "I was the first Air Force guy to make that team in like five years. I don't know why I made it, to tell you the truth. Other people were better qualified—kind of luck of the draw."

So finally, against all odds, he had a chance to become a pilot.

And he got his dream plane—the F-16.

He had great fun at Luke as a B-courser. "I was dating around a lot. If it had a tail, I chased it. I didn't catch many, but damn, I tried. As far as flying, I was an average swimmer. I should have tried harder here—but instead I partied like a rock star."

He had his sights set on Korea, the "last bastion of the fighter pilot—which means it's the last place you can act like a fighter pilot and not get arrested, because your buddies will take care of you."

Bailing out of a crippled jet at Luke proved ideal preparation for Korea. "First couple of months were rough, to say the least. I was swimming like a dog against the current. At first, I was a weak swimmer—no doubt about it. After a couple of months, another guy showed up who was dumber than I was and I got out of the wedge."

Still, the parties in Korea were everything an honest-to-God, blow-stuff-up fighter pilot could ask for—hilarious, drunken binges overlooking a stinking tidal flat that faces China to the west and North Korea to the north. The America base butts up against the DMZ, which means the North Koreans would obliterate it almost immediately in the event of war; the pilots there are essentially well-armed hostages to guarantee U.S. intervention if the North Koreans ever come swarming across the line. Almost all career F-16 pilots rotate through Korea, where they get at least a taste of a frontline lifestyle.

"North Koreans are very well respected—they're tough—fucking tough," says Punch. "Old-time tough. They're not going to roll over like the Iraqis—they're little itty-bitty killing machines. They've been fighting for three generations and digging in like moles. If we ever go in—or if they cross the line—it would be a bloodbath."

As it happened, Punch had met the woman who would become his wife just before shipping out, and she came to visit him in Korea. "She loved it. She had the time of her life. It was like a big, huge family—the college experience I'd hoped to have, but with adults."

The drinking was legendary. "At Kunsan, there are guys who drink so much and do stuff so stupid, it's tough to stand out on stupid. And one guy—Augie—just eclipsed the whole standard of dumbness. He'd walk into a bar and seek out the nearest Weapons School guys—young Turks with $8 million worth of training—and start flipping them shit. He'd do some pretty funny things—and he was a big dude, pretty tough to control. Fortunately, he was kind of a friendly drunk."

After Korea, Punch rotated to Cannon Air Force Base in New Mexico—which was miserable, mostly because they had too many wingmen. He flew only 83 hours in his first year there, completely losing his edge. His second year at Cannon he flew 112 hours, still not enough. Might as well be in the North Korean air force. So he bought his own plane and flew on his own. On the other hand, he was married now and his wife lived on base, so they had plenty of money. They even bought three horses, and his wife became a riding instructor while working at a Western clothing store. "She was in heaven. She cried when we showed up there—it looked so remote. But then she really did cry leaving—the people were so nice. But I was not flying. My skills were degrading."

That's the thing about being a military wife: you get dragged along behind the pickup—down whatever raggedy-assed dirt road the Air Force decides you should visit. The pilots get the credit, the glory. But the wives make it possible—packing up, leaving friends, quitting jobs, raising the kids.

Finally he got his shot—half a war—deployment to Prince Sultan Air Base as a squadron flight leader in the summer of 2000, helping run Southern Watch. "Totally cool. We'd fly over Iraq every night and get shot at. You'd see sparkles, but I'm 6 miles up. Mostly they'd miss by miles—but there's always that golden BB"—with your name on it.

Most of the missions didn't amount to much. They'd fly for ninety minutes just to reach the patrol zone, then spend the day keeping the Iraqi air force in its hangars. They'd refuel a couple of times and return to base with all their bombs still fastened to the underside of the Viper.

They spent a lot of time wishing some MiG would have a go at them. "They'd launch aircraft and the AWACS would spot them right off, but they wouldn't come south. One time we had a MiG 25 take off from Baghdad, head south, and climb up to like 70,000 feet. He's up there on the edge of the airspace heading south and if he gets by you, the next thing he can hit is the tankers," notes Punch. "If you miss, the tankers are screwed."

The MiG 25 is one of the fastest fighters ever built. It's dedicated to shooting down other planes and doesn't have to carry bombs and extra gear for bombing, like the F-16. So it's faster than the F-16 or the F-15. But it has always been limited in its conflicts with the USAF by the off-setting advantages of U.S. pilots: intensive training, flexibility, and the embrace of the initiative. Other air forces that use the MiGs—like the Iraqis and the North Koreans—can't match the costly training of the American pilots and so generally opt for rigid ground control of fighter formations. Moreover, the overlapping coverage of American AWACS planes and satellites almost always give the American pilots far better information on the movements of their enemies. As a result, American pilots have always dominated enemy pilots, even when they're flying top planes like the MiG 25.

As the MiG 25 climbs and turns toward the tankers, Punch realizes he's got a problem. "I'm at 30,000 feet and I'm not as fast as a MiG 25, so I've got to shoot him in the lips," says Punch, referring to a head-on missile shot. For a few years, the Americans had the only air-to-air missiles that could make a head-on shot—which gave them an enormous advantage. Now, the Soviets have developed an "all aspect" missile of their own, which they have sold to client states.

But the MiG pilot turned away—too fond of living.

"I don't think he would have gotten through, but if you fuck up he might get a shot and take down an AWACS with thirty people on board. Of course, we'd run him down and kill him—but it gets your pucker factor up."

On another Southern Watch mission, Punch flew support for some bombers trying to take out an antiaircraft battery hidden in the middle of a residential area. "That's a standard Iraqi tactic—to hide something in the middle of a neighborhood. So we're diving in there and you see bombs going off and cars are driving off the road—these poor schmucks just trying to get home. You feel bad for the bystanders, but the Iraqis are using that equipment to target us and you've got to crush them. Then the city goes dark. I don't know if we hit something, or if they turned off the lights."

He also got a crash course in the complexity of combat missions that depend on precise coordination and constant refueling in the air.

One night, his operations commander—a veteran of the first Gulf War—took gas from the wrong tanker. During the Gulf War, the tankers orbited at the edge of the conflict and fighters could gas up from any tanker open for business. But the tankers were much more carefully rationed during Southern Watch. Each one had precise assignments. "But the commander is used to the Gulf War, so he just slides up and takes some gas. And right away, everyone's screaming. 'No. No. Don't take the gas.' Turns out, he'd taken the gas intended to refuel the AWACS controlling the whole operation, so now they can't get their gas—and it caused the whole mission to get cut by two hours, so they didn't get the aerial photos they'd gone in for. We ridiculed that poor colonel for about two months after that. Our weapons officer back in the control center was standing next to the general who is yelling, 'Who the hell is that?' It was pretty funny. Flash took the ribbing pretty well. You don't want to fuck up in a fighter squadron, because you'll be ridiculed until someone fucks up worse. But that one little thing cut the mission, like, in half—kind of makes you think. It got written up by our weapons officer. He has this little story with cartoons and a little bubble with a two-star general screaming, 'Who the fuck is stealing my gas!' Poor Flash. That guy couldn't get a break."

Punch spent 110 days away from his family, flying into Iraq and getting shot at every night.

"It was awesome. I loved it. I flew a lot. Carried live weapons. There were actually aircraft out there I could shoot down if they crossed the line. The base had a great gym. That was before they blew up the USS *Cole,* so those were happy times. We weren't that intense. Roller hockey and soccer every night I wasn't flying. Got a good tan—if my wife had been there, it would have been perfect. Of course, it was tough on her, but she bore up pretty good."

Once he got back, he rotated to Luke to become an instructor pilot—partly because he was one of the first pilots to gain a lot of experience with night-vision goggles. He had wanted to try his hand at teaching. But he might have gotten in on the actual invasion of Iraq if he'd remained with an operational squadron. "I'd be breaking things and killing people right now," he says, regretfully. "Sorry? Hell yeah. Kills me. I missed Allied Force. Desert Fox. Desert Storm. Desert Storm II. It's luck of the draw. They're doing a great job over there. I mean, the Iraqis didn't even come up to challenge them. Dropping a bomb is great, but killing somebody air-to-air, you're going to be immortal. That's just so rare now. It's just mano a mano—no doubt who the Good Guy and the Bad Guy is.

But they didn't even bother flying against us—which I guess is the ultimate goal," he says regretfully.

Still, he loves Luke—and teaching. He helped design the training course for the night-vision goggles, which have helped guarantee American air supremacy at night. The goggles impose a bug-eyed tunnel vision and require extensive practice to avoid disorientation, but they transform the once dangerous business of night flying—especially in formation. Night flying is notorious for inducing disorientation, as pilots jockey into position alongside another fighter or an air tanker, cross-checking between the faint running lights and the HUD. But viewed through the goggles an unlit F-16 glows brightly in the pitch darkness. The development of the night tactics, the use of the goggles, and the spread of GPS-guided bombs has dramatically increased the accuracy and safety of night flying—while the ground defenders remain blind.

Punch says the B-coursers now are a lot better than when he went through. He's only had to take the jet once while flying the backseat, when a student got within about six inches of another jet. The training squadrons use specially modified F-16s with a back seat for the instructor, mostly at the expense of fuel capacity. Juggling the scheduling of the limited number of two-seat Vipers with the larger number of regular Vipers provides one more complexity for the schedulers. "I just took the jet and then gave it back to him. You cannot get upset or lose your cool. They take whatever you're doing—and whatever you say—and multiply it by ten. So you panic and start pinging, they're going to ping ten times worse. I always hate it when I hear people yelling on the radio. I've never seen a problem get better when you get upset."

On one night flight, he watched a student get disoriented. "I told the kid to get in close on the tanker's wing. He didn't. He was losing his visual references, so he started a slow roll. I waited to see what he was going to do. Right as I was about to take it, he says, 'Sir, I'm all fucked up.' I said, 'Yeah, you are.' I rolled him away left. So he learned why I told him to snug in there close so he wouldn't lose his orientation instead of guessing at the tanker's position and then trying to close up. He thought the tanker was in a turn, but it wasn't. He was watching the plane, not the instrument."

So Punch takes punks just as seriously as Iraqi SAMs.

Except when he's teasing them or buying them beers.

But now he's got to prepare a briefing for the start of the Air Combat Maneuvers phase—the most dangerous portion of the training. He starts writing the briefing parameters on the board, getting ready for Beaker—thinking as he writes how he'll do the briefing. Beaker's a challenge. He's so eager and smart that it always seems like he's getting it in the briefings. But then he gets tentative in the air. Punch gnaws on the problem as he prepares the boards.

Beaker comes in precisely on time—absolutely ready. Focused. It's impossible not to like Beaker—thin-faced, kind-eyed, faintly geeky, with his receding hair and pleasant features and faint air of "gee whiz"—kind of like Opie on the Andy Griffith Show. He's cast against type as a fighter pilot, but there's no mistaking the intensity of his ambition and concentration now. The air-to-air training has gotten pushed up another notch, with the emphasis on fighting as a wingman in a two-ship formation.

The IPs at Luke teach the basics of the complex, shifting roles that have evolved in air-to-air combat, all based on the advantages of fighting in units of two, which are used to build formations of up to twenty-four jets.

At this stage, they're focused on fighting as a two-ship formation against a single enemy jet. The flight lead takes the offense, while the wingman provides backup. In more advanced tactical doctrines, the two jets shift back and forth easily from offense to defense. But that requires flawless coordination and flying. In the B-course, the IPs train the students for a much simpler two-ship tactic in which the flight lead engages the enemy jet and the wingman drops back. At that point, the wingman scans the skies for another enemy jet, stays out of the way, and waits for an easy kill as the enemy maneuvers desperately to escape the flight lead. If the enemy fighter manages to gain an advantage, then the wingman must jump in and take over the attack to prevent the enemy from killing his partner.

So Punch explains the complexities of that shifting of roles for their upcoming fight against one of the IPs. Punch makes sure he creates pictures, so that when Beaker sees the jets align in the air he'll have that life-saving click of recognition. Beaker must also learn the terse but vital radio vocabulary with which the lead and wingman coordinate their actions in the bewildering swirl of combat. He's building on the pictures of the one-on-one dogfighting they've just completed.

"All right, so we have 'fight's on,' and break left, and I can't get behind him—he's moving to my six. I say, 'Bogey. Six o'clock. No joy. Bogey switch.' We just had a role swap," says Punch, because the enemy fighter has shifted to the offense and gotten behind the flight lead. Once Beaker jumps in, Punch can reposition and wait for a shot. "What kind of fight are you going to have?"

"A rate fight," says Beaker uncertainly, which means he should try to get inside the enemy's turn circle to get into position for a gunshot.

"I'm going to let you do it and just hang out there, watching," Punch says. In other tactical formations, both fighters would seek offensive positions. Veteran pilots argue endlessly about the proper role of the wingman. But they agree that a fluid, two-ship offensive formation demands intensive training and specialized communication. With the B-coursers, they'll be lucky if the wingman doesn't crash into the other planes or offer up a free shot to the enemy fighter as he loiters at the edge of the fight.

Punch knows that the wingman is often tempted to enter the fight by going straight at the enemy, rushing to get into position behind the Bogey. That's usually a mistake. Odds are the wingman, who has been up high, saving his energy, will shoot past the sharp-turning Bogey. And once Beaker is following the enemy jet around in a turn in a "one circle" fight, Punch will have fewer shots that don't risk hitting Beaker. Instead, Punch urges Beaker to seek a two-circle fight, by starting his turn circle away from the Bogey.

"Cool. Once we got the role swap, I'm going to assume you're blind— can't see me at all. So I'm going to talk and be your eyes. I'm going to say, 'Mud Hog One [the flight lead], Bogey switch—Mud Hog Two [the wingman] is engaged,' " says Punch, to signal the wingman to jump in and take over the fight. "What is your normal walk-out-the-door game plan for a high-angle merge?"

"Two-circle fight," says Beaker.

"Two-circle fight," confirms Punch. "Now, what if we get in a prolonged engagement and you're losing the offensive. What is a good call?"

"Neutral," says Beaker. That call would tell the circling Punch that Beaker has lost the offensive.

"Good. Hopefully I should have a good idea of who's who," he says.

Not a small point.

Keeping track of a swirl of fighters at 350 knots poses a problem. That's especially true in training, when pilots are usually fighting other F-16s. The supporting fighter can't just hover out there watching. He's flying at 400 knots himself, turning constantly to keep his position above the fight as the other two planes roll, bank, and turn furiously. It's hard enough to sort MiGs out from F-16s; it'll give you a migraine trying to keep two F-16s sorted in a 6-g turn when your head weighs about 150 pounds. "Sometimes in the training world, it's hard to keep them straight," says Punch. "Now, in this kind of high-aspect turn fight, that's where some dudes have trouble with g's," he adds.

Prolonged high-g turns are brutal, smashing every inch of the body with nine times the force of gravity. Only the 30 degrees of recline on the pilot's seat in the F-16, the constantly inflating pressure suit, and reflexive breathing and tensing make it possible for the pilots to pull 9 g's without passing out. But the sheer physical strain of high-g maneuvers extracts a considerable toll—especially if the pilot must constantly move his head to keep track of other jets. That's why fighter pilots almost all work out obsessively and why you'll never see a chubby pilot in an F-16 squadron. "The g's will bite you more because your attention is back over here where you're getting away from the fight. So you see a juicy opportunity and you whip it around," piling on the g-forces and maybe blacking out.

"I know two guys that smacked the water because of that," cautions Punch. Deaths in training are an inevitable fact of life. "So if you're getting tunnel vision—feeling any of the symptoms—you just say 'status'—that's the best thing you can tell me," says Punch earnestly—knowing that the macho instincts of these fighter pilot cubs make them reluctant to admit to any weakness.

In this exercise, the circling wingman should ultimately make the kill—which means he can't just hang out and watch the fight from afar. But Punch knows the B-coursers have trouble knowing when to jump into a swirling fight 2,000 feet below and 2 miles away. At least initially, the IPs are happy if the circling students don't get in the way or drift in front of the enemy jet, offering a free shot.

"Just don't be the high-speed cheerleader right through the middle of the flight," cautions Punch. "You've got to always be thinking in three dimensions—and relative roles. So if you see him turn and give you a shot, take it. If you can't take the shot right away—don't wait around hoping it will sweeten up. Reposition. Get back to the perch. You've got to know that I'm in the fight—I'm not watching you anymore. It's your job to deconflict."

"Is it a hard-and-fast rule that if you go low, never come back through the horizon?" asks Beaker, pondering what to do if he comes off his perch, misses a shot as he dives past the fight, and ends up low. How does he get back on the perch to take a shot again?

"Don't be crossing in front of him when he's in the fight and give him a free shot. But he may have assumed you're going to stay low—so maybe he turns his back on you and you can go high. Very good question."

Beaker nods.

Punch grins.

Good question. Punch loves good questions.

It suggests that he might have a wingman on his hands.

And he is, after all, in the business of handcrafting Viper wingmen.

14

AND THE BUSTS KEEP COMING

THE AIR COMBAT MANEUVERS phase takes its toll.

On the other hand, no one's dead.

And Rex hasn't washed out yet.

And now he's got company. Several of the other B-coursers who watched him sympathetically (and with small prayers of gratitude that they weren't him) are now dog-paddling furiously, trying to stay afloat.

The IPs are starting to sort the strong swimmers from the dog-paddlers.

To everyone's surprise, Igor and Stihl have come on strong. They haven't busted a single ride and pick up each new brick with enthusiastic ease. They both came to Luke with spotty records at IFF—but have accelerated here. Who knew? Neither had military in the family history, so they struggled to adjust. And neither seems particularly good at bending to authority. But that's not necessarily a bad thing in a fighter pilot. Truth is a fighter pilot has to be confident to the edge of arrogant. It's like Olympic downhill skiing—you're on a team, but you get the gold medal individually. Neither Stihl nor Igor did well in IFF—the pilot's equivalent of boot camp, with its institutionalized abuse. Lacking a military background, they didn't see the motivational benefits of abuse and humiliation. But as soon as they got to Luke, where the IPs treated them like pilots rather than washouts waiting to happen, they took hold. Leastwise that's one theory.

Igor has undergone the most marked blossoming at Luke, thriving on the expertise of the IPs. The IPs noted his heavy, blocky features and his slow, friendly, deliberate manner, and figured he was going to drag along behind the jet. It didn't help when he got the nickname Igor. But they reserved judgment—partly because of the whole going-through-the-cockpit incident. Good thing. Every flight now, he gets better. Maybe that was because Ship made a conscious effort to build him up, taking special care to give him compliments. Ship had a gut feeling the cockpit-smashing incident hinted at a natural flier under Igor's deliberate manner. After all, the guy had worked as a bush pilot in Alaska—landing God knows where in God knows what kind of weather. Best to give him a chance. And sure enough, Igor got off CAP quickly. He displayed a natural ability to prioritize tasks in the cockpit, a crucial asset for a fighter pilot. The single hardest thing about flying the F-16 is handling the bewildering onslaught of information. The HUD displays twenty different key bits of information about the airplane, from headings to weapons locks. The switches on the stick offer about sixteen choices at the flick of the thumb. The radio buzzes and chatters with calls from every jet in the air, not to mention crucial instructions from the ground and distant AWACS controllers. Igor quickly demonstrated that crucial ability to pay attention to everything, all in the right order.

On the other hand, Rex, Gimmie, Pong, and Pap are all struggling.

Of course, Rex is still flying drag and still on CAP. Mercifully, he hasn't busted a ride lately. He's got a little Houdini in him—picking the lock just before his oxygen runs out. He's keeping himself in the game through sheer guts and determination. Normally, that doesn't work. Normally, the harder you concentrate, the more you screw up. But it seems he can absorb the pressure—even the knowledge that they all expect him to fail. "When they gave me the name," he says, "I figured I had two choices. I could either prove them right, or learn from it."

Gimmie had a rough time in the air-to-air dogfighting phase. She often seemed half a beat behind in her decision making. It doesn't take much—an extra second in which you doubt your instinct. In that moment, the IP, deft as a sword juggler, has turned. Suddenly, he's behind you. She's in no danger of washing out right now. They put her on CAP after she busted two rides close together. But then she settled down. She never complained, never flurried. She just mocked herself, with that small, wry grin. Then she hit the simulator. She hung out with Stihl and Igor—picking their brains. She watched the tapes of her mistakes—then took that into the simulator and practiced the same maneuvers. She sought out the IPs and got additional, informal tips. She did what she has always done—flew under the radar, kept her cool, made no fuss. So she quit busting rides. She still doesn't have the instincts of Stihl or Igor, but she's not making dumb mistakes. She's still getting gunned, but she's making decisions and following through. So they took her off CAP. She knows some of the IPs figure she lacks the killer instinct for an air-to-air knife fight—being a woman. That's bullshit, of course. But it's the accusation that hovers just out of sight when pilots talk about the question of letting females into the fraternity.

Other B-coursers are having more trouble killing IPs in dogfights than she is—no one wonders if they lack a killer instinct. Well. Maybe Beaker. He doesn't seem like much of a killer. But whenever that thought occurs to Gimmie, she just sets it aside. People are going to think what they think. That's not her problem. Let it go. Like always. There's only one answer to the unspoken question. It's in the simulator. It's in the debrief. It's on the tape. It's waiting up there over the range, next time some IP willing to underestimate her calls "fight's on."

Pap has been struggling as well—which surprised the IPs. Early on they figured he'd be among the strongest swimmers. He aced the academics. He had a knife-edge, buttoned-down military bearing—despite the handicap of having attended frigging West Point. He's an enthusiastic team player—always helping the other pilots, getting people home from the bar, helping with studying. He's eager for information. He has a great attitude—never defensive, determined to learn from mistakes. He's always "Yes, sir" and "No, sir." He wants to fly so bad you can feel the heat coming off him. But he's been kind of distracted. His timing deteriorated during the air-to-air phase. Maybe it's because some of his best friends from West Point are over in Iraq—getting shot. One buddy got shot all to hell in an ambush. Pap has been keeping track of his classmates from West Point over there by email. And it's eating him up. He feels guilty—being here all comfortable and excited about flying while his buddy lies over there in the hospital—missing pieces of himself. Pap should have been over there. Secretly, he wonders whether his shift to flying represents some failure of nerve—some lack of character. He remembers the decision-making process. He just wanted to fly. He wanted the challenge. It wasn't because it was somehow safer, cleaner, further from the ambush. Was it? He can't remember ever thinking that dropping bombs from 25,000 feet would be safer than walking around like a bull's-eye in Iraq. But maybe he did—somehow—in the back of his mind. Certainly his buddies are now in the shit and he's safe and sound in the middle of the wrong desert. Or maybe that's not it—maybe that's not what has cost him the edge with which he entered the program. But there's no doubt he's struggling. On one busted ride, he took off and leveled out at the wrong altitude. His airspeed fluctuated. He had trouble working the weapons selection. He set off on the wrong heading. He went into a dogfight without switching his target selection from air-to-ground mode. He lined up a shot, then hit the wrong button, and ended up not even firing. It was a mess.

The other B-coursers have been hit and miss—average.

Jack presents the IPs with something of a riddle. A third-generation pilot, with brothers, parents, cousins, and friends already flying, he's eager, likable, comfortable in the military setting. He has a country-boy charm, and big, eager, friendly eyes. But he's unpredictable. Some flights, he floats—running through the checklists and handling his plane with casual perfection. But then, suddenly, he'll unravel. Make careless mistakes. Forget stuff he seemed to have down cold. "It's like he's snake-bit," notes Ship. "I can't figure it out. It's one of those plague things—an unconscious thing." So Jack will be sailing along—then suddenly have one bad ride after another—then suddenly he's just fine again. It's like a jet that has a critical malfunction warning light that blinks on and off—no matter how many times you tear down the control panel and recheck it. But Jack never downplays his mistakes, he always puts out maximum effort, and he mixes easily with the B-coursers and the IPs. He's got all the attitudes and the underlying skills of a great pilot. But then the red light comes on—without explanation.

Beaker, although he's a captain with many hours in the air as a C-130 navigator, has not distinguished himself. The IPs consider him an "average pilot," lacking that killer edge of confidence. He second-guesses himself—taking the desired self-criticism a step too far. Ideally, pilots learn from mistakes without doubting their skills or their judgment—because hesitation can easily prove fatal. It's one reason the IPs can almost always kill the punks if they try. The experience of the IPs allows them to instantly process a change in the outline of the enemy's jet and react instinctively. The punks still have to notice the change, decide what it means, and then consider their alternatives. An added moment of second-guessing in the midst of that already difficult process is a killer. Hopefully, once Beaker gets his confidence, he'll take hold. Certainly he's a hard worker with a great attitude. He's prone to small mistakes, like flying through the floor. Mostly, that's because he hasn't yet absorbed the mechanics of flying so well that he doesn't have to pay conscious attention. So if he's working on a new skill—like locking the targeting circle in the center of the HUD to track an enemy jet—he'll lose track of his altitude and fly through the simulated floor. He has quivered at the edge of busting rides, but hasn't quite stumbled over the trip-wire yet. However, he also hasn't provided the kind of leadership for the other B-coursers that the IPs expect of a captain.

In the meantime, the divisions that have fragmented the B-course have hardened. They're not pulling together; they're going off in different directions. The hard core of single guys went off to Las Vegas for a long, wild weekend—renting an RV and plodding up there to blow off some steam. That was good. Fighter pilot stuff. But it only reinforced the division between them and the married guys, who are trying to keep their marriages afloat despite the long hours and their families' struggle to adjust to Phoenix and the long, hot, suspenseful interlude of the B-course. They can't really settle in—because they know they'll be gone in six months. But six months is a long time to mark time, especially when your spouse is gone for fifteen hours a day. Especially when you're just getting used to the idea that your spouse is going to fly an aging, single-engine fighter jet for a living. So the married pilots mostly have a lot of propping up and making up to do. They love flying—it's the dream of a lifetime. They burn with ambition. But already they're starting to miss those moments with their families, and are struggling to make it up to them.

The dream costs.

And it's not just the pilots paying the bill.

15

BOMBING AND FIGHTING:
ANOTHER BRICK

IN TRUTH, MOST VIPER PILOTS WILL SPEND their careers dropping bombs. They all yearn to kill MiGs, rolling into two-circle fights that will make them aces. But that doesn't happen much anymore. Instead, generations of targeting pods and smart bombs have turned the lightweight, nimble F-16—designed to outturn MiGs in the skies over Europe—into the most flexible bomber and SAM-killer in the USAF inventory.

So Major Chris Ashby—"Crash"—takes very seriously the upcoming briefing for a four-ship bombing mission involving Punch, Gimmie, Stihl, and himself.

Crash's nickname is misleading. You'd think it would refer to some fireball of a crash. In fact he fell off a roof. He was up there with a couple of other wobbly fighter pilots with a worrisome blood alcohol level taking part in one of the proudest traditions of a fighter squadron—a roof stomp for a new squadron commander.

A thirteen-year veteran, Crash spent the first interminable chunk of his career teaching punks how to fly T-38s. Life got better once he finally moved on to F-16s, but now he's got a realtor wife and two teenaged girls who don't want to have to move—again. The family had a great time during the three years they spent in Germany, touring the continent while he flew with Danes, Poles, and Germans. He was among the first

U.S. pilots in Poland after the Soviet Union dissolved and the Polish air force was integrated into NATO.

That gave him a chance to fly mock dogfights against all the MiGS—23s, 21s, and 29s. None of them proved much of a match for the Americans, in large measure because of differences in tactics and training. The MiG 23 could outrun and outclimb the F-16, but it couldn't maneuver as well. "It's built for low, fast, straight flying—so air-to-air with a MiG 23 isn't much of a challenge," Crash says. "If he tries to fight, you can outmaneuver him. If he tries to run, you can missile him."

The MiG 29 is a fair fight for a Viper. "It's going to come down to who's flying the jet," he says.

Some of the Europeans—most of them flying F-16s—can match the U.S. training. "A lot of the European countries—Denmark, the Netherlands, Belgium—are like how our air force used to be. They fly, and that's all they do—putting all their time into flying and tactics instead of getting bogged down with two or three ground jobs, like everyone in an American squadron. We get bogged down with all the crazy stuff coming along, like total quality management—instead of thinking about the mission."

His dad was an enlisted man in the Air Force during Vietnam, loading bombs onto jets in Thailand. Afterward, he stayed in the Reserves and worked as an Illinois state cop. Crash thought about becoming a cop, but got into engineering in college. A ROTC colonel talked him into the officer-training program in college, which provided a scholarship with a four-year commitment. Crash figured he could be a pilot—since he'd always half-dreamed of being an astronaut.

After graduation, he had to wait for a pilot spot to open up before he started training. So in the meantime he sold lawn and garden supplies at Sears. That cinched it.

When it came to combat, his timing was good—and he got in on both Northern and Southern watch—plus Bosnia and Yugoslavia. All told, he flew seventy-three combat missions, just under 300 hours.

Northern Watch in 1997—designed to protect the rebellious Kurds in northern Iraq from Saddam Hussein—was a bore. He spent six weeks flying F-16s looking for SAMs to kill. "We would be protecting everyone else—flying four or five hours for forty-five minutes in the airspace, then back to the tanker, then back in for another forty minutes, then back home. No one ever shot at us. It was pretty simple."

More of the same in Southern Watch—a similar mission designed to protect the Shiites in southern Iraq. The fighter jets mostly flew boring missions intended to keep the Iraqi pilots on the ground and away from the Shiite areas. Sometimes, Iraqi fighters appeared on the radar, well away from the edge of the no-fly zone. Sometimes, some frustrated Iraqi SAM operator would fire up his radar. Mostly, they just patrolled the desert, between trips to the air tankers. "We flew a lot of that at night—just flying around in circles in case something happened. That nonsense went on for about twelve years."

He was based in Turkey, which was good: the base had its own movie theater and pool—with parties going on all the time. Just off base, they'd buy Turkish rugs and Turkish shotguns and all kinds of strange stuff. "The Turks appreciated our business," he recalls, but then they didn't interact much with the locals.

When Operation Allied Force broke out in Bosnia, Crash's squadron was moved virtually overnight from the U.S. to Italy. They crossed the Atlantic in a huge fleet, clinging to the air tankers and topping off their ravenous tanks every thirty minutes on the nine-hour haul.

He worked in a four-ship hunting SAMs. Two of the Vipers carried HARMs, 800-pound missiles that home in on the SAM radars. The other two F-16s tagged along to provide cover. Mostly, they just kept the SAMs shut down by being there. "If they know we're up there and they don't turn their radar on, then we've done our job. SAM operators are fairly smart. They know if they turn on, they're going to get some ordinance coming their way. And if they turn on the radar and start lobbing missiles, they're going to get swacked pretty good. So if they know you're in the air, they won't turn on their radar."

Using the high-tech targeting pod for the HARM took a lot of practice. "It's got some pretty cool receiver stuff built into it to display where the SAM radars are. So you can find the radar and put a cursor on it. Normally, we can get off a shot before the SAM can even lock a target. It takes about two months and about fourteen training rides to learn how to use it."

Most of the pilots tried to read up on the intricacies of Balkans politics once they got to Italy—but much of it defied comprehension. "They all hate each other," Crash shrugs, "but they're all living in the same chunk of land there. So the Serbs are going down there beating up the Muslims or whoever—taking their houses, shooting them, throwing them in ditches. We would watch CNN every day from the hotel room to find out what happened today and what's happening tomorrow. Most pilots are going to do what we're told, but if we can find out about it, we will. Regardless of what it is—someone tells us to do it, we're going to do it. Truth is, it's not all that hard to figure it out from the air. You see them down there burning down houses, and trucks driving away from it. You see that. You see the stuff on the TV. It's not that hard to get behind the cause."

On the first night, Crash was handed command of a four-ship, although he was only a captain. So he plunged into the planning. They were providing cover for a bombing mission, mostly Canadians. The initial goal was to blast the Serbian army to force them to break off the ethnic cleansing that had been underway despite NATO threats.

"The Canadian F-18s were hitting some factory or something, and we're sweeping out about 10 miles ahead of them for SAMs."

Everything starts off running like a Swiss diver's watch. They take off, link up with the tankers, top off, and push into Bosnia. "Pretty much as soon as we get in country, the AWACS tell us we've got MiG 29s airborne. So we arm up. It sounds like the MiG is about 60 miles north of us. But just one MiG. Pretty soon we hear the Dutch F-16s up there talking to the AWACS, and the MiG turns away. Then we hear the Dutch F-16 call 'Fox three—shooting an AIM-120.' After that, we get 'Splash one,' which is a hit. I'm looking and I can see a flash when the missile hits it—sparks trailing out in the distance all the way down to the ground. I don't think the pilot got out. The Serbs lost several MiGs that night. We only lost one in our package—one out of like thirty."

His four-ship shot only one missile that night—a long shot at the radar position of an SA6 SAM site that hadn't locked anyone up. The signal went off the air and didn't come back on; Crash doesn't know if they killed it. Later, they figured out that the SA6 site they shot at was drawing a bead on the Dutch F-16s that killed the MiG.

"I saw the SA6 on my scope about the same time as my wingman, flying trail about 5 miles back. So Zar and I start talking about it, trying to figure out whether it's worth shooting or not. I go, 'Well, that's kind of in tomorrow's target area.' But we're not sure—it's a long way and the HARMs are like $250,000 a pop, so if I'm going to shoot one I want it to be a fairly reliable shot. But we decided to go ahead. So all I'm thinking is, 'Please don't let me screw this up.' So I quadruple-checked what I was about to do. But when I hit the pickle [to launch the missile], nothing's happening. I looked out at the HARM on the wing, just about the time it leaves the wing and starts climbing. They climb, tip over, and start looking for the target. So it comes off, goes up and I haven't said anything at this point. I haven't called 'Magnum,' I haven't called anything. My wingman sees this huge, bright flame near my jet and thinks I've been shot."

They orbited the target area while the Canadian F-18s went in, staring down at the mushrooms of flame on the ground, where Serb soldiers were getting incinerated.

"Went back to the hotel, drank a beer—pretty exciting. Couldn't wait to do it again," recalls Crash.

After that, they fell into a daily routine.

He outturned dying a couple of times.

Normally, they operated in a four-ship formation. They would set up over a target area ahead of the bombers, flying a track carefully designed to avoid smashing into the incoming bombers. Usually, each two-ship unit was flying in an opposite direction at any given moment, so someone would be pointing at a SAM site no matter where it was located. An elaborate cat-and-mouse game developed between the pilots and the SAM operators down on the ground. The Viper pilots always worked the timeline, knowing exactly when the bombers would be coming in on their precisely defined tracks. "You've got tons of papers and maps and everything else on your leg—you just have to read faster than you can fly."

That's why the combat-veteran IPs drill the B-coursers so hard on learning to fly by reflex. They know that a single-seat Viper pilot will have layers of critical tasks in combat and so can't afford to devote much brainpower to just flying the jet.

One day, just as the incoming bombers report they've been spiked—probed by ground radar—Crash's computer sounds a warning that he's been locked up on someone's targeting radar. At that moment, he sees SAMs launch from the ground at the incoming bombers. The bombers—a pair of F-16s with ground-oriented targeting pods—hit afterburners to maneuver. Surviving a SAM lockup depends on going head-on to the missile and then wrenching violently to the side to break the missile's radar lock at the critical moment. But with the incessant warning that he's also locked, Crash can't afford to level out long enough to launch a HARM against the SAM site.

"I start maneuvering my jet, calling out that I'm defending. I end up turning sideways to the threat, pulling my nose downhill and rolling out, using my chaff and my ECM [electronics countermeasures pod]. As soon as I roll out, I see an SA3 that I didn't know was there shooting from right below me. So I was locked by two missiles at the same time."

They both exploded in the air just below him, detonated by his countermeasures.

His wingman rolled in, locked up, and put a HARM on the SAM site.

"Another four seconds, they would have had me. Seeing the SAM site blow up, it looked like the Death Star in the first *Star Wars* movie. Things were shooting out of it, and it was roiling and bubbling as it exploded. But you can only even think about it for a couple of seconds, because they're launching more missiles. We really didn't say much about it. But back in the hotel bar it was, 'Holy Shit, man.' That was close."

All told, he had fifteen SAMs shot at him. In most cases, the SAM operators launched the missile to explode at a preset altitude without guiding the missile actively to him with their targeting radars. They knew that if they held the radar lock on his jet long enough to guide the missile all the way to him, they'd draw a lethal HARM missile from the circling Vipers. "They just set them to detonate at different altitudes, to try their luck. I was using countermeasures and maneuvering the jet, but when they're throwing up all that stuff at once, it makes it tough. Some missiles are more maneuverable than others, but they're moving really fast—so if they go past you, they can't do a 180-degree turn and come back."

His closest call came later, when seven SA3 missiles rose up toward him one after the other in a 20-minute sequence that demanded extended violent maneuvering, with missiles exploding in the air all around him. The Vipers finally silenced the tenacious, even reckless, battery with HARMs—and in the meantime absorbed all of the attention of the missile batteries. The bombers got through unscathed.

"Every time we turned to try to take a shot, we'd get two more missiles. We kept bleeding altitude to avoid the missiles until we got down low enough that we started seeing the triple-A coming up from the guns on the ground. That's kind of their tactic, to make you maneuver down low where the triple-A can get at you once you're out of energy and can't climb up out of range. But no one in the squadron got shot down."

In fact, despite heavy antiaircraft defenses, the allied forces lost only two jets over Bosnia. One was an F-117 stealth fighter-bomber—a lucky shot. The other was an F-16 caught by a SAM while flying blind too close to the top of a cloudbank.

Crash was part of the exhaustive search for the F-16 pilot during the week he was missing, hiding in the underbrush to evade the Serbian search. "We were just coming off the tanker when we got the call to fly CAP [combat air patrol] for the rescue, since they were moving SAMs in. On the radio, we can hear them coordinating the rescue. Could hear the downed pilot talking into the radio trying to describe where he is. At one point, he can see people coming—he can hear gunfire coming his way. So the sun starts coming up, and we're wondering if they're ever going to get him out of there. But he hears the helicopters coming and vectors them in pretty good. They see him and pull him out just as the sun's coming up. The helicopters take a lot of fire going in and coming out. But by the time we got back to the base and have breakfast, he was already back in his squadron. We went over there to welcome him back, shake his hand, talk to his buddies in the flight."

Looking back, Crash loved that war.

"It sounds stupid, but I actually had fun flying those missions. It's what you train to go do. When you actually get to go do it, it's going to be enjoyable," he says. Now he just tries not to think about missing Iraq. Everyone's doing that. All the time.

But that combat experience now animates his work as an IP. "You bring it back and pass it along. You just have to help them build that picture that's going to keep them alive. Of course, it's not much of a challenge dogfighting these guys. But you have to build them up. So sometimes, you're going to let them shoot you—so they start to see the picture, start to build some confidence."

Of course, as soon as they get the picture, it's time to drop another brick on their heads.

So as soon as they get used to fighting one-on-one, they've got to learn the wingman's job. Soon as they get comfortable fighting two-on-one—they add another jet, so now they're flying in four-ship formations, fighting two or four opponents.

The IPs say it's like piling bricks on a sheet of plate glass. You put on a brick. Wait a minute—listening for that cracking sound. No crack. Put on another brick. Wait another minute. Maybe you don't tell the punks how big the pile of bricks is. They won't even know how ignorant they are until they get to their operational squadron.

So now Gimmie and Stihl sit quietly, stretched like trip wires, ready for the briefing. They flash through the operational details that used to consume an hour—alternative runways, weapons loads, ground operations, navigational points, weather, emergency backup plans, formations, routes to and from the range. Gimmie gives a crisp, professional, calm summary and details the weather report. You can hardly believe they're the same pilots, having absorbed the jargon and the quiet confidence that oozes from the IPs.

Gimmie has started to pull out of the tailspin of her air-to-air phase. She's popular with the ground crews; she learns their names, chats with them, and compliments them. Sometimes she picks up that undercurrent about her sex, even with them. But she never bridles at it. In fact, she includes them in her self-deprecating humor. She hangs out with the young single pilots, going on their adventures and often ends up as the designated driver. She is "one of the guys," although she maintains a certain reserve.

Stihl is one of her friends among the B-coursers—but then, everyone feels like Stihl's one of their friends, except maybe the captains who pulled rank over the base assignments. Stihl continues to amble along, his abashed, ironic, laconic manner inviting underestimation. He hasn't had a single bust. Not even close. The IPs all say now that he's a "strong swimmer," although they laugh and scratch their heads when they say it. It still seems like some kind of mistake—some kind of fraternity prank in which they elect the geek as president. It's weird. At first, it seemed some kind of fluke. Certainly that's the way Stihl presents it—like he went to pilot school as a lark, and gee, guys, it's not too bad. But increasingly he seems like that rare commodity—the natural flier. Most of the B-coursers excel by dint of willpower, obsessive work, and aching ambition. Stihl just takes to it, like a sea lion slipping into the water for the first time.

But even for Stihl, the latest load of bricks—flying in a four-ship formation—causes a spidery network of cracks to appear in the glass plate of his awareness.

The training has now built up to the heart of the F-16 mission: flying to a target in an exquisitely planned four-ship formation and dropping bombs, all the while ready to engage enemy fighters. Designed as a cheap fighter to match the Soviet hordes, the F-16 has morphed into a flexible fighter-bomber—for both day and night. The key to that flexibility remains the four-ship formation, which enables the speeding jets to provide their own air cover and hit a variety of targets with precision.

But that flexibility comes at a cost—mostly the bewildering layering of tasks pressing down on the single pilot. The radar has half a dozen different modes: some scan for enemy jets, some lock up targets on the ground. The buttons on the joystick offer a mind-numbing array of options—missiles for dogfighting, aiming pipers for cannons, launches for a range of bombs. Some fall with gravity. Some steer themselves to the GPS coordinates preprogrammed. Some home in on radar signals from SAM sites. Some follow the pointer of a laser beam. Some can be directed from the cockpit by a TV camera mounted in the nose of the plummeting bomb.

And that's just for starters.

The Viper pilots also must master the tactics of fighting as a four-ship unit—which are exponentially more complex than when fighting alone or as a two-ship.

First and foremost, the B-coursers have to master the art of flying in formation, even when maneuvering, without smacking into each other. Initially, that means clinging to their flight lead like a tick on a bloodhound. That works for a while, leaving the complex maneuvering and coordination tasks to the experienced IP flying in the lead. But even if the punk manages to stay slotted in behind and above the flight lead, and to keep adequate track of the skies around and behind the formation, just clinging to the flight lead eventually develops bad habits. Some of the B-coursers have lost track of the flight lead during some severe sequence of maneuvers and wound up wandering completely disoriented—not even sure where the target is anymore. That's a busted ride, a round of beers back in the squadron, and major humiliation at the Crusades—although the tradition of the Crusades has all but vanished in the past few months.

Of course, like almost everything else in the B-course—the goal is to make flying in a four-ship formation so routine that it doesn't require much concentration. Ultimately, the wingman has to develop his own understanding of the mission and his own picture of the sky.

In dogfighting, the four-ship formation dramatically increases the swath of sky the formation can cover. The leading jet concentrates on the target while the other three jets watch for enemy fighters. They cover one another's blind spots, with each jet separated by several miles. That leaves the fourth jet in the formation vulnerable to attack from the rear, but minimizes the danger to the rest. In enemy territory, the two lead jets will sometimes turn and fly back on their own trail, so their radars can scan the skies for 50 miles to the rear of the formation. Ideally, the four-ship flight will also be protected by a distant AWACS controller with a flight of orbiting F-15s ready to kill approaching enemy fighters before the Vipers' radars even detect the bogeys. At the very least, the distant AWACS controller will give the Vipers a warning and permission to shoot down an approaching blip when it's still 10 or 30 or 50 miles away—the exact range remains classified. If they're unlucky or the situation is confused and fluid, the Vipers might have to close to within visual range to identify the target before shooting.

If the four-ship does face enemy fighters, the lead pilot assigns targets to each of the other jets in the formation—sometimes "sorting" each two-ship element to designated targets. Often, the formation's lead pilot directs one fighter to dive toward the bogeys and flares the other jets to the side, bracketing the enemy formation. In theory, one fighter risks that flash past the unidentified jets to make visual identification. If the lead calls "hostile," the other fighters start shooting their assigned targets. That sounds simple enough, but it requires a complex orchestration of jets closing toward each other at 10 miles a second.

For now, Crash wants to make sure that Gimmie and Stihl—working with Punch—can maneuver in a four-ship formation without disaster. "You three are wingmen for me, so don't hit me—and don't hit each other either," he says.

Naturally enough—it's not that simple.

Because they're flying in formation, the wingman has to make the same turns—this time at low altitude for a bombing run—as the flight lead. That's fine if they start the turn in perfect synchronization. But if the wingman doesn't recognize the small wing-waggle that signals the onset of the turn, he could react a beat or two late. In that case, he'll have to turn more sharply than the flight lead to stay in perfect formation. When a wingman gets behind the curve, his turns can quickly get very sharp—piling on the g-forces.

"So what are the chances of g-locking today?" asks Crash. He knows that even a momentary loss of consciousness in a 9-g turn can prove fatal.

"Pretty good," says Stihl, typically laconic.

"Why?"

"Low altitude," says Stihl, with a faint smile.

"How far you going to turn?" asks Crash, checking to see if Stihl remembers the training rule designed to minimize the chance of g-locking. Some veteran pilots argue that the accretion of safety-oriented training rules have insidiously undercut training—leaving pilots less prepared for real combat. On the other hand, training-related deaths have declined significantly in the past decade.

"180 degrees," says Stihl.

"Right. No more than 180 degrees. Can you still g-lock? You bet you can. Make that breathing pattern your habit, so it will just become natural to you. How about collision avoidance? Each other—obviously— but what about all those doctors and lawyers flying back and forth to Los Angeles? They are taking off from Deer Valley [airport]. Taking off from Glendale. They're everywhere," he says, knowing that an F-16 can overtake a turning Cessna like a race car hitting a tortoise on the highway. "You just have to keep your eyes peeled."

He checks his notes and continues. "Everything should come off the jet today. Make sure of one of those magic numbers, 3,000 feet, 300 knots," he says, a rule designed to make sure they have enough speed and altitude to maneuver a sick jet. "Bottom line is, don't do something stupid. And if you've got a problem—the needles start to split and show red fuel gauges—tell somebody. Don't keep any secrets. As we're going out and coming back, make sure you're searching in the blind spot. If you see anything within 20 miles and 5,000 feet with 20 degrees aspect or better and I'm not talking about it, then talk about it." This is to keep another plane from flying into the formation, with potentially disastrous consequences.

"Don't hit the ground today," says Crash, referring to the artificial ceiling. "You'll bust the ride if you hit the ground—either because of a visual illusion problem or you're distracted—channelized on something else. You're not going to die from Punch or myself shooting electrons at you," he says of the computer-simulated death by dogfight.

Next, they discuss setting the computerized warnings on the radar, so that Betty's insistent voice will warn them when they're getting close to the ground—in this case he tells them to set the ground warning at 7,000 feet, about 5,000 feet above the top of the tallest mountains on the range.

Crash moves on, a machine-gun rattle of information. "Birds: don't hit them. But you're at low altitude, so have your helmet visors down. You're going to need the visor anyway, because of the sun. Say you're cruising along at low altitude and there's a turkey vulture right in your face, what are you going to do—climb or descend?"

"Climb," says Stihl, "because they'll dive." He sounds confident, although he's making this stuff up. You never know what an IP will ask in a briefing—so you always try to sound confident, but not arrogant. Who knows, you might be right.

Not today.

"They have no capability to outclimb you," says Crash. "But can they penetrate your canopy?"

Stihl looks uncertain.

"The canopy is that thick—no kidding," says Crash, demonstrating a comforting thickness of several inches with his fingers. The F-16 canopy is a marvel—offering perhaps the best visibility of any fighter, able to withstand huge impacts and crafted to avoid visual distortions despite its curvature. "That buzzard would have to be frozen pretty hard to break the canopy. But if you climb, it can get into the engine. I'd probably bank and turn. In another squadron, an IP took a turkey vulture in the left side of the nose and it entered the cockpit from the footwells. No kidding. Blood and feathers all over. It was nasty and smelly and there was stuff flying up at the guy—so keep the visors down"—so you don't get blinded. "When we do this high-low transition, you're going to hit 550 knots," he says.

Now he reviews the big threats—all of which relate to the pilot falling behind the jet and doing something stupid. "Channelized attention, task saturation—those are the things you're going to want to avoid today. Now, you have to look for those mental pictures. You're flying in formation, so you can kill somebody if you become channelized." A wingman who gets mesmerized by the flight lead while trying to stay in position can lose track of everything else—and fly into the top of a mountain or into another jet.

Moreover, a strange and poorly understood loss of spatial orientation poses a constant danger—even for veteran pilots. Denied normal visual and physical clues, a pilot can lose any sense of up and down and relative motion. He can descend, but think he's climbing. He can move toward another jet, certain he's moving away. Even veteran pilots sometimes simply fly into the ground. Most inexperienced wingmen focus their attention on the flight lead. But even that can deceive. "Sometimes, you're looking at the lead and all of a sudden you can't tell if you're looking at the top of his plane or the bottom," warns Crash. "So, let's not get spatially disoriented. If you do—if you even think it's happening—climb to 15,000 feet and we'll come and get you."

That's hard advice for Gimmie or Stihl to take. None of the B-coursers wants to look weak.

"OK. What's your minimum airspeed?"

"350 knots," says Gimmie.

"You're cruising along at low altitude, how far can you turn?" asks Crash, reviewing that crucial rule.

"180 degrees," says Stihl.

"How about role reversals? At low altitude, can you?" asks Crash, referring to the essential, split-second coordination of roles between a lead and a wingman in a dogfight. In theory, the lead is "offensive," with primary responsibility for engaging the hostile fighter. The wingman provides support, looking for a shot and fending off any other enemy fighters. But if the enemy fighter gets the advantage and the lead fighter loses his offensive position, the lead calls for a role reversal—so the wingman will swoop in to pursue the enemy fighter while the flight lead escapes, repositions, and assumes the wingman's "defensive" responsibilities.

Stihl look at him quizzically. Obviously, he hasn't a clue.

"No. Not at low altitude," another training rule designed to limit the loss of punks, since the violent maneuvering involved in a role change might drive someone into the ground. It's an unavoidable risk in real combat, but not in training. "So he spits out the back and you go, 'When am I going to go kill him?' Can you reverse roles? No. As soon as you turn that maximum 180 degrees, start rocking your wings and that will stop you from turning," which will break off the simulated combat. The combat veteran IPs chafe at the restrictions, knowing that real dogfights often degenerate into quick-turning fights close to the ground. Practicing such fights realistically would give a pilot an edge close to the ground. But the Air Force decreed it was losing too many pilots and jets in training close to the ground. So rules were adopted to raise the simulated floor and impose turning and tactical restrictions.

"Also, remember, make sure you climb above 1,000 feet before you start shedding chaff and flares—we don't want to set anything on fire."

More restrictions.

Today, they'll fly to the range and drop bombs. Sometime during the flight, they'll split into two two-ship elements and fight each other. Crash and Gimmie will be "blue"; Punch and Stihl will be "red." But each team will have separate altitude blocks to avoid air-to-air collisions. Mostly, they'll launch simulated missiles and let the computer call the kill. "Red will be imitating the MiG 29. If you're killed, there will be a quick terminate after that. Don't keep quiet back there. It's more important to deconflict than to get a kill," he says, making sure they know they all have a responsibility to keep people from flying into each other.

Moreover, they have to watch out for slow, low-flying A-10s practicing on the gunnery range, flying out of Tucson. "There will be A-10s out there. So multiple groups could be on your radar."

All that traffic could limit their options once they spot each other on radar at 10 miles and turn to close. Ideally, fighters spot the enemy first and sneak up from the rear. But this time, they'll rush toward one another head-to-head—like knights with lances on horseback. In fact, head-on fights often work spectacularly well for American fighters, who have "all aspect" missiles capable of a nose-to-nose shot. The U.S. monopoly on such "all aspect" missiles guaranteed air superiority in the first Gulf War. But this fight assumes the fighters will flash past each other to make a visual identification, then maneuver for position. Normally, training rules require them to pass each other with a comfortable margin to avoid colliding. But the constricted airspace today might require a closer approach, notes Crash. "We know the area is so small it's almost impossible to get enough offset anyway—so wherever you start from, hopefully I'll have the skill and daring to offset the other direction."

Now the briefing splits, so they can talk about their tactics for the return to Luke during which they'll fight each other. Gimmie and Punch—the Red Team—depart for their own briefing, leaving Stihl and Crash to work one-on-one.

Crash outlines the rules for the fight. "If you say the K-word, you'd better mean it, or it's going to cost you five bucks, and that's with valid ID." The pilot calls the kill in the air, but later the cockpit tapes reveal whether he actually got a kill. Pilots who get a kill without calling it don't suffer damage to their cool. But a delusional hotshot who yells "kill" into the radio and is later proven wrong is going to get lots of shit and buy lots of beer.

"When we're looking low today"—trying to pick out the mottled gray outline of the jet against the ground—"it's going to be very hard to see them, even if they're dirty," and still loaded up with bombs and missiles. He suggests they narrow their radar beams, to improve resolution and reduce "clutter" from radar signals bouncing off the ground.

Two-ship tactics should guarantee that they're always scanning in different directions. "So if I target someone at 25,000 feet," says Crash, "it's automatic for you to search low. If I target you to a group below 25,000 feet, then I'll automatically search high." If one pilot is concentrating on scanning the skies above and in front, he'll see any additional enemy jets. By dividing the tasks, they reduce the chance of surprise. But it takes clear communications and discipline for the wingman to scan the empty sky instead of focusing on the approaching enemy.

"We're going to be working mostly at 1,500 feet in the target area. The floor is 500 feet—no one below 500 feet. As we come off target, we're going to be fuel-critical and we're going to have to come home. If someone is in our way, we're going to have to engage them. Targeting and sorting are standard. If something pops up inside 10 miles, then probably whoever attacks it first is going to be engaged [offensive], because we're not going to have time to swap. If we end up high and you're looking down, it can be quite challenging. Don't be surprised if your radar is not seeing what you expect. Maybe you'll have to hold back and do another sweep. How long does it take to make a 40- to 50-mile sweep?" he asks, referring to a single scan by the radar of a wedge of sky off the nose of the jet out to about 50 miles.

"Four seconds," says Stihl.

"Four seconds for each sweep," says Crash, correcting. "So about twenty seconds for a complete sweep."

"So when we come off target," continues Crash, "they'll be waiting. We're going to offset and determine their awareness," changing course to see if the radar images on their screens adjust to the new course—in which case they've been spotted. "We're going to offset," separating so they can't be shot down by the same jet. "When we engage, we're going to bracket them," splitting to fly one on each side. If the enemy fighter turns to fight one of them, the offset wingman has a perfect kill shot. If the enemy fighter plunges through between them, they'll both have a chance to slide in behind for a perfect shot. Normally, the two-ship formation that brackets first wins the fight—which is why the American use of AWACS planes and intricate communications and radar nets have guaranteed complete air supremacy in every combat since Vietnam.

"So when do we bracket?"

"Ten miles," says Stihl.

"If we do it at 10 miles, we're really late," corrects Crash. "For me, ideally, everything happens at 15 miles. When we execute this offset against this bogey group, and he seems to be unaware of our position, at 15 nautical miles I'm going to make the decision. I'm going to tell you to 'Target group bull's-eye for one,' " which tells him which plane Crash will lock up. "All you have to say is—two," which means Stihl should track the wingman. "Don't just float to my six o'clock—get over there aggressively," even if the violent maneuver causes him to temporarily lose the radar lock. "Better to get over there fast. The computer should find them again and you don't have to spend a lot of head-down time," trying to keep the target lock centered while moving into the right position. "What is that good deployed position?"

"Two and a half to three miles," offset from the flight lead.

"Right. What is different for WEZ [the weapons engagement zone] for that low-altitude environment?"

"It's going to be shorter," says Stihl. The ranges at which a missile can track and lock up targets will be compressed by the proximity of the ground.

"Right. The WEZs are going to be compact—so things are going to happen faster. Don't get outside two miles from me. If we're at 25,000 feet, what would you not have to worry about?"

"Hitting the ground," says Stihl with that charming grin that says he's having fun here.

"Right. Hitting the ground—because right in the middle of this is this mountain," he says, referring to a map of the range. "So there you are, 15 miles, I have sorted you in there to your target. You say, 'Veer one is tally one,' meaning you're sorted and on target. I'm going to say 'fox,' or I'm not going to say 'fox.' If I don't say 'fox' right after that—you're cleared to hammer down," and take a shot. "And then hopefully he's going to blow up. On the other hand, suppose either because of my buffoonery— or because he's aware of us—we get to 15 miles and can't get them locked up. Let's say I dick it up and fly right across his nose—I'm going to say 'bracket.' A little harder for you actually. You're going to go up, you're going to go . . ."

"We're going low to high?" asks Stihl.

"We're doing low to high," confirms Crash, meaning they're going to target enemy jets flying above them.

"What are you going to shoot?" Crash asks. "What's your first choice?"

"AMRAAMS," says Stihl—radar missiles.

"Most of the time, AMRAAMS are going to be your weapons of choice," confirms Crash. "We'll be doing different sets—so you're going to be flying three roles—engaged, supporting, and then a defensively engaged position," he says. "If you're the supporting fighter, you're responsible for deconfliction," to avoid midair collisions. "After that, you're responsible for taking shots of opportunity. If you're the defensive engaged fighter, because you're the guy that gets spiked by the radar of the fighter, what's your main responsibility? Number one: do not hit the ground. I'd rather sacrifice the perfect notch than have you steer yourself too low. This is only training, so don't hit the ground. Then pitch back in when you reposition."

Stihl nods. Fighter tactics depend on this complex coordination of roles. In time it becomes second nature—but for now, the B-coursers can hear the plate glass crack.

"Let's say we have a single unaware group out there—they haven't spotted us. I'm turning at 5 miles in absolutely the perfect position. Then, suddenly, when I get closer so I'm visual, lo and behold, we've got two of them down there—I say 'tally two' for the second bad buy. Who am I sorted to right now?"

"Whatever our sorting plan was," says Stihl.

"You see him on the radar, you're going to want to get a lock. If I can tally two and target my guy, in a perfect world, what do you think will happen?"

"You're going to ID your guy as hostile and shoot."

"Right. I shoot the far guy. What's the quickest way to get your sort to find your target?"

"Watch who you merge with."

"But I wouldn't look down at 4 miles. You can always just shoot him with a heater (heat-seeking missile). I'm going to ID him as I go by. You're going to do whatever it takes to deconflict from me and shoot this guy. What if you can't? What's your responsibility? Who's engaged here?"

"You."

"Right. I'm the engaged guy. I'm going to share with you because I'm a sharing guy—but what's your number one responsibility?"

"Deconfliction," says Stihl, in the rhythm of the questions now.

"Deconfliction," says Crash, bouncing on the balls of his feet. "Because if he's not turning, I may take 'em both. And if there's only one guy out there, leave him alone—he's mine."

Now he moves to the contingency plan. "Let us say we're making this conversion, diving down on them. And these guys start turning—and I miss this shot. And you're trying to shoot your guy—and you miss that shot. So now they're turning into us. Now what's going to happen?"

"We're going to go into air combat maneuvers," basic dogfighting.

"Go into two-circle fight. But by the time I turn around to shoot him again, you've probably already turned 180 degrees—so the fight's over," according to the training rules. "Knock it off. Nothing more embarrassing than shooting him when he's rocking his wings saying the fight's over. I'm going to terminate the fight when we get stacked at low altitude, because it's just not what we're looking for," he adds. Every mission in the syllabus is designed to teach them the heft of one particular brick. No point in spinning off into freestyle dogfighting.

"In the perfect world," continues Crash, "they're unaware and easy kills, and I want to be an ace, so I kill them. But if this guy shows any awareness—at 15 miles—then we blow the lead guy up. He's gone. Now what do we do?"

"Double up on the next guy."

"What are the options? I will be able to preserve range—and then we'll be able to determine—based on the bogey call—what to do. You keep him spiked [locked]. I may tell you to stagger, ever heard that?"

"No, sir," says Stihl, abashed.

"Dddddddddddddddddddddddddddddddd," stammers Crash, feigning amazement. "Well, you wait about fifteen seconds then you pitch back. If it's far enough out, we'll either go to the left—then engage off the nose at about 7 miles. I'll probably say 'bracket,' which means at least get away from me, outflank them on both sides. And then we'll engage at the merge."

He continues. "Now the worst case is, the group coming in has spiked us with radar missiles. You're going to pop out chaff. And get in the notch. How long you going to keep at it?"

"Four times the spike range," says Stihl, the standard flare and chaff sequence to frustrate both radar-guided and heat-seeking missiles when Betty detects the enemy's targeting radar lock and calls out in alarm.

"Don't be in a big hurry to jump into this notch," by turning across his nose, cautions Crash. "You need to execute. If you go naked, at some point you're going to have to pitch in with flares and fight your best one-versus-one. Hopefully, I'll kill him while you're turning. If I get spiked and I go into the notch—then you're going to have to execute the same thing."

Stihl gets it. They're synched.

16

───❦───

Behind the Jet

Rex has busted his fifth ride. He rolled in over the gunnery range, lined up with his lethal cannons, and slaughtered the wrong target. Completely wrong target. Lord.

What's more, the inspectors have arrived.

And Buster's worried. The stress has accumulated throughout the squadron. You can hear the creaking of the bulkheads—the popping of the rivets. And Buster's worried that maybe it's his fault.

Maybe it's a morale issue.

The Crusades are a dim memory. No time these days—with all the maintenance-related jinks in the scheduling that have forced frequent Friday flights. But it's also the quick change and the drift of leadership. Each flight commander must knit together the IPs and punks in his flight. That's one key function of those rowdy, weekly gatherings that made them feel like shit-kicking fighter pilots flying the best jet ever built into the Wild Blue Yonder, upside down at 9 g's. Without the Crusades, that fighter jock spirit has gone underground. The lack of squadron-level bonding has allowed the underlying division among the punks to fester. They have fragmented. Most of the married B-coursers head home quickly after their flights, while the hard core of the unmarried punks goes barhopping. That often includes the married Gimmie, who maintains her "one-of-the-boys" friendships, but rarely

191

gets drunk or loses that quiet reserve that protects her in this aggressively male world.

Moreover, the squadron has been straining to prepare for a base-wide inspection. The inspections, which are critical for career advancement, threaten to create a bureaucratic Perfect Storm. For weeks IPs have been staying late cramming for the inspections. For instance, every IP maintains a thick briefing book, with hundreds of pages of the latest rules and regulations. Mostly, it's basic stuff the IPs can recite upside down in a barrel roll. But the details change constantly, so before the inspection the IPs laboriously compare their individual briefing books to a master briefing book—page by page by page—to spot outdated pages and insert the updates. It's a tedious, time-consuming process, but all over the squadron you find brooding, mumbling fighter pilots updating their books.

So far, the inspection has gone well.

Except, of course, for the Rex situation.

Rex has been on CAP ever since he got into the program. Every time he's about to come off the extra supervision, he busts another ride. He rarely busts in a spectacular, oh-shit-get-him-the-hell-out-of-the-cockpit fashion. He just struggles along on that ragged edge of task saturation. Inevitably, Rex responds to a bust by ducking his head, taking the hit, and redoubling his effort. He's bruised, eyes swollen shut, weaving—but he won't go down. The IPs admire his grit, but they're frustrated. They don't know how to pull him away from the edge.

Naturally, the glinty-eyed inspectors notice that Rex has been on CAP ever since he arrived at Luke.

That's misusing CAP, they say. You're supposed to use it for a short-term intervention, then throw the sucker back into the pool with all the other baby sharks. If you nurse a guy along on CAP all through the B-course, he's just gonna hit the fan when he goes operational. These days, F-16 pilots could get hurled right into combat—tooling around Afghanistan and diving on downtown Baghdad—trying not to hit the friendlies. They don't have CAP in operational squadrons. He's going to get his damn fool self killed. Worse, he could get his flight lead killed, or bomb the Good Guys. So the inspectors grill Buster on the logic of keeping Rex on extra supervision. Shouldn't it be a case of fly or crash at this point?

Buster says Rex is a special case—the IPs figure he'll get it eventually. He's got a great attitude. Has shown continuous improvement, but somehow times his bad rides so the CAP never quite comes off. Buster reassures the inspectors that Rex hasn't busted a ride in a while—so he'll no doubt come off CAP soon. What no one's saying is that the Air Force is short on pilots—especially in the Reserves—now that we're bogged down in a couple of countries and flying the occasional fighter air patrol over New York, Chicago, and even Phoenix. Besides, the taxpayers have already invested something like $4 million in teaching Rex to fly F-16s. Best to give him every chance to catch up.

So the inspectors shake their heads and make notes and wander off to study the IPs' briefing books.

And the next day, Rex strafes the wrong goddamned target.

Mercifully, he didn't go after the manned observation post where the range officer conducts traffic and scores the bombing runs (although he wouldn't be the first B-courser to take a run at the observation post).

So now a couple of IPs have gathered in the ready room with Buster to figure out what to do about the Rex problem.

"I got strafed," says Buster of the discussion with the inspectors. "They didn't even like putting him on CAP at the start based on the evaluations from IFF," grouses Buster. "But it's like—you can't win. If a guy comes in with marginal evaluations and you don't put him on CAP and he screws up, then they're going to say, 'Why wasn't he on CAP?' And of course, if he gets off CAP without screwing up, then they're going to say, 'Why the hell was he on CAP?' "

Of course, Igor was on CAP when he came into the program—based on problems in IFF. But he hasn't busted a ride and has surged into the lead among the B-coursers, in his low-key, unflappable way.

"What I told them," continues Buster, "is Rex has just kind of been hit and miss. We've got eight students—three have had no trouble whatsoever—the other five have needed a little more supervision—usually three or four weeks. They'll hit a wall and get behind. So we give them a little extra attention—some continuity."

So now Rex has busted five rides. One more bust and he has to go before a review board, which usually means washing out. So he's staying on CAP—inspectors be damned. Of course, no one really expects Rex to make it now. He's run out his string. No way he can finish out the course without one more bust. Still, they're not going to let the inspectors pressure them into pulling the handle of his ejection seat.

Then right in the middle of that discussion, in comes Punch and AWOL—trying to figure out whether to bust Stihl, who just more or less blew his silly self up on a bombing run.

In combat these days, most F-16 pilots drop some variety of "smart bomb." The GPS bombs use satellite signals to home in on GPS coordinates. Anti-radar missiles home in on signals from SAM sites. Laser-guided bombs seek a pinpoint of light held steady by either the pilot or a ground spotter. Some bombs have TV cameras in the nose so the pilot can guide them from the cockpit right through the freaking picture window of Saddam's summerhouse. But the punks don't use those fancy and expensive bombs in practice. They blow stuff up the old-fashioned way: flying in low, popping up at the last minute, turning upside down so they can keep an eye on the target, and then diving at a very particular angle. Once released, the bomb hurtles toward the target with the momentum of the jet. Meantime, the pilot yanks his jet up and away to escape the lethal shrapnel from the bomb's explosion. While he's at it, the escaping pilot throws in a series of jinks and maneuvers to throw off any knucklehead on the ground with a shoulder-launched SAM or a triple-A battery or a frigging SAM site. It's actually a lot harder than the modern task of dropping bombs in the real world. But it's great practice, since it demands intense flying skills. It's also the most dangerous single thing the punks do in the whole course, since a mistake or a blown engine at 400 knots 1,000 feet off the deck can easily prove fatal.

Of course, usually the punks don't drop real bombs—just little concrete simulations. That enables the guy in the observation post to score the shot, with minimum expense and risk. The bomb run requires precise control of the plane's speed, course and dive angle. Too shallow and the bomb will miss. Too steep and the jet will end up inside the blast radius of the bomb.

So now Stihl—the grinning, laid-back surfer dude who hasn't busted a single ride—has flown through his own simulated blast pattern.

Should they bust him?

"He was, like, 5 degrees steep on the dive," says AWOL.

He should have noticed he was steep and not released his simulated bomb. But he hit the pickle button anyway.

"That's surprising," says Buster. "He seemed to be excelling at weapons delivery."

"He's been above average to slightly above average," says AWOL, which in IP talk is high praise. "I was surprised too. It was his very last run. He saw it at the last minute—and over-checked intentionally to try to correct it. But he still ended up at 27 degrees."

"What was his action range?"

"On this first run, he went too steep. On the subsequent ones, he caught it and floated back up a little bit," says AWOL, referring to the height above the ground.

"A little bit? Like 500 feet?" asks Buster.

"Like 500 feet. Standard student attack—eating up his brain bytes concentrating on pickling. It was an average kind of student mistake, going through with the attack. I talked to him to emphasize that you need to go dry if the angle is wrong. They get a little anxious carrying bombs the first time. I was surprised when the subsequent attacks went steep."

Punch chimes in. He was the flight lead. "Stihl said, 'I knew I was steep, I had no idea how steep I was.' " It's a key point; at least he had an idea he was pushing the envelope.

"So he's got four more rides, two dedicated to medium altitude. This is the last dedicated low-altitude ride where he can work on it," Buster ponders. If they bust him, he has to repeat the ride. That would crunch the schedule and spoil Stihl's perfect record. "So what do you want to do?"

"He's going to get more low attacks—so maybe we should just press on with additional training in the simulator—with an IP," says AWOL.

"What would you do?" Buster asks Punch.

"I kind of lean the other way, I think," says Punch carefully.

They call in Opie for an opinion. He's also flown with Stihl. Opie never swaggers. He's utterly confident, but moves quietly through the jostling egos in the squadron. He's also one of the most respected pilots. He lacks the outgoing charm and humor of Doughboy or Bongoo—but he's like a Jedi in a jet. He also has an uncanny knack for guessing what's going on in a student's cockpit and intervening with a question or suggestion at precisely the right moment.

Opie favors not busting him and not making him repeat the ride; he can rehearse hitting the dive angle at low altitude in the simulator.

"I'm kind of leaning towards the Santa Claus technique," says Buster, figuring not busting Stihl would be a gift—since he's been more nice than naughty. "Stihl has some aptitude. Besides, we've got four days of eight studs [students] going out in seven-ships," he says, knowing that with all of the malevolent bad luck of the last month, they'll be lucky to get the class through on time. "But I'll support the recommendation either way," he says, handing the issue back to the flight lead.

On cue, in strolls Rage, the flight commander.

"Stihl fragged himself," says Buster.

AWOL repeats the summary—two steep dives into the fragmentation pattern—but notes that Stihl immediately recognized the mistake and flew an otherwise flawless mission.

"So he noticed what was happening?" asks Rage.

"He didn't notice he'd fragged himself. He didn't climb out of the frag."

"And he wasn't helping out AWOL in the air," interjects Punch. "He wasn't giving AWOL a clue what the fuck was going on so he could help him out."

"He was right on for one of the four. Initially, I was thinking I don't want him going to the next sortie—but then we remembered he has some other low-altitude rides coming up."

"You've always got the low option on SAT 7," notes Buster in reference to an upcoming bombing mission. They all know the syllabus cold. It's like manipulating a Rubik's Cube—getting all the skills lined up with the rides.

"I'd go either way," says Rage. "If you want to hook him, we can hook him. Or put some red Xs on the grade sheet."

"You can have red Xs on the grade sheet and not on the board?" asks Buster, new to the complexities of rating punks. A busted ride goes on the board—for everyone in the squadron to study. Only a handful of IPs see the grade sheets.

"Yeah," says Rage, "you can have all the red Xs on the grade sheet you want. Do I think he's going to wash out? No way. Will hooking him do him some good? Maybe."

AWOL's not sure. "You hook them when you need to stop the training and make sure he has something before you let him go on. I'm not for hooking him to send a message. I don't think you need to send him a message—he's already pretty down on himself."

In fact, Stihl's first major screwup has hit him hard. His surfer dude manner actually conceals a true fighter pilot ego—and a ruthless capacity for self-criticism.

The discussion has forced Buster to do some soul-searching. Training fighter pilots is a tricky business. You can't just operate off a checklist. Basic pilot training does that—but they're trying to get rid of weak pilots. They're trying to pile on the pressure and make them crack—to save lives down the line. It's like boot camp so you can blast the punks out the back of the jet like chaff. But once they get to Luke, the goals change. Now you want to turn them into fighter pilots—not weed them out. Part of that's just hard work. They memorize books bulging with information. They demonstrate this whole progression of skills. They say the right stuff on the radio—hit the right buttons, toggle the sixteen different weapons settings. Part of it is just drill and practice. But there's more—something much harder to define. It has to do with trying to help them balance on that knife-edge between essential confidence and deadly arrogance. It's like a high-wire guy juggling knives on a unicycle. Yeah, it depends on practice and skill. But more than that, you have to believe you can juggle knives on a unicycle on a high wire. Flying an F-16 isn't actually that hard, thanks to the vigilance of the computer that keeps you from asking for impossible maneuvers. But being a single-engine, single-seat fighter pilot—well, now, that's a different matter. The minute you doubt yourself, you're dead—all the knives come down at once. You're frozen on the centerline, staring into the headlights. So you want these kids to believe they can do it, to come barrel rolling right up to the edge of arrogance. You've got to be arrogant to fly an F-16. You've got to believe you can do anything, kill anything, and escape any missile. More to the point, you've got to believe the engine won't choke, the radar blip really is an enemy fighter and not your wingman, and all those little dots on the ground aren't a bunch of marines in your crosshairs. Then again—you always have to entertain the possibility that any of those things might happen, so you check, and cross-check and adhere to routine—except in the moments when the routine will kill you.

So you don't want to cost Stihl the edge that promises to make him a great pilot.

And you want to give Rex a chance to gain that edge—to visualize himself in such a way that he will live up to the picture.

It's more art than science.

And what makes it even more complicated is that great pilots aren't necessarily great instructors. Certainly, that seemingly inborn instinct helps. Certainly the students respect a great pilot—and hang on his utterances. But then, they're just punks—they don't necessarily know a great pilot from an experienced pilot. In fact, a great pilot can be a terrible instructor. The kind of ego often found in great pilots may not help them when it comes to teaching. It's like anything else, you've got to burn to be a great instructor, it's got to haunt you. Most pilots end up being IPs at some point, either at Luke or in their squadrons. Most pass through and do a good job. Some have a gift for it, an instinct for what the student needs. Opie has it. So does Bongoo. And Punch. And Rage.

Buster wants to learn it—but he's not sure yet. He remembers one instructor in particular. The guy was a mediocre pilot, but he yearned to teach like some guys want to kill MiG. So he memorized his briefings and practiced them in front of the mirror. He would go to the briefings of the IPs he admired. Every time he got a tough question, he'd go out and buttonhole other pilots and do research and try it out in the simulator until he had a great answer. He was always pestering the squad's weapons officer for tips and the latest technical data and advice on how to explain something. He'd seek out the best pilots and get them to teach him their best moves—so he could incorporate that into his briefings. The guy got to be a better pilot as a result— although he never did acquire the instincts and split-second reactions of a great pilot. He did, however, turn into a great instructor. So now

he's Buster's role model, helping him rise to his leadership responsibilities in the squadron.

So he gives Stihl a pass.

And he busts Rex and leaves him on CAP.

Inspectors be damned. He's the operations officer now.

17

⸺❧⸺

The Future of Blowing Stuff Up

The B-coursers don't know it yet, but it's possible they're the last generation of fighter pilots. By the time they finish their careers in twenty or thirty years, we may not need daring hotshots at all.

It's a depressing thought for the fighter jocks, especially the veterans like Doughboy.

But, alas, he has seen the future.

And it's complicated.

Doughboy got a glimpse of that high-tech future while working in the computerized future command center for the war in Afghanistan.

He volunteered just before the bombs started falling in Afghanistan, and his combat and electronic warfare experience got him a slot normally reserved for a colonel. The Air Force plucked him from his F-16 squadron and sent him to Saudi Arabia to work in the command and control center. The air war over Afghanistan completed the long, dramatic transformation of the Air Force since Vietnam—changing some things utterly, and others not at all.

Doughboy worked almost around the clock in the Coalition Air Operations Center, a cavernous building dominated by two 60-foot-wide, 30-foot-tall projection screens, each split into quarters. All of the information from Afghanistan flowed into the center through satellite links, so the air war unfolded in real time through the blended transmissions of satellites, Predator drones, jets in the air, and spotters on the ground. The command center coordinated strikes by the Air Force, Navy, Army, and allied aircraft—and coordinated those strikes with intelligence from the ground.

"I was one of two time-sensitive targeting cell chiefs—which I'd never even heard of before. We would focus on high-value targets, like Bin Laden and his chief deputies. We actually had guys on horseback calling in coordinates—literally—and then sitting there and waiting and reporting where the bomb hit. We were working twenty-hour days and sleeping under our desks—targeting hundreds of sorties and thousands of bombs. But every time we started to get tired, someone would just say, 'It's better than being a New York fireman on September 11,' and everyone would get quietly back to work."

The targeting officers had to figure out new procedures on the spot. Historically, mission planners pore over satellite photos and make complex calculations to establish targets before passing them along to the pilots. But now they had Army and Special Forces spotters on the ground with handheld GPS markers, calling in target coordinates—often changing those coordinates on the fly. The targeting planners agonized about how much to rely on such on-site targeting without satellite backup.

"At first, that was a big issue—would we allow the guy on the ground to call in coordinates to an airplane dropping a GPS bomb? I said, why not? The admirals and generals were not comfortable with that. But we went through a three-day process of proving that the coordinates from the guy on the ground were just as accurate. So we'd have jets leaving carriers and flying for two hours to a target, then having the ground spotter say, nope, it's moved, and giving us new coordinates."

Moreover, the precision-guided munitions dramatically improved the effectiveness of many aircraft. Before the invention of self-guiding bombs, Viper and F-18 Hornet pilots practiced for hundreds of hours to achieve a pale shadow of the same accuracy—and the big bombers like the B-52s just dropped masses of bombs that obliterated whole areas. Suddenly, the fifty-year-old B-52s could drop bombs with such pinpoint accuracy they could provide close air support for troops on the ground.

"Used to be, you'd have to roll in and visually acquire the target. That takes a lot of practice. Now we can have any old kind of airplane up there that can drop a GPS bomb."

Of course, precision bombs still kill the wrong people. The fury of war inevitably breeds mistakes. One army unit called in a strike on itself. The handheld GPS unit the army spotter was using went dead, and when the spotter replaced the battery, he forgot that in some situations the reset instrument would give its own position, rather than the position it had displayed before the battery died.

Much of their information flooded in from unmanned Predator drones, flying slowly over the battlefield, uplinked to satellites. Besides burying the targeters under information, this real-time linkage to the battlefield created new opportunities for generals and politicians to try to direct the war from Washington, bypassing the commanders in the field.

"The feed is going all over the world. So you can have some guy sitting in the Pentagon watching in real time what's happening on the battlefield. So the generals want to reach out and grab control. One Army commander got fed up and called back to the Pentagon and said, 'I'm the commander on the field, and if you want to do it, get out here—otherwise shut up.' "

The flood of information can also create the illusion of control and understanding. "All of us in the trenches are running around with our heads chopped off trying to get the guys in the field what they want—and trying to keep the generals happy. They want more information to make decisions on, but you're looking through a soda straw. You don't really have the big picture on the ground. But the people on the ground are also just seeing this little portion of the picture too."

That glimpse of high-tech warfare, and the growing role of the Predators, offered a veteran fighter pilot a sobering vision of the future. Already the plodding Predators carry missiles. Already, the most advanced air-to-air missiles carried by the F-16s and F-15s can outrun the fastest jet and kill the best pilot. Manned fighter jets can only do 9 g's in a turn. Unmanned drones and missiles can pull 50 g's. After the guidance systems in the missiles improve for another generation or two, fleets of cheap, disposable Predators guided by satellites and AWACS planes could probably shoot down the most advanced fighters, with the best-trained pilots. That's one reason the Air Force invested in the costly "stealth" fighter, the F-22 Raptor—and has plans to replace the F-16, F-15, and F-18 with the stealthy Joint Strike Fighter in the next decade. The Air Force hopes stealth technology will protect another generation of fighter pilots from the increasing lethality of radar-guided missiles. Still, fighter pilots like Doughboy who have seen the new technology in action cannot suppress the uneasy feeling that they're training the last generation of fighter pilots—before the drones take over the world.

Of course, the Air Force reverted to all its old worst habits in designing the latest of manned fighter jets. The plans for advanced fighters with radar-confusing elements now total somewhere between $300 billion and $400 billion.

The F-22 Raptor is already in production. Intended as the dogfighting replacement for the F-15, the Raptor ended up with bombs tucked into little bays to keep them from sticking out into the wind and giving enemy radars a return. The Air Force wanted 750 planes, but as the cost ballooned they settled for half as many. The Air Force says the Raptors will cost about $134 million each; the General Accounting Office puts the ultimate cost at $200 million apiece.

Meantime—naturally enough—the Navy wants its own stealth fighter. So it will spend $100 billion for a Raptor competitor, loaded up and gold-plated just like the F-18 Hornet, the spawn of the plane that lost the Air Force design competition to the F-16. So now the Air Force is buying the F-22, while the Navy pours money into its own stealth fighter-bomber plus more billions for 548 souped-up, F-18 Super Hornets.

Having won approval to build the horrendously expensive F-22, the Air Force has begun cannibalizing other programs to fund the Raptor. Once upon a time, the Fighter Mafia outmaneuvered the brass and got the cheap, flexible, and lethal F-16. In something of the same tradition, the Air Force started work on a cheaper replacement for the F-16, the F-35 Joint Strike Fighter (JSF), when the Raptor's cost went stratospheric. Inevitably, task inflation set in. Now various versions of the JSF will supposedly land on aircraft carriers, take off vertically, provide close air support, and dogfight anything except the $200 million Raptor—all for $50 million per plane.

Just to prove they're serious—the Air Force has stopped buying new F-16s—like Cortez burning his boats before he marched on the Aztecs.

Dumb move, say critics.

For one thing, the F-16s and F-15s are still working just fine, thank you. No other air force can challenge the U.S., although a resurgent China presents a smudge of a cloud on the horizon.

Meantime, Vipers have won every dogfight they've entered and no one else has a fighter on the drawing board to effectively challenge it, or the aging F-15. Moreover, smart bombs have dramatically increased its bombing capabilities. Hell, B-52s can provide close air support—who needs a $200 million fighter jet? Critics point to the B-2 bomber, a radar-evading stealth bomber intended to replace the venerable B-52s. The B-2 ended up costing $2 billion per plane and has been plagued by mechanical problems. Designed to penetrate thousands of miles of dense, integrated Soviet air defenses, the B-2s now end up flying halfway around the world to blow up some frigging concrete bunker a Viper could kill with a smart bomb. The critics point out that the U.S. now spends more on its military than the next twelve biggest-spending nations combined, which has bought air supremacy with existing jets for the foreseeable future. Besides, say the green-eye-shade types, smart bombs and armed drones have changed everything. Vipers no longer need to penetrate a hail of antiaircraft fire. They can go lolling in at 30,000 feet and take a shot from 10 miles off with a 2,000-pound bomb outfitted with a $25,000 GPS adaptor kit—easily destroying a target that required a twenty-four-plane strike package in the first Gulf War. Why spend $400 billion on a new generation of stealthy fighter jets when the Eagles and Vipers can keep flying until the drones take over?

Maybe manned jets have entered the death spiral of an obsolete weapons system—as did armored knights and battleships. George and Meredith Friedman, in their disturbing book *The Future of War*, compare the costly embrace of stealth technology to the construction of the massive dreadnoughts after World War I just before the appearance of aircraft carriers. Once World War II started, the battleships on which the aging admirals had pinned their hopes and strategy proved fatally vulnerable to small planes with torpedos. It could be happening again, as computers make possible lethal smart missiles and unmanned drones. For instance, the stealthy B-2 bomber does the same job as the ancient B-52, delivering about 50,000 pounds of bombs some 7,000 miles. But the B-2 costs $2.2 billion per plane—ten times the originally promised cost. Certainly, the B-2 has a much better chance of surviving long enough to nuke Moscow. But, critics insist, even at such a horrendous cost, the stealth aircraft won't remain "invisible" for long. Already the Russians say they can detect incoming stealth aircraft. The U.S. is also actively developing detectors that can spot the difference in temperature between the radar-evading plane and the surrounding air. So should we spend $2.2 billion per bomber to improve the odds of getting past radar-based defenses for the next ten or fifteen years?

Then again, perhaps the critics miss the point, never having strapped on a Viper and read a radar screen. Spotting the enemy a long way off determines who wins in the air. Stealth technology combines innovative design and radar-absorbing materials to absorb or deflect radar signals, dramatically reducing the radar signals that bounce off the jet and back to the enemy's receiver. The non-stealthy Vipers and Eagles romped across Iraq with minimal casualties in part because the stealthy F-117 Nighthawk fighter flew into Baghdad on the first night, unescorted, and decapitated the Iraqi air defense and command and control centers. A handful of Nighthawks struck the nerve centers of the air defenses and the hardened hangars hiding the Iraqi fighters, apparently all but invisible to the Iraqi radars. Perhaps stealth aircraft could not easily penetrate cutting-edge air defense systems. But then, we can always send long-range missiles against those targets. In the meantime, the stealth technology ensures another generation of absolute dominance against second-string air defenses in places like North Korea, the Balkans, Iraq, Iran, Syria, and almost any other plausible target.

All the F-16 pilots say they're eager for the new technology—much as they love their Vipers. Even a frigging punk on his third dogfight understands that the battle usually goes to whoever gets off the first shot. It gets back to that discouraging statistic—the 90 percent ambush rate in air-to-air kills. So if you're flying a radar-evading fighter and can consistently spot your enemy 20 miles sooner than he can spot you, you're gonna kill that sucker every time. Moreover, they know that the next generation of ground- and ship-launched antiaircraft missiles will prove lethal for a non-stealth fighter. Even today, F-16 veterans who have flown in exercises against U.S. carrier taskforces say a conventional plane can't get within 100 miles due to the air defenses. "It's suicide flying against carriers," says Doughboy. "You'll never even see them on your radar. It's murder."

Plus, you can't keep a fighter jet in the air forever, no matter how good the ground crew. Already, many of the F-16s are flying at twice their design life, thanks to continuous reinvention. The average age of the 6,300 planes the Air Force owns is about twenty-two years—twice as old as the average airliner. As a result, readiness has dropped 25 percent in the past five years, and the cost of an hour in the air has risen 45 percent. Worse, the accident rate has soared. Almost all of the more than ninety U.S. fighter pilots who have died in the cockpit of an F-16 have died as a result of training accidents and engine failures. The Air Force reported thirty-five major accidents in 2002, which partly reflected a 200,000-hour increase in hours in the air from the previous year. The accident rate's much worse in the Army, Navy, and Marine Corps.

At Luke, three Viper pilots have died as a result of crashes, which remain common. During the B-course, two jets crashed within days of each other. One sucked in a turkey vulture, which trashed the engine. The second involved a mechanical failure in an overstressed piece of the engine. That resulted in the grounding of a host of F-16s with the same engine part from the same factory, while ground crews worked feverishly to replace the suspect part. Ingenuity has kept the aging Vipers and Eagles in the air for the past two decades—with escalating costs and risks.

So proponents of the F-22 Raptor and the F-35 Joint Strike Fighter say they'll not only assure another generation of air supremacy, but also cut hourly flying costs and increase reliability. The stealth fighters may cost twice as much as the planes they're replacing (maybe more), but if a handful of Raptors can obliterate any enemy air force, they'll be worth every penny to the grunts on the ground.

Yeah. Well. In theory. So long as we don't go broke, like the Soviet Union. Except they went belly-up keeping up with us. We're on the road to broke keeping up with ourselves. For instance, one B-1 bomber crashed in the middle of flying halfway around the world to bomb some frigging caves in Afghanistan. That one bomber cost half of Afghanistan's gross domestic product. Seriously.

The effort to design the successors to the F-16 and F-15—politically convoluted, full of stops and starts, and characterized by incestuous military-industrial connections—has illustrated all of the awkward trade-offs and problems the Fighter Mafia battled. Pilots report that the $200 million F-22 flies brilliantly but suffers from an onslaught of bugs—like software glitches that keep shutting down the Raptor's radar. But the Raptor's main problem remains its staggering cost. Currently

F-15s mostly protect air tankers, AWACS planes, and bombers. The 300 F-22s on order will be stretched dangerously thin in an actual war.

That brings up the JSF, the cheaper replacement for the F-16 Viper and the F-18 Hornet. The JSF poses a much tougher design problem, and so far the specifications seem to resurrect past Air Force design disasters. Hopefully, it won't turn out like the Navy's stealthy A-12, which was supposed to take off from carriers, flit past radars, and provide close air support for troops. Developed as a classified project, cost overruns and technical problems doomed it before it ever reached production. The fiasco cost taxpayers billions.

The Air Force version of the JSF adhered to many of John Boyd's principles of Energy Maneuverability design, but the imperative to create versions that land on aircraft carriers and take off vertically has spawned expensive design nightmares. Aircraft design demands trade-offs. Agility comes from sticking as big an engine as possible on as light a frame as possible. The range, payload, turning radius, and acceleration of a plane all interact. You can design a solid, slow, durable, reliable jet to blow up tanks and loiter around to support ground troops (like the A-10), but that jet won't stand a chance against an F-15 in a dogfight. You can build a jet to carry heavy bomb loads and land on carriers (like the F-18), but only if you give up range and agility. In the same way, you can buy a jeep and go off-roading, or you can get a Corvette and corner fast—but you can't do both. The poor, freaking JSF is supposed to replace the F-16, the A-10, the carrier-based F-18—and take off vertically like the crash-prone British Harrier.

Oh yeah, and it's also gonna be cheap and reliable and have a long range.

Right.

And that assumes that by the time they get done adding stuff, redesigning it, testing it, canceling it, reviving it, and parceling out the juicy subcontracts, someone hasn't invented an alternative to radar that will make the stealth planes easily detectable. Or, worse—the stupid scientists haven't done away with pilots altogether with unmanned drones. The Pentagon's working on an unmanned "UAV" about the size of an F-16 that's supposed to fly by 2012. It's all very classified stuff, but presumably this offspring of the Predator drone will sport the latest air-to-air missiles and links to the AWACS and a guy on the ground peering through the cameras and putting the damned thing through 50-g turns that would squash the most peerless of pilots. Freed from the need to keep the pilot alive and conscious, such a drone could fly inverted circles around some poor fool in an F-16. While the budget for the JSF has already climbed over $65 billion, the research budget for the drones stands at about $2 billion annually. The Air Force recently ordered sixteen faster and more heavily armed and sensor-equipped Predator Bs, at a cost of about $9 million each—already twice the cost of the earlier version. The Air Force has also ordered up larger Global Hawks, high-altitude surveillance drones that can fly 12,000 miles to provide real-time views of the battlefield. The Air Force hopes to have about twenty-seven in its inventory by 2007—part of an eventual fleet of fifty-one, costing $57 million each. So much for cheap little drones—although still a bargain compared to $2.2 billion bombers.

The recent air wars in Afghanistan and Iraq demonstrated how quickly things are changing, even without the next generation of fighters and drones.

Just ask Doughboy.

The scene in the command center running the bombing of Afghanistan yielded a sobering view of a costly, high-tech future, even against the low-tech Taliban. Often, Hornet pilots would launch from carriers in the Persian Gulf on fourteen-hour missions with repeated midair refuelings to drop bombs on trucks and caves. Sometimes they couldn't find anything to bomb once they got there.

"The big heroes of Afghanistan you never hear anything about are the tanker crews," says Doughboy. The tankers would orbit for hours, sometimes leaving their safe orbits to fly deep into the danger zone when fighters and bombers ran critically short on fuel.

The Command Center included its own staff of tanker liaisons. "So I'd go to the tanker guy and say, 'We have to move a tanker—we need 150,000 pounds of gas so I can orbit this B-52 for another two hours waiting for a target. And, by the way, I needed that an hour ago, is that OK?' But they had to keep it all straight—because the Navy and the Air Force use different refueling equipment—so you've got to make sure everyone can link up."

He recalls one strange incident involving a soldier serving as a roving, undercover forward air controller. The guy dressed up in robes and rode around on a horse loaded with communications gear, so he could set up on high ground with his binoculars and his laser pointer and his GPS equipment and call in targets. But then his saddle broke and he got thrown. The horse ran off, loaded with classified communications gear. The spotter called the command center in a panic, fearful the gear would fall into the hands of the Taliban. But the Northern Alliance guy said not to worry—the horse would come home for dinner. Sure enough, the horse came home. So the Air Force airlifted the guy a new saddle from Texas. "The general stands there shaking his head, saying, 'I never thought I'd see us airlifting saddles.' "

The new technology also brings the ethical dimension into sharper focus. Suddenly the Predators and the camera-fitted bombs make the kill personal. "At the time, you're so intent on your job, you're not thinking too much about it. It's not until you leave the target area that it really sinks in. I had a friend flying an A-10 in Desert Storm and he was strafing a column. So he sees a guy running away from the column. He starts leading him and squeezes off a couple of seconds of fire. And he was shooting people who are running away. They're still legitimate targets, but he's thinking, 'I should just blow up their trucks and leave them alone.' We did a lot of that in Afghanistan. I mean, most of those people we were fighting were really bad people, but we wanted to rescue the good people. We did all kinds of things to mitigate damage—we'd always have a collateral-damage estimate, which became a nightmare. So we'd have F-16s with laser-guided bombs blowing up buildings in downtown Kabul and we'd have them set the fuses so the bomb would go through the building and blow up under it, so as to not damage the building next to it. You'd watch it on the feed and it was just amazing—it was like you took an eraser and erased that house. We went to all kinds of trouble. So if something moved 50 feet, we couldn't bomb it because you had to redo the collateral damage estimate. I mean, we could have carpet bombed the whole country, but you can't do that because you're trying to rescue the people who aren't bad."

So you have to put it out of your mind, sometimes. "I remember in the Gulf War, I shot this one missile that just totally took off and I have no idea where it went. But I can't spend the rest of my life wondering whether it landed in the ocean or on some guy's house. Our job is to kill people and break stuff. If we could do the job without killing people, we'd be happy. But there are evil people out there. And we could bring every American back to the United States and they'd still be after us—they're just like that. They're very weird."

For the most part, the B-coursers have resolved not to think about such issues.

"Making that decision is for people making a lot more money than me," says Jack. "I trust the guys making the decision are going to make the right decisions, based on the intelligence they have—not what I have. That said, you know that when you go in, some people are going to get killed that shouldn't have. I don't like the idea of it, but I guess that's the greater good."

Igor notes, "I may be called upon to put my life at risk to defend the lives of Americans and take the lives of people who fight against us. Did I grow up thinking, I want to be a fighter pilot so I can kill people? Nobody thinks that. Well, actually, there may be some nutcases that think that—but I wasn't one of them. War is an ugly thing. You're killing people. You're destroying things. There's nothing beautiful in that. And no war will ever be surgical—the war in Iraq is the closest we've come. We lost like 100 Americans invading an entire country. It's almost obscene. But I don't make the policy on who tells me where and when to go. It's my job as the go-man to say, 'Yes sir, boss. Right away.' I mean, I've talked to guys who have been around a while—who used to do the nuke routine—knowing the odds are if they ever dropped they were going to be killed in the blast. But you do what you're trained to do. The cockpit is a very sterile, desensitized environment. At 30,000 feet, you pickle off a bomb that targets on a laser point—and you may not see the explosion. All you hear is the sound of your breathing and the radio transmissions."

18

⸎

LEARNING TO KILL PEOPLE
AND BREAK THEIR STUFF

THE IPs KEEP PILING ON the bricks—listening for the sound of cracking.

As soon as the B-coursers learn the basics of flying to the range, lining up on a target, flying in under radar, popping up, rolling over, and diving in toward the target at just the right angle—they up the ante. In the final missions of the air-to-ground training, the IPs throw in some simulated MiG fighters, waiting to pounce soon after the F-16s deliver their bombs.

The F-16's evolved flexibility makes it one of the most useful jets in Air Force history. The development of smart bombs has made the F-16 a lethally effective bomber—especially in close air support. Once, it took fighter-bombers and B-52s dozens of missions dropping hundreds of bombs to destroy a specific target—like a bridge. Now, four F-16s can destroy almost any target for which they have coordinates. Of course, versions of the F-16's GPS bombs can also be dropped wholesale from B-52s and strike fixed targets with the same transforming accuracy. But B-52s and other dedicated bombers remain vulnerable to fighters and so require heavy escorts of F-16s or F-15s. By contrast, not only can the Viper precisely deliver bombs, it can outfight virtually any other jet—with the exception, over long ranges, of the F-15. Moreover, F-16s have also largely taken on the Wild Weasel role, so they remain the primary

213

SAM-killers—likewise able to fight through enemy fighters while loaded with bombs.

All of that has complicated the already complex job of the F-16 pilots. They must learn most of the tactics and weapons used by the dogfighting F-15 pilots, plus the complicated bomb-delivery tasks of the bomber pilots—all without a navigator, a weapons officer, or a backseat pair of eyes. As a result, although the F-16 remains one of the easiest planes in the world to fly, it's one of the toughest to employ.

As the B-coursers have discovered with each new layer of bricks.

In this case, Igor and Jack learn how complicated and unpredictable the task of dropping bombs gets when you've got MiGs—even F-16s acting like MiGs—laying an ambush on the escape route back to base.

The plan is simple enough. Fly to the range. Descend to 500 feet for a breathtaking hurtle along the sun-blasted desert ridges below enemy radar to within 100 miles of the target. It takes about ten minutes to cover 100 miles in an F-16, tooling along without afterburners. Near the target they will climb to 20,000 feet and then dive toward the target in an inverted arc, to release the bombs at a precise heading and angle. It's not as gut-wrenching as the low-angle attacks they've been practicing, but it more closely resembles a real-world mission—since smart bombs and SAM-killing Wild Weasels have mostly eliminated risky, treetop approaches.

Then all they have to do is get home without getting shot down.

Igor and Jack do all the mission planning: programming the navigational steerpoints, precisely plotting the path the jets will follow on the map, drawing the diagram of the bomb run, complete with the precise speeds and angles. The plan builds in deconfliction to minimize the chance of a midair collision. When they started, it would have taken them six hours to develop the mission plan. This time it takes just ninety minutes. The IPs can do it in half that.

They'll be bombing three bermed fortifications suitable for basing SAMs. The plan calls for two jets to hit the center target, with the other two jets splitting to hit the revetments to each side. They're treating the target like a SAM site, with a central van containing the targeting radar and the missiles themselves splayed off to the side. The plan choreographs the arrival of the jets so they don't fly across one another's path on their approach—when the pilot's attention will be focused on the target.

The takeoff proceeds flawlessly, each two-ship lifting off in formation. Once, every takeoff required intense concentration and anticipation. Once, working out the details of ground operations—taxiing, accelerating down the runway, lifting off in formation, turning to the precise headings necessary to avoid other jets and the subdivisions sprawling out beneath them—seemed a major accomplishment. Now, it's all routine, like the stretch from the garage to the freeway on the morning commute.

Approaching the target, they follow the steerpoints programmed into the ship's computer on cartridges prepared during the mission-planning phase.

The cloudless sky arching over the canopy is brilliant, blue and featureless. The horizon stretches out beneath them, brown and rumpled, the edge between tawny earth and brilliant sky clearly etched. Flying an F-16 remains exhilarating—when the pilots have a moment to pay attention between checking the radars and the steerpoints and their position in formation.

Igor flies with his habitual, methodical care—attending to the mantra of "Near rocks, far rocks." The pilots have learned to shift their attention constantly, a habit intended to make sure that no critical task slips out of their "situational awareness." So Igor moves his eyes deliberately to the closest mountain ridges, making sure he's on the preprogrammed flight path and has plenty of elevation to clear the "close rocks." Then he shifts his attention to the higher, more distant mountains—the "far rocks"—to quickly calculate whether he needs to change altitude or direction. Now he shifts his attention inside the cockpit, to check the radar that would warn him of approaching planes. His eyes flick to the speed, altitude, and the time and distance to the next steerpoint. But he only lets his attention remain inside the cockpit for a few seconds before shifting again to the "near rocks," then over to Opie, flying lead. Now he turns and looks back over his shoulder, the wingman habit that could save all their lives in combat. Then his attention shifts again to inside the cockpit. It's all a matter of intensively trained routine—the distillation and reiteration of lifesaving habits of vigilance and double-checking. At the beginning of the training, the B-coursers could only really pay attention to a few things on each mission. Often when flying in formation, they spent all their time just maintaining the proper position off the wing of the lead fighter. The lead could fly into the side of a mountain and the punk would follow him in, never taking his eyes off the wing of the doomed jet. Now, the flight formation is just one item in the ceaseless cross-check.

Soon, they approach the target, marked by the splitting of a dirt road skirting the edge of a wash between two low, saguaro-spiked, sun-bronzed mountain ranges. Igor recognizes the topography immediately from the aerial photos he studied before the mission. Rex's humiliation in strafing the wrong target gave them all a walking-past-your-grave chill. Ever since, they've all been studying their targeting photos with extra intensity. They're all proud, self-critical overachievers—with a horror of failure and ridicule. Even the unflappable Stihl felt like he wanted to crawl into a hole and hide after nearly busting his recent bomb run. They each dread the thought of anyone ever talking about them with that kind of pitying condescension most of them employ already when talking about Rex. All of which makes Rex's dogged, uncomplaining persistence the more remarkable.

Igor lines up the small smudge of the SAM site on the canopy rail of his cockpit, using those visual clues to guide his approach. He double-checks the target, which lies at the end of a three-pronged side road. In studying the photographs, Igor had already cautioned himself not to mistakenly target a different series of mounds on a four-pronged fork off the road that led him in toward the SAM site. As he approaches, the target begins to disappear under the nose of the jet, so he shifts to the right and rolls halfway over so he can keep the target in sight. He manipulates the control stick intuitively now.

The jet seems an extension of himself, thanks to the computer-mediated controls. Originally, the engineers made the stick itself solid, unmoving, since the computer could translate the pressure on the stick from the pilot's hands as easily as the stick's actual movement. But the pilots hated that. They wanted to move the stick, to gain that sense of control. Now F-16 pilots often wrestle the stick, sometimes straining their muscles in the violent maneuvering of combat, although the computer pays attention to only the first few increments of that pressure. But an experienced F-16 pilot flies the jet with a light touch, never looking down. Sometimes, it almost seems as if the jet is reading his mind—straining like a racehorse at the slightest shift of the reins. Moreover, the enormous thrust of the Viper creates its own gravity and orientation. So as he rolls into his turn, Igor instinctively puts just enough arc into his turn to press his body into the seat at about 1 g, even though he's three-quarters upside down. This manipulation of g-forces often makes it feel like the F-16 isn't really turning or climbing or diving or rolling at all. Rather, it seems like the world is shifting—twirling—out there beyond the bubble arch of the cockpit. The horizon shifts to vertical, then becomes the floor. The earth tilts and becomes the sky. And all the while, the force of the jet's path makes it seem like he's sitting comfortably in level flight.

Igor comes out of the rolling turn so that now he is flying at a carefully calculated angle to the target, keeping it in sight for the final 10 miles of the approach.

Suddenly, Opie's calm, but penetrating voice sounds in his earphones.

"We have a lock and a SAM launch at your five o'clock," he says.

Of course, it's not really a SAM lock. But the rules of the mission include maneuvering to evade a SAM strike. So Igor veers abruptly into a violent, classified maneuver designed to break the radar lock of a SAM missile. Usually, the antiaircraft missiles follow a radar signal from the ground, so if the ground station loses the radar lock the SAM will go off course or explode prematurely. Essentially, the evasion involves abrupt, gut-wrenching maneuvers to turn the jet edge-on to the radar signal from the ground, breaking the lock. The maneuver, which depends on the agility of the F-16, proved effective repeatedly in Bosnia and Iraq. Opie studies the sequence of Igor and Jack's violent evasive maneuvers until he's satisfied, then declares that the missiles have missed.

"You're still alive," he adds helpfully.

They reassemble. Early in the course, simply corralling four jets in so vast a sweep of sky and precisely matching their headings and speed would have been a major focus of a whole flight. Now it's done in an offhand way, in the midst of more important tasks.

When it's time for the bombing run, Opie rolls in first, followed by Igor and the other two jets in sequence. The jets execute a "Pappy Peel," named after World War II ace Pappy Boyington: a line of jets plummeting toward the target in single file.

The first pass goes off smoothly. Each jet must dive at a 45-degree angle at 430 knots and release its bomb at precisely the moment the computer calls the shot. Every jet hits the right dive angle, releases right on time, and then banks away from the target—ready for more evasive maneuvers if Opie calls another SAM launch.

Igor imagines himself hurtling down at the target on an imaginary wire strung tight at a 45-degree angle to the ground. He knows he can drift to 48 or 50 degrees, but flattening to 35 degrees will make it harder to hit the target, and going steeper than 55 degrees will take him into his own blast pattern—either way, he will bust the ride. During the mission planning, Igor spent twenty minutes calculating the dive angle and speed for his assigned weapons and altitude. "Then you go out there and make those numbers work," he says. "You measure to a millimeter, draw with a crayon, and hack with an ax," he jokes.

On the first pass, he's 50 feet too high, but right on a 45-degree angle, when he drops the bomb. He looks at the airspeed indicator and notes that he's just 5 miles per hour too fast, so he pickles and drops the 24-pound concrete-filled steel bomb. But he screws up. He looked at the airspeed indicator, which gives his absolute speed relative to the ground; he should have looked at the Mach airspeed indicator, which gives his speed relative to the speed of sound. The speed of sound varies significantly with altitude—as it propagates through the different densities of air. The restrictions on the release of the bombs are based on Mach speed, which more accurately indicates the pressure of the air on the jet and the bombs slung to the underside. In fact, if Igor had checked the Mach speed indicator, he would have seen that he was diving so fast that he would have been in danger of ripping real 500-pound bombs off the pylons on the underside of the wings. He flirted with the limit that would have automatically busted the ride—but "by the luck of God and the grace given to fighter pilots," he didn't exceed it.

As he goes around for the next pass, he recognizes his mistake. Shaken, he prays the tape will show he didn't quite screw the pooch—then steadies himself and fixes his concentration on the Mach speed indicator. Of course, that's the whole point of training. Hopefully, the peerless young hotshot is completely humiliated and busted because he's looking at the wrong airspeed indicator. And that burns the distinction between the two gauges into his brain. As a result, he'll never make that mistake again—when it counts and the bomb slung under his wing really could kill him if he went in too fast.

Every other pass is textbook—within 10 miles per hour of the right speed, within 3 degrees of the right angle, within 100 feet of the right altitude for the drop. He's got it nailed.

Every bomb hit inside his targeted revetment—even the first one.

Several days earlier, Igor and Stihl had made a jaunt down to the firing range, waiting for a lull between runs. They went out onto the range to look at a cluster of rusting, armored half-tracks they'd bombed the day before. Stihl located the truck he'd hit with his 24-pound steel bomb—which had plunged down through the hood, punching a hole the size of a person's head.

Very cool.

"When you drop a bomb with a fragment pattern of 3,000 feet," says Igor, "and you drop it within 50 yards of your target, you're going to kill it. Last pass, no kidding, hit dead center of where it was supposed to hit. That feels pretty good."

After finishing their runs, Opie calls for a range check. The range sprawls for hundreds of miles along the Mexican-U.S. border. The Border Patrol crackdown on the major crossing points like San Diego, Nogales, and El Paso have driven the smuggler networks into the vast, unpatrollable stretches of the desert—especially in the millions of unpopulated acres devoted to the gunnery range. During the great western immigrations of the 1800s, this stretch of desert was dubbed the "Devil's Highway" for its killing heat and the lack of water. It was littered with the bones of reckless and unprepared California gold seekers. Now the F-16 and A-10 pilots who practice on the range regularly report groups of people and bodies, sprawled, shriveled, and twisted in the sand. That's a pain. Usually ends up shutting down a chunk of airspace for hours, as the Border Patrol heads out into the desert to round up the illegals or recover the bodies—nameless people risking death to pick lettuce and wash dishes.

No one has cleared the range for a couple of hours, so Opie and Igor swoop down low and scrutinize the territory in an outward spiral—looking for any furtive motion among the rocks and saguaros and thirsty green Palo Verde. It's a kick, whipping along at 800 feet, eyes fixed on the ground—flying the jet by instinct in tight, terrain-hugging patterns—the proximity to the ground giving them the sense of speed normally elusive in the featureless sky.

Opie pronounces himself satisfied. Igor did blow the first run, but he recognized the mistake himself. "If a guy has no idea what was going on, then when you say, 'How was that attack?' you don't hear anything. What was your dive angle? You don't hear anything. That means he was pretty far behind the jet. No SA [situational awareness] on how his pass went."

The whole training has been leading up to this point. Most F-16 pilots want to become aces—go tip to tip with a MiG. But they'll spend most of their careers training intensively for combat most will never see. And if they finally go into combat, they'll mostly drop bombs. Partly, that's because the F-15s dominate the dogfighting mission. But mostly it's because no other air force in the world stands a chance against the U.S. in a dogfighting war. Even in fights with substantial air forces in the years since Vietnam, the U.S. fighters established complete air supremacy within days. As a result, the F-15s mostly end up boring holes in the sky, while the F-16s blow things up.

The sequence of missions builds a mental picture in the minds of the B-coursers, stacking one brick atop the next as they acquire skills. "First, you just learn to get to and from the range," says Igor. "Then you're building this mental picture. You're on the first pass to put the bombs on the target and kill it. You're thinking, 'Holy cow,' because the real picture is so much smaller than the aerials. But mostly you're trying to keep the navigational system up to speed and fly formation and put the target in the steerpoint. By the third [air-to-ground] ride, you can kind of breathe a little bit. By the fifth and sixth rides, you have a grasp of the big picture—and you can do three different things at the same time without even really knowing you're doing them—like updating the navigational system, staying in formation, listening to the radio. You have an idea where you are, where you need to be, what side to be on—like in chess, where you have to think ahead of where you're going."

"Then we add more stuff," says Opie. "Let's see, can he fight his way in and deal with some air-to-air threats, getting jumped on the way out of the target? Every time they get comfortable, we task them with something else. So maybe I'll call, 'Break right, bandit at six o'clock,' and see how they react. The key is, they've got to stay ahead of the airplane. I know they're having a rough day if they're drifting out of formation. They're not saying anything on the radio. They're freaking falling behind the aircraft."

Gradually, flying becomes automatic. "It's like when you're driving down the highway on a four-lane road," says Igor. "I drive down the road and I know who's in front, how fast I'm closing, who's behind, who's in either lane on either side. You have a 360-degree picture—so you can react and avoid getting into an accident. And if you mounted a radar detector, you'd be checking for cops. And looking at all the underpasses for speed traps. Meanwhile, you're talking and listening to the radio. Same thing when you're flying. Whenever you're doing a turn, you're checking to make sure it's a level turn—so you're not running into the ground or changing altitude. You automatically check, thinking, if I turn that direction, can I hit anything? Am I going to hit anything going this direction—yeah—but I have twenty seconds, so I can look behind me. So you look back, and then check left and right—it's just a fluid environment. You're doing what you need to do.

"When we first started in T-38s in basic," adds Igor, "we were flying at 1,000 feet—that was really impressive. Then we dropped down to 500 feet at 360 knots. That was really impressive. Then you get here and do it at 420 knots at 500 feet—that was no different. Once you're going fast, a little faster is not a big deal," says Igor.

"I had a blast today," he says of the flight. "It was a ton of fun, it's a great feeling, being ahead of the jet. You've got everything waxed. You're in perfect position—and here's Interstate 10 so you do a little wing flash for the civilians. Or you're going to split a mountain—that's sweet. You just put that mountain right between your jets. You get so you can do something most people would say is insanely dangerous and enjoy it. It's way crazy cool. Your mind is operating so fast you can count fence posts at 5,000 feet and 500 knots. You fly over I-10 and you can just in a flash see the blue car with a semi behind it—and twelve or fourteen cactus on top of that mountain—and a bird went by just above to the left while I was doing my radar fix. Your cross-check is so reactive and automated that you don't miss anything."

The danger adds to the thrill. That includes the possibility that someone out there wants to kill you.

On the way out through "Bad Guy Land" a cluster of blips suddenly appears on the radar screen, a flight of jets at 22.5 miles, angling across the path of the returning flight of Vipers.

"Nacho three," says Opie, calling Crash's attention to the radar image. Crash is the flight lead of the second two-ship element, with Jack as his wingman trailing 4 miles to the rear. Each of the four ships in the flight has a code—Nacho one through four. "Target group Bull's-Eye, 260. 55.

15,000," Opie adds, giving the group's altitude and a steerpoint as reference. The "Bull's-Eye" refers to a reference point, in this case the Gila Bend airport, and the "55" is the distance in miles from that point. The code allows pilots to describe over the radio the position of anything relative to a known reference point rather than their own positions; any pilot who knows the Bull's-Eye point will understand. In combat, Bull's-Eye is kept secret and shifted during the engagement, so that enemy pilots can't figure out the position of the U.S. jets by listening in on their communications. So now Igor knows that Opie's talking about the contacts on his radar flying at 15,000 feet 55 miles from the Bull's-Eye on a 260-degree heading.

"Three's targeted," says Crash, as soon as his tracking radar locks the still invisible jets.

"Nacho two, sort, 260, 56, 15,000, west," says Opie, telling Igor to track a specific aircraft in the group on his radar. The radar now shows four "bogeys" in two groups. Igor will track the group to the west and stay with them if they split. If they spot the approaching four-ship, they will probably try to outflank Igor's flight.

Jack, flying on Crash's wing, now starts scanning the sky anxiously for enemy fighters, especially anyone creeping up from behind. He's trailing the formation, covering the vulnerable six-o'clock position for Opie, Igor, and Crash, which leaves his own rear area dangerously exposed.

"Targeting" Crash to that group makes Crash and his wingman responsible for killing them if they prove hostile. By sorting Igor to the western two-ship in the group, Opie has made sure Igor will stay with that group if they split. Until such a split takes place, and the bogeys remain a single group, Crash will control who takes a shot.

Now the eight jets converge. The four bogeys remain on a steady heading, now moving away from Opie's four-ship. But the Vipers have a 100-knot speed advantage and quickly close the distance. Igor's fingers move constantly on the control stick, shifting radar views and getting his air-to-air missiles ready as he continues the habitual cross-checking—near rocks, far rocks, check your six.

Opie lets them converge. He has lots of options now. Having made Crash responsible for taking the shot, Opie can maneuver for position or close in for a visual identification. Since Opie has sorted Igor to keep track of the western group, the flight should react smoothly to a split by the enemy jets. So far the enemy jets give no sign they know they're being stalked, although Opie's flight has closed to within 15 miles.

Suddenly Igor's computer sounds a warning tone, indicating that he's just been swept by the enemy's radar—followed by Betty's soft but insistent warning.

"Three's targeted," comes Crash's voice. "Group. Bull's-Eye, 262, 40, 15,000. Declare," he adds, asking Opie to declare the unidentified jets hostile so Crash can kill them.

"Badger declares group Bull's-Eye 265, 40, 15,000 hostile," says Opie, filling in for "Badger"—the AWACS plane that would sort out the bewilderment of aircraft during a real engagement. The comprehensive coverage by AWACS controllers at the edge of the battlefield has played a crucial role in every major air engagement since Vietnam, dramatically increasing the advantage American pilots already enjoy.

"Nacho three, Fox three," says Crash, indicating he has launched a simulated air-to-air missile.

"Nacho four, Fox three," adds Jack, having been sorted to the western set as well by his flight lead.

Crash and Jack each launch two missiles—with perfect parameters. The four unidentified jets fly straight and level to their deaths. Of course, they were just four Vipers on their way to the range—with no idea they'd just been incorporated into Igor and Jack's training.

Still, it's a kick—killing the bad guys. Of course, next time, the bad guys will shoot back. The easy days of turkey shooting have ended. The Large Force Deployment looms now, the culmination of the training.

This time, the best IPs will be doing their level best to kill the punks. And anyone else who gets in their way.

19

⸙

MIDAIR MELEE:
LARGE FORCE DEPLOYMENT

THE COURSE HURTLES NOW TO ITS CONCLUSION, in the shadow of the large force deployment—the culmination of their training. All the skills come together now: flying in formation, bombing, communicating with the AWACS and one another, spotting lurking enemy fighters, dogfighting, two- and four-ship tactics.

They spend two days in the planning. The "safe"—the locked room full of maps and computers where they do the mission planning—brims with B-coursers and IPs, feverishly drawing together all of the bits and pieces of the mission, which will involve up to sixteen Vipers attacking a coordinated set of targets and then fighting their way home past IPs posing as enemy MiGs.

They even plan in relays. First the overall briefing involves everyone; then they'll break into four-ship and then two-ship elements for additional details.

On the screen in the front of the room is one of the many pithy fighter pilot mottos: "Kill something every day, no matter how small, just to keep in practice."

No doubt these fighter pilots are nice young men. Disciplined, bright, funny, and patriotic. But they're also killers—and proud of it. They have cut and trimmed and trained and forced their minds and their hearts into their mission. They'll go out and kill anyone the President targets. They yearn to kill something—to drop real bombs, destroy real targets. They all hate missing any combat. Anything.

And now they get to practice killing something.

Each other, to be specific.

Buster offers the overall briefing, since he'll be leading the attack. "Here's the Big Picture, what you guys can expect. The Nation of Pronghorn has violated UN sanctions, by expropriating natural resources," he says, straight-faced. The mission is obviously designed to echo Saddam's invasion of Kuwait—but there's a dig at pronghorns thrown in there. The last few, struggling herds of Sonoron pronghorn antelope in the nation live on the gunnery range. Mostly, they wander in the vast, empty stretches that don't get bombed. In fact, the preservation of so much empty space has probably prevented the extinction of the pronghorns, although some environmentalists question whether the roar of the jets reduces reproduction or limits their wanderings. Much of the bombing range is also a federal wildlife refuge, so the movements of the tiny herds can affect operations.

"The Nation of Pronghorn is threatening a SCUD launch," Buster continues. "They've got MiG 29s carrying Archers and Alamos"—heat-seeking and radar-guided air-to-air missiles that can hit a target fired head-on. "Air defense—triple-A, SAMs. We'll have sixteen ships. We have prestrike tankers. Adversaries will be F-16s simulating MiGS—so be craniums-up on like aircraft," he warns. Often these milling, sprawling dogfights spawn mass confusion, since the "enemy" MiGs look just like the friendlies, except for orange paint on their dummy missiles.

"Objective," Buster says, "destroy fragged targets with no losses, mutual support, no unobserved or unreacted to threats, clear, concise com. We'll deploy as strikers—with the four-day operation to wage a full campaign against the Nation of Pronghorn. Day one, we render the airfields unusable and attack SAM sites," he says.

An all-out attack on the air defenses in the first moments of any conflict now constitutes USAF doctrine. Despite the lessons of blitzkrieg in World War II, the U.S. neglected that approach in Vietnam. USAF planning now stresses taking out enemy air defenses on the first day of the war—as the Israelis did with devastating effect in the Six Day War, and the USAF did in the opening phase of both wars against Iraq.

Buster continues, noting that each flight will develop its own plan to carry out its piece of the mission. "Set up the game plan so the mission commander can quarterback and get the tasks done." Orchestrating an attack with so many planes requires mind-numbing layers of planning, including ordering up the right weapons, programming all the cockpit computers, coordinating with the tankers, developing elaborate contingency plans in case of mechanical problems or weather issues, and timing the bombing runs so that jets don't hit each other. The key to success lies in this cascade of responsibilities, starting with the mission commander and flowing down to the last plane into the target.

"After you have your individual spins, we will have a coordination brief with all players. But we've still got to cover the B-course instructions and limitations. We'll have an intel [intelligence] update, so things may change. Provide all 'lessons identified' within twenty four hours.

"For you B-coursers—here's a refresher on how to be a kickass wingman in life," continues Buster, knowing that many of the B-coursers are white-knuckling it right now. This exercise offers them the best opportunity to screw up—and maybe kill themselves—in the whole course. Mostly, they're worried about getting lost, shooting down their flight lead, or hitting the wrong target—humiliations that will get replayed over and over to hoots and toasts in the bar. But Buster's worried about the very real possibility that in that crowd of jets some B-coursers will zig when the plan calls for a zag and slice through the wing of his flight lead. Almost as bad, they'll be bombing close to the ground with other jets diving in behind at precisely choreographed intervals, so they could easily get disoriented and fly into the ground.

"Stay visual—make your flight lead's job easy. Don't try to do too much . . . That's huge. Stay visual and fly formation. If you get task-saturated and you need to get closer to your lead, go ahead. If you're losing the visual and getting spread out—just let some of those other tasks drop out and fly formation.

"After that, hit your target—big to small. Study the target the day prior, in the brief and in the jet. Be able to draw the target area. Be the bomb. But remember—big thing—it never goes as planned. So know that route, the flow itself. Know it cold. Know the steerpoint numbers. Just go straight to the target area—all you have to do is stay visual and fly the plan. Everything's going to change once things start happening.

People die. People get shot. You end up coming from different headings. So you've got to know the numbers—not only the primary attack, but the backup attack as well," he says, moving down the list of mission priorities. "Number two—don't get shot. Have the best visual look in the flight. If you start threat-reacting by diving into the notch, you have to know where the threat is and where you need to be—so when you come out of that threat reaction, you start looking for the lead," he cautions.

He knows what the B-coursers only dimly perceive: it's absurdly easy to get lost in a sky full of F-16s—half of them trying to shoot you down. Flying along fat, dumb, and happy in a flight of four, they'll explode like quail out of brush if they get a radar lock warning. Experienced pilots maintain an awareness of the geometry of the sky, and the actions of their wingman, even in a violent evasive maneuver. The B-coursers will probably get completely flummoxed. Odds are, they'll try to do a rejoin on a pair of enemy fighters.

"Number three—keep SA. Study the map, know the flow—know the Bull's-Eye points. Your primary job is going to be dropping the bombs. There will be a sweep out there helping you out with the threats. So there's no reason to be cranium-down in your radar looking for these threats. Keep focused on your business, narrow down to your own little world. Fly formation, stay visual, and drop your bombs."

Now he shifts and addresses the IPs running each flight. "If you're the mission commander, then here are the ten steps to being a successful mission commander.

"Step one—have your shit together. Recage your brains. The most important day is the planning day.

"Step two—stick to the timeline. Hold people to it. Get routes early.

"Step three—delegate. You worry about the overall problems and put someone else on the rest of it.

"Step four—what if your plan goes to hell? Think of every possible contingency and how you would handle it.

"Step five—brief the pain-in-the-ass stuff.

"Step six—deconfliction. Brief a thorough flow plan, lateral, vertical, timing deconflictions.

"Step seven—solid tactical plan. Make it simple. The idea is to show these guys the whole concept, no need to get enamored with the tactics.

"Step eight—brief as four-ships—how to find and hit the target, the flow, the plan, deconfliction," he says.

"Step nine—it's your game plan," continues Buster. "Be the ball," he adds, harking back to his football days and the sport analogies that pervade fighter pilot thinking.

"Step ten—debrief. Tie it all together. No need to stick around for six to nine hours with the nit-picking stuff. But have everyone look at their shots and attacks prior to the debrief."

Now Doughboy rises for the safety briefing.

Seeing him, Gilligan yells, "Be safe."

Rage calls, "Fly safe."

Opie calls, "Think safe."

Doughboy rolls his eyes and gets the laugh.

Then he shows a video, with "Viva Las Vegas" playing as the soundtrack. The video shows a horrifying succession of crashes, most into the ground, some air-to-air. It's a sobering chain of carnage, captured by ground-based cameras, wing cameras, or targeting cameras from other planes. Most end in fireballs, with no sign of a parachute. Some capture midair collisions. The video appears to show the last moments of more than a dozen pilots' lives—a fatal succession of miscalculations. A jet tumbles on landing. A jet maneuvers so violently that a wing clips the ground, triggering a pinwheel of flames. A jet suddenly fills the view of the HUD from inside the cockpit, followed by a flash of flame and a dark screen. A bomber drops a string of bombs and another jet flies into the shrapnel. A jet swoops low, climbs, and hits a ridgeline in a ball of flames. A jet wobbles, loses control, and plows into one of two motels sitting side by side.

The room is silent after the lights come on. The B-coursers, arrayed as usual in the back, look grim.

"So what's the moral of that story?" Doughboy asks.

"That hotel—on the right—that's the place to stay," quips Bongoo.

The laugh breaks the tension.

They are—after all—fighter pilots. Never show fear. Use it. Channel it. Outflank it. But don't show it. Not in a briefing. Besides—the possibility of instant, flaming death gives flying fighters its thrill. Plus the women love it—except the wives. They hate it.

Doughboy continues. "On Friday night when this is all over and we're all drinking at the bar, we ALL want to be drinking at the bar. So don't get so carried away being cool that you do something stupid out there," he says—nailing it perfectly. He understands all about being cool—that inarticulate and irresistible yearning to be the best.

Buster takes the podium again. "You know what it was like out there in a four-ship, with two bad guys popping up out there. Well, this is going to be sixteen good guys and eight bad guys. So if you guys do nothing but keep in sight of your flight lead and get your bombs on target—that would be a huge success. Don't get shot down, that would be nice as well—but primarily stay with your flight lead, drop on target, and survive. This should be a blast for you guys, you should have fun—and I think you'll do great." The briefing breaks up into four separate four-ship briefings, which will in turn splinter into two-ship briefings in the exhaustive, top-down planning process that ensures each two-ship fits into a larger picture but also remains flexible and coordinated.

Rage leads one of the breakout briefings, for the eight-ship unit.

"All right," says Rage briskly, moving down his checklist. He covers the "motherhood" issues quickly—the stuff that used to consume two hours of briefing time and constitute the main purpose of a training mission. Now those basics take a few minutes—more of a reminder than a briefing. Still, Punch notices that the plan doesn't give them quite enough taxi time for the 11 a.m. takeoff—illustrating the exhaustive detail in which every one of the pilots studies the mission plan. Getting eight planes into the air quickly enough for them to form up and fly in formation requires some extra planning, down to where they'll park on the taxiway awaiting takeoff.

"If we can get all eight back together and you're 4 miles behind on the way out, but correctly aligned, that would be great," says Rage. "But if we're two four-ships—that would be fine too. Could be some situations where we're completely fucked up. If you find yourself with a different flight by the time you come off target or rejoin after a scrap, then come back with whoever you line up with. If you're down to a three-ship in your flight, fly fluid three—wingman, you may be flying in the number three position."

He gives them the radar settings, tells them they'll be working with AWACS controllers dispatched from Oklahoma City, who will have to declare as "hostile" any unidentified plane before they can kill it.

Rage machine-guns the key points, knowing that the punks have learned the vocabulary and the concepts. To an outsider, he's no longer speaking English as he bombs through checkpoints, backup plans, code words, radio protocol, and a host of technical points.

He concludes, "Don't hit the deck. Don't hit another jet. Stay visual. Stay in formation. Bombs on target. Kill the Red Air [the enemy fighters]. Your priorities are in that order."

He knows the B-coursers will feel overwhelmed with so many jets in the air and they'll be doing well just to get their bombs on target and not get scattered trying to get home. The whole plan depends on daunting, split-second timing, with layered link-up points.

"The com can get completely dicked up," says Rage, referring to the chaos that can prevail on the radio in such a large-scale engagement.

Just to make it more interesting, they'll face simulated SAM shots on their way to the target. "Those suckers are mobile—they have the ability to be mobile. So if you're spiked, react accordingly and sing out, like, 'Mud six, south, weaving 120. Singer south, defending, blah blah blah,' " he says, assuming that they've now mastered the communications and tactics to react to a SAM attack.

"Everyone is going home by flowing out through the steerpoint nine on the way back to bed, so let's not go there and hang out until someone runs into us. Flow back and flow out, even if we haven't all rejoined."

Now they discuss tactics for dealing with enemy ships on the way out. They'll be arrayed in eight-ship lines, with each four-ship ready to react as a unit. Doughboy's eight-ship will fly a different path out, and face different enemies. Each set of eight will have four IPs, each with one of the punks as his wingman.

"Expect that as twos and fours you will be targeted into those hostile groups, with the element leads picking up any spitters [single fighters] or nontargeted guys. I'd like to work a bracket game plan, with us having about 10 to 15 miles separation between us. It will look like an eight-ship wall, although we'll actually be deploying as two four-ships."

The B-coursers listen intently. Beaker jiggles, his leg moving ceaselessly. Pap chews his fingernails. Igor sits quiet, almost expressionless, with a look of intense concentration.

Now Rage turns to the rules for shooting down enemy fighters, which gains the full attention of the B-coursers—for dogfighting remains the

Holy Grail. He reminds them that they can't shoot down any radar blips until the AWACS controllers declare it "hostile," or until they get close enough to eyeball the orange-painted missiles slung on the underside. "If you've been targeted to one of the bogeys, you want to wait for the 'hostile' declaration. If you think one of the bogeys is targeting you, or someone else in the formation, then sing it out."

Then follows a technical discussion on the rules of engagement—an increasingly critical element of modern combat. Once, fighters rarely killed enemy fighters or bombers until they'd gotten close enough to see the distinctive outline of the other plane. Close-up, it's hard to mistake a jetliner for a Soviet bomber—much less a MiG. But these days, most air-to-air tactics rely on killing the enemy before you ever see him. That means most American fighter pilots go after targets determined by AWACS controllers and fire their lethal missiles before they get the bogey in sight. That makes the discipline of declaring a radar-screen blip "hostile" crucial. Usually the AWACS will make the call in the real world.

So they spend a long time talking about the process for declaring a radar blip killable. Then they discuss several levels of contingency plans for dividing up the enemy fighters should they close to knife-fighting range.

Rage notes that on the way in to the target, the AWACS controllers will probably call the opposing fighters "hostile" before they get to within visual range. But on the way out, the rules require the Viper pilots to make a visual identification of the enemy fighters before killing them.

"The air-to-air scenario is going to be a little different because we have a lot of airplanes up there and so it's going to be kind of a hairball," says Rage.

Next, they discuss the bomb run on the simulated SAM sites, complete with several backup plans in case something goes wrong. As with a real mission, Rage doubles up on the SAM's command center to guarantee its destruction, relying on formulas developed from hundreds of actual missions. If someone misses his target, that two-ship flight will have to go around again, which means they may have to get back to base on their own. If the rest of the flight waits, it will just attract enemy fighters and hidden SAMs.

He also warns them against sharp turns when they're loaded with bombs. "Be aware, for the simulated weapons we're carrying you can't pull more than 5.5 g's, so be aware in your turns on your air-to-air threat reactions. Don't over-g your airplane or simulated weapons."

"Stay visual," he says, again stressing the mistake most likely to actually get them killed—a midair collision. "Don't go blind. Don't go blind. Don't go blind. We have too many airplanes out there to have little singletons running around out there trying to get back together. Fly the plan. Flow the ingress. Fly the attack. Fly the egress. Yes, there will be times when we're off the plan, but look for those key times: the push time, the IP time, and getting back to your hacking place so we're back together," he concludes.

Now, they break up once again.

They've briefed as an eight-ship.

Now each four-ship element briefs.

Beaker and Gimmie pair up with Punch and Rage for a further level of planning for their four-ship element.

"OK," quips Punch, "on with our 'Death by Briefing.' Any needs of a nonsexual nature that need to be accomplished before we brief this?"

Gimmie and Beaker grin wearily.

The briefing zips along, full of technical detail, backup plans, discussion of the weapons. They hurry through one item after another that once constituted the core of a whole training mission. They cover backup airfields, the g-limits for the weapons slung under the jet, radio com settings, codewords—a daunting and bewildering blending of jargon and technical detail. Once the B-coursers struggled with each item; now everything blends together seamlessly—a dazzling display of crisp efficiency. Gimmie and Beaker seem barely recognizable as the hesitant, baffled, white-knuckled kids who started the program.

The convergence of so many jets flitting along at 400 miles per hour brings special dangers. So Punch warns the B-coursers—the wingmen—to mostly keep their mouths shut. Up until now, the IPs have often talked to the students during the flights and encouraged them to continually provide updates on what they're doing—so the IP can judge the student's task saturation. But that won't work on this mission, since it would overwhelm the radio connecting the sixteen attacking and eight defending jets with chatter.

"If there's a safety factor—like you almost hit somebody—call a knock-it-off in the clear. You want to stay in close. In the real world, you'll have a lot of weapons on the underside and you'll be heavy and you'll fall out of the sky if you don't stay close to your flight lead. When you're just hanging on by your toenails—you may have 1,000 feet of separation— you can lose that in a flash with Mark 82 [bomb]."

He spends extra time on the bombing run, since they have more experience bombing targets as a two-ship than as a four-ship.

"We're in a spread-four formation, pushing line abreast. As soon as we cross steerpoint three, you're cleared to move to the other side," of the flight lead. "I may direct you to get to the others side, or Rage may—then we'll all start collapsing in on the target. I only want to be 250 to 500 feet away from you at roll in. Sure, it increases the chance they'll hit one of us—but to get bombs on target it should be, no kidding, stack, stack, stack. You should be able to look down 45-degree angles to the canopies of all four jets lined up down to the target. Weapons of mass destruction live in there," he says, pointing to a building on the aerial photo. "We'll use a Mark 82 with the airburst to incinerate every bit," he says.

He covers the attack itself, trying to create in their minds the picture of the target, the formation, and the attack itself so it will seem familiar when they do finally roll in. That's really the point of the whole laborious mission preparation and all the layers of briefings: to make even the first attack on the target seem familiar. They'll be rolling and diving at the target in sequence, which means a different altitude and angle of attack for each of the ships to minimize the risk of a midair collision as they come off the target.

"Number four," he says, "you're going to wind up damn near upside down. I have seen a student do this, does a full roll and does this," he says, corkscrewing his hand through the air with lots of body English. "It was hilarious—don't do that—although we were all very impressed," he laughs.

"We'll be a four-ship strung out—two plus two for geometry—you can kind of keep it tight, rejoin to the inside." Maneuvering in formation requires position changes in a turn. If the wingman is splayed out to the left and the lead starts a turn to the right, the wingman slips across behind the lead, instead of getting whipsawed like the poor kid at the end of the line in Crack the Whip. Formation flying demands effortless coordination and hours of practice. "This is going to be tough, because the sun's going to be right over here," he adds. Basic fighter tactics stretching back to World War I stress the value of rolling in on the target out of the sun, to gain that knife-fighter's edge. Mission planners always consider the sun's position in lining up an attack or preparing an ambush.

"I expect you'll be blind coming off the target," says Punch, knowing that between the sun and the sharp pullout away from the target and the lurking SAMs, they won't be able to keep the flight lead in sight for that moment. "But that's the one time I'll give it to you. If you are unsuccessful, then call 'chum' on Victor [the ship-to-ship frequency]. If you are successful, don't say anything. If you need a re-attack, you're going to say 'Rapid Two needs a chum.' If you chum, you're going to have to do it again."

Inwardly, Beaker takes a breath—picturing the humiliation of that chum call. In the real world, missing the target on the first run can have fatal consequences. It probably means both the lead and the wingman have to go around again, with the defenses fully aroused. It might also mean going home through the enemy defenses as a vulnerable two-ship instead of a relatively safe eight-ship. In this exercise, missing the target won't be dangerous—just humiliating. About the only thing worse than calling "chum," and declaring yourself a fool to the whole world, is to not call chum only to have the squinty-eyed IP review the tape and see that you should have called chum but were too far behind the freaking jet to know it.

Now Punch moves on to the challenge of getting home after a successful attack.

"What about a wounded bird?" he asks rhetorically, referring to a Viper damaged by ground fire in the attack. Fighter pilots need to think about the possibility—since the USAF mostly flies deep into enemy territory. Sometimes they wonder about getting shot down— and winding up beaten, brainwashed, and tortured, like the legendary Vietnam-era pilots. But in truth, most fighter pilots don't think seriously about crashing. They sustain a personal conviction of invincibility. But they do dream about being one of those fabled wingmen who stand by a fallen comrade. Every fighter pilot knows the story of the shot-to-hell Phantom whose wingman tucked in behind and literally pushed the crippled flight lead almost back to the American lines. They finally both ejected over mostly friendly territory after the wingman used up his fuel.

"If we had a wounded bird in the real world, we'd assess defensive and offense capabilities. Then decide whether we're going to go line abreast getting out," he says. "It would be far more interesting in the real world."

Next he covers the possibility that they'll get impossibly scattered in the bombing run. "If the re-form plan is all fucked up, it's probably because we're blind. The key is to call it and then head back at a predictable speed and altitude until we can re-form."

Now he moves on to the possibility of fire from the ground.

"Surface-to-air threat reactions—two things you can do. You can weave—like at low altitude. Puke a little chaff. If I get a full lock warning on the radar—five tones—I've got all this canopy space to look for it. If you're full-up locked, what are you going to call?"

"Launch indication?" says Beaker. "Rapid Two, Singer Six, defending 330," which will tell his flight lead that he's trying to shake off a missile at a bearing of 330 degrees.

Punch corrects him. "Rapid Two, Singer Six, *southwest,* defending 330," since adding the direction will help the flight lead spot the threat. "I'm going to get my flight completely out of the way. You're going to do your Funky Chicken, trying to keep everybody in sight. Try to look for the next missile."

Now he moves to the dogfighting—the heart and soul of the fighter pilot world, and something a USAF Viper pilot will probably never do for real. Basically he tells the B-coursers to keep their mouths shut unless they see something approaching on the radar that no one else has noticed. In that case, they should ask the flight lead to declare the blip hostile. "I would never harm a wingman for speaking up in that situation. You may save the day. If you say, 'Rapid Four, declare,' I'm going to go, 'Holy shit, Rapid Four is talking—I didn't know he was in the same airspace.' As soon as you call 'Declare'—one, I'm targeting it and two, I'm killing it."

Now he shifts to the alternative scenarios. "When he's in our area, what are we going to do? Four-ship bracket. We're going to have way too many aircraft for everyone to be freelancing," affirms Punch. "You're used to just two bad guys and two good guys—but we could have six or eight planes hitting the merge where the fight starts. So let the IPs worry about doing the shooting."

Standard tactics call for splitting the formation to bracket the bad guys. Usually, the first group to get to a flanking position survives because either way the outflanked fighter turns, someone shoots a missile.

"If he gets a radar lock on one of us—you jump in the notch," says Punch, meaning that the wingman will twist into turns designed to stay just outside of a missile range—and occupy the attention of the enemy fighter. If the enemy doesn't jump into the lethal turning battle, the wingman can whip around behind and kill him. So in theory, the enemy will get into a turning fight.

"Then I go in and kill him," says Punch. "That's the most complex thing we'll see today. Air-to-air game plan. Me and Rage have seen this once or twice, so we'll be pretty standard."

Rage adds his advice. "Just hang on—seriously. If at the push on into the target you find yourself trying to catch up, just push for the IP. This is going to be a hoot guys," he says.

Yeah right. Easy for him to say. A hoot unless they make complete, flaming fools of themselves—bust the ride, crash the jet, run into the freaking flight lead, say something stupid on the radio, shoot down a friendly. Oh yeah. A hoot.

20

LARGE FORCE MISSION: CLUBBING BABY SEALS

IN THE VERY BEGINNING, everything looks good.

The jets line up.

The B-coursers perform their ground operations flawlessly.

They lift off in pairs—two sets of eight flying roughly parallel missions. After days of preparation, they've completed the three levels of briefing and have spent hours studying the detailed topo maps of the approaches and the aerial photos of the targets themselves.

They form up a few miles from the runway—each eight-ship arranged in two sets of four. The flight leads connect with the AWACS controller, watching the coalescing formations from hundreds of miles away. Everything's running smoothly, much to the relief of the IPs. They know that training accidents and ordinary mechanical failures have killed far more Viper pilots than real enemy fire.

But from the first crackle of the radio, with the strange voices and mission-specific codes, the B-coursers realize how confusing this day will become. But they don't know the half of it.

The mission will hurl two independent flights into the range—one led by Doughboy, the other by Rage.

Doughboy's Blue Air flight will attack three targets—all simulated air defenses they must knock out on the first day of the "war." He's leading two four-ship elements. Doughboy will have Rex on his wing and AWOL will fly with Pong in the lead four-ship element. Coming behind them, Bongoo has Igor on his wing and Ship has Stihl. They face just two enemy jets. That sounds like an overwhelming advantage, but Buster and Festus will be flying the "Red Air" jets—two lethal veterans, who will "regenerate" themselves to multiply the number of enemy jets. So the punks have a doomed feeling—like a saloon full of gunfighters facing off against Clint Eastwood.

Meanwhile, Rage's Blue Air flight of eight jets will fly into the bombing range on a different heading at a different time—operating completely independent of Doughboy's mission. Rage has Beaker on his wing and Gilligan and Pap in his four-ship lead element. Just behind them, Punch will lead the second four-ship element, with Jack on his wing. Crash and Gimmie will round out the flight.

They know that they'll face three enemy Red Air jets—flown by Old Man, Ozone, and Opie.

In the real word, coordinating a two-wave attack by sixteen Blue Air jets would offer a routine challenge, even when you throw in five enemy fighters and a thicket of SAM sites. But with B-coursers flying eight of the jets and a single AWACS plane staffed by trainees, it could get hairy. Besides, they've got to get past Old Man, Festus, Buster, and the rest of their crew, which includes some of the most accomplished killers in the known universe. Granted, the good guys have a big numerical advantage. But we're talking punks up against veterans. They'll be outgunned.

Rage's flight of eight goes in first. They're operating as two four-ship formations separated by 10 miles. In the real world, they'd probably stay closer together, but here they want to limit the risk of midair collisions, especially over the target or in the welter of a dogfight. The separation gives them a view of a large swath of sky and makes the lead element almost impossible to ambush from behind.

Rage has Beaker on his wing and flies in formation with Punch, who has Jack on his wing. The second four-ship formation trails. Gilligan leads the second four-ship, with Pap on his wing. Crash will fly in formation, with Gimmie on his wing. Ordinarily, a flight of bomb-laden F-16s subject to attack by enemy fighters would come sweeping in behind a screen of F-15s, outfitted strictly for air-to-air combat with their long-range radars augmented by the AWACS umbrella. But in this exercise, the Vipers work without the F-15 CAP (Combat Air Patrol).

Short of the range, Rage gets a radar contact approaching, low and slow. The rules of engagement won't let him take a shot until the AWACS controller declares the radar blip "hostile." Rage calls in the sighting, but the AWACS controller seems confused and indecisive. Rage makes a mental note and groans inwardly. The AWACS controller must be a newbee—a damned punk. This could turn into a mess.

At that speed and course it's probably civilian traffic. They're not even over the range yet—not quite. So Rage glumly watches the radar blip approach. It could be Old Man posing as a Cessna—trying to sneak in and bounce them the minute they cross over into the airspace—maybe even get in a cheap shot. Of course, if it was enemy fighters and they were flying along fat and happy, they'd probably be dead by now—waiting for the AWACS punk to figure out the deception.

In the end they do nothing. Rage keeps scanning the sky on the heading of the bogey until he sees a leer jet ambling along. In a real war it would have taken an enormous exercise of discipline to let that dude get close enough to eyeball. Then again—that's why fighter jocks sometimes shoot down airliners—getting light on the trigger. Besides—if it had been Old Man, Rage would have had the space of the radar lockup warning tone to react—AWACS or no.

So Rage's flight crosses over into the airspace, still in formation with a 2-mile spread between each jet, which means they're visually sweeping a swath of sky 8 miles wide and 10 miles deep—with radars scanning some 50 miles in all directions.

Of course, the trip to the target is the easy part. The ground rules require the Red Air F-16s to transmit certain codes that will identify them as "hostile" to the AWACS guys. Ordinarily, the AWACS's radars and computerized identification programs read the subtle variations in radar signal, speed, and configuration to identify the type of plane. Since today involves a brawl composed entirely of Vipers, the rules require the enemy Red Air fighters to give themselves away by broadcasting a signal the AWACS can pick up. On the way in, the rules allow the AWACS to call the Red Air planes hostile as soon as they decipher the identifying signal—which means Rage's flight should get clearance to shoot while Old Man's fighters are still beyond visual range. No problem.

Suddenly, the AWACS controller's calm, crisp voice sounds in Rage's headphones, warning him he has three bandits approaching, nearly head-on. Rage shifts his radar to air-to-air mode, narrowing the search beam to scan the heading transmitted by the AWACS. The other ships in his flight do the same. The three bandits are hurtling straight at them, with a closing speed of more than 1,000 miles per hour—but they're still out of effective missile range. The AWACS controller calls them hostile and the fight is on.

Rage holds his missile fire—knowing he's at the limit of effective range, and expecting a trick from the shrewd Old Man. He sorts the approaching fighters, assigning one to each of the jets in his flight. But he tells them not to fire yet. They have already discussed the plan for this situation, designed to take advantage of Gilligan's four-ship element coming up behind. If Rage's four jets in the lead can force the enemy fighters into defensive maneuvering, then Gilligan's guys can sweep in and kill them as they're turning to attack Rage's lead element. Fleetingly, Rage's radar lockup warning sounds as he and Old Man hurtle towards one another. Still, he holds fire.

Sure enough, Old Man suddenly turns violently and reverses his course 180 degrees. Had Rage's missile been in the air, the maneuver would have broken the lock—and left Rage vulnerable to a follow-up shot by Ozone, Old Man's wingman. At the same moment, the remaining bandit, Opie, turns in an attempt to flank the flight to the south. The AWACS controller reads the split perfectly and radios precise headings. Rage's fighters take their shots, each having been sorted by Rage to targets. The computer records kills with two of the four missiles, eliminating Opie and Old Man.

As soon as Rage's flight launches their missiles, they go into violent maneuvering to frustrate a missile lock. They have the luxury of going defensive because a friendly four-ship is already in range. Sure enough, Old Man's wingman, Ozone, shoots through the suddenly scattered formation—without a good lock—and dies a moment later in a barrage of four missiles from the second four-ship.

Nice work.

The B-coursers did their jobs—and kept their mouths shut. Only one small flaw: Beaker pulled 7.5 g's in his defensive maneuver to avoid a missile lock. If he'd had real bombs slung under the jet, such a maneuver might have ripped one of the 1,000-pounders loose from its pylon.

But as they re-form for the rest of the run to the target, small problems start to propagate. They have switched positions as a result of the dog-fight. The four-ship unit led by Gilligan, which includes Pap, Crash, and Gimmie, now takes the lead. Meanwhile, Rage's four ships take time to reform, having been scattered across the sky in the dogfight.

Over the target, Gilligan's four-ship makes a perfect bomb run—with all four ships hitting their targets. Pap and Gimmie heave a huge sigh of relief. They've survived the trip in, hit their targets, and not made fools of themselves even once. A good day. Maybe they'll even start having fun now—knowing the worst is over. Only great discipline keeps Gimmie from hooting into the radio, she's so happy. Pap mostly just feels relief. He didn't want to screw up—let people down. But lately, bombing has gotten complicated for him. He keeps getting progress reports from his buddy in the hospital—blown to hell in Iraq. So sometimes in a moment of calm, he thinks about them—down on the ground, under the bombs. That occurs to Pap in just a flash, as Gilligan and Crash lead the flight off the target to re-form for the trip back.

Rage's flight rolls in just behind Gilligan's at precisely choreographed speeds, altitudes, and angles. The image of the target looms in the HUD, with the numbers indicating speed and dive angle flickering past at the edge. Unaccountably, Rage's attention wavers. Truth be told, he's already worrying about getting everyone back into formation once they come off target. Rage wrenches his focus back to the dive angle, only to realize he has drifted from the precise path. If Rage drops now, he'll miss. So he doesn't hit the bomb button, but yanks the stick to veer away from the bomb run and any ground fire. "That was just buffoonery," he says later. "I was too far ahead, thinking about what was next."

Behind him, Beaker rolls in for what starts out as a perfect attack. At just the right moment, he hits the bomb release button on the joystick. In the real world, the jet would lurch as 3,000 pounds of bombs drop away, but Beaker's dropping light concrete dummy bombs. So he squeezes the bomb button, but releases it before the numbers flash on the screen indicating a successful, simulated bomb release. So he never actually drops the bomb. Instead, he goes through dry, but doesn't realize it until too late.

Fortunately, Punch and Jack, coming down the tube next, deliver their bombs perfectly. Still, only half of the jets in Rage's flight have hit their targets.

Now Rage faces a dilemma. He can't go home when two planes have missed their target—leaving the SAM site operational. He and Beaker will have to re-attack—which in the real world would dramatically increase their chances of getting shot down as they went back over the fully alerted SAM operators and triple-A batteries. Of course, in the real world they would have used GPS bombs dropped from a couple of miles away at a nice, safe 25,000 feet. But never mind—the rules of engagement control here. He could have Punch and Jack fly a big circle and wait for Rage and Beaker to re-attack. But that would burn up their gas and expose them to a substantial risk from either additional SAMs or Old Man's lurking fighters—who for the purposes of the exercise have come back to life to attack them on the way home. On the other hand, that means Punch and Rage will go back separately. That makes them each a much more vulnerable two-ship until they meet up with Gilligan's flight of four, now heading for the rendezvous point.

But they worked the re-attack plan out ahead of time—so Rage doesn't hesitate long. Rage sends Punch and Jack back toward the rendezvous point to hook up with Gilligan, Pap, Crash, and Gimmie. Meantime, Rage and Beaker circle around to line up their attack again.

This time, Rage and Beaker deliver their bombs perfectly. But by the time they finish the bomb run, they're some 30 miles behind Punch and Gimmie—beyond effective support.

Soon the AWACS plane warns Punch of two approaching bogeys. On the trip to the target, the AWACS gave Rage's flight a "hostile" declaration beyond missile range. But on the way home, the rules change to favor Red Air. The AWACS controller flips a coin to decide whether to give a "hostile" declaration beyond visual range. The flip goes against Rage's flight. So the AWACS controller just tells them that two unidentified jets are closing from just off their noses. They can't take a shot until the bogeys shoot at them, or until they get close enough to see the orange markings on the enemy Vipers.

A moment later, the AWACS warns them of another pair of jets approaching from a different heading, 10 miles east of the first group. This time, they declare the jets "hostile."

Suddenly the separation between Punch and Rage looks potentially fatal. Rage kicks up his speed, trying to close the gap in time to fend off the second set of fighters.

But now something very strange happens.

Punch ignores the AWACS's warning about the second, "hostile" set of fighters and turns with Jack to face the two, unidentified jets.

Later they learn that the AWACS controller warned Rage about the second set of declared hostile fighters, but did not directly warn Punch. Apparently, the AWACS controllers assumed Punch would be eavesdropping on the warning to Rage and so didn't repeat it. The controllers should have used Punch's call sign and gotten an acknowledgement from Punch. Unfortunately, in the intense concentration of sorting for the first, unidentified set of fighters, Punch didn't hear the exchange between Rage and the AWACS guy about the second set of bogeys.

It's a perfect illustration of the fatal "fog of war."

To make matters worse, the radio suddenly crackles with multiple overlapping conversations. First, the radio carries talk about the developing battle into which Punch is flying, half-blind; Second, the radio carries calls from Doughboy's distant flight; Finally, the AWACS trainee makes several garbled and confusing declarations and headings. So Punch misses the confusing AWACS call identifying as hostile the approaching group, still beyond the range of his radar. As a result, Punch and Jack turn unknowingly across the path of the hostile fighters—which turn out to be Ozone and Opie—and toward the "bogeys"—really Old Man.

As Rage would explain later, "Due to com errors with AWACS and their task saturation, the leading two-ship was unaware of the hostile group. It got said, but it didn't get processed."

Rage and Beaker, having just come off the target and shifted their radars and radios over to air-to-air fighting mode, can see Punch and Jack turn but don't understand the consequences.

So Punch and Jack get a nasty surprise when their missile lock warnings scream in their ears. Both hurl their jets into violent defensive maneuvers—punching out flares and chaff as they skid sideways through the sky, putting themselves at right angles to the approaching missiles—coming at them from behind. The maneuver comes too late. They both die. Well, actually Jack dies. The computer later shows that Punch probably turned quickly and sharply enough to have evaded the missile. However, Punch thinks he's dead, since the missile-lock warning was sounding in his ears when he heard Opie call a kill. So Punch straightens out and looks around to deconflict—no point running into someone once you're already dead. He is in a delicate position—involving the finer points of fighter pilot ego. If he'd been dead and had ignored the kill and gone jetting about killing MiGs, he would have looked silly when they rolled the tape. He would have owed some huge number of beers, and come in for an outlandish amount of ribbing. Of course, giving up and acting dead when he's still alive will occasion some ridicule, but it beats looking like a bad sport. So he considers himself dead. Turns out, the kill call he heard on the radio was Opie killing Jack.

Thinking himself dead, Punch levels out. Behind him, Ozone's still maneuvering for a shot. Suddenly, it looks easy. Ozone looks the gift horse right in the mouth—and shoots him in the head. He fires a second missile—laughing—figuring out already what happened. This will make a great story.

Poor Jack—blown out of the sky by a jet he didn't see, which is what happens in 90 percent of air-to-air kills. Jack levels out and contains his disappointment, cursing himself inwardly—but not too bitterly. Truth is, dead or not, he didn't do anything egregiously stupid. Technically speaking, it was not his fault. Sometimes there's comfort in being a wingman.

Rage and Beaker both hear the fight on their radios. "I'm going, 'Oh, man, they're both dead,' " says Rage. "Got to get back to our base. So away we go, me and Beaker—we don't see each other, but know that we're close—trying to get our mutual support back together. Can't dillydally around, and we're still too far away to do anything for Punch."

Within minutes, they've come within radar range of the fight that "killed" Punch and Jack. Rage can make out five fighters milling about on his radar, but can't at this point tell his dead friends from the Red Air. Rage seeks directions from the AWACS—still hoping for a clear hostile declaration with a heading. The AWACS controller calls the fighters circling at 18,000 feet "hostile," but that makes no sense. Rage searches his radar desperately. He can't find any fighters at 18,000 feet—although he's got some ominous-looking contacts at 28,000 feet. But maybe that's Punch and Jack. Wouldn't do to kill his own guys. What the hell is going on?

"So I'm swearing to myself going, there's no way the Red Air guys are at 18,000 feet. They're in the exact spot the AWACS is saying, but at the wrong altitude."

Given the conflicting information, he can't take a shot until they get close. They'll have to get their kill the old-fashioned way—eyeball to eyeball in the merge. They know that Gilligan's four-ship is still out there somewhere, perhaps converging on the fight. But it's all a big, frigging, confusing mess—with the AWACS adding to the confusion with all the bad calls. In the real world, they might have turned and run for it—although they'd be offering free shots to the pursuing enemy fighters. But then again, the Red Air jerks did just kill their buddies. Fighter pilots take that personally.

So they approach the unidentified jets warily, still fatally handicapped by the rules of engagement and the AWACS calls. The unidentified jets split, two veering to the north. Rage and Beaker now close on the closer pair. They're not sure why the other two unidentified fighters have bugged out. They don't seem to be trying to bracket Rage and Beaker—they're just leaving the battle.

Maybe that's Punch and Jack, heading home.

Or maybe they're Bad Guys heading off to intercept Gilligan's four-ship—somewhere off the radar, but probably hurrying to help Rage and Beaker as a result of calls from the AWACS.

In any case, Rage decides to close with the two remaining Vipers.

Immediately, they get a missile lock warning, so Rage begins maneuvering violently.

The two Red Air jets—now clearly hostile—go after him. Beaker takes a quick missile shot with a good lock. But he holds off on a second shot, waiting for a better angle. Because he was carrying bombs, Beaker only has four air-to-air missiles—so he hoards them. The Red Air jets each have six simulated air-to-air missiles, which gives them an edge in a dogfight. But saving that extra missile proves a fatal mistake. Although Beaker thought he had a lock when he fired, the computer declares it a miss.

Rage goes after the first Red Air fighter—Opie—hoping he can get a kill before he gets double-teamed. He makes a quick turn into the approaching fighter, moving to his three o'clock, on the edge of a firing solution. But Opie maneuvers sharply, trying to stave off the shot long enough for his wingman, Ozone, to kill Beaker and then jump Rage.

Meanwhile, Beaker maneuvers to a perch away from the fight—the classic wingman position. He has both Ozone and Opie in sight. For a glorious moment, he thinks he might kill them both and save Rage. He'd be a hero. He'd have a story he could tell his grandchildren. Well, maybe not his grandchildren—but the other punks. God. To kill Opie. Or Ozone. To save Rage. Glory to God on high.

Just as he gets ready to shoot Opie, who is starting to lose a vicious turning fight with Rage—Beaker's radar-lock warning tone sounds incessantly. Preoccupied with getting to a good defensive perch without losing sight of the dogfight, he doesn't notice that Old Man has doubled back after seeming to have left the fight heading north. It takes hundreds of hours in the air—and many mock dogfights—to remain aware of the whole sky while focusing intently on the fight just under your nose. Beaker can't do that yet.

Alerted by the radar-lock tone, Beaker reacts a beat late, throwing himself into a sharp turn—hoping to break the lock. But Old Man has anticipated the maneuver and, in a flash, Beaker and Old Man are in a classic one-circle fight, shedding altitude and energy, each trying to lure the other into overshooting or bleeding off too much energy.

Abruptly, the distant AWACS controller calls terminate, since training rules require the fight to end once a plane has made a 180-degree turn. The mission is designed to teach them large-force deployment skills, not to stage individual dogfights. The odds of a training accident are too high with a sky full of twisting, turning Vipers in a fight to the death.

Later, Beaker concludes the AWACS called the fight too soon. Just as well, he admits—Old Man would have killed him in another minute.

On the other hand, the tapes suggest that Rage was gaining on Opie when the fight ended. However, Ozone—freed from concern about Beaker by Old Man's appearance, had moved to a perch from which he would have almost certainly killed Rage if he had won his turning fight with Opie.

"I was offensive," says Rage, "but there was another guy quickly closing on me. If it had gone for another forty-five seconds, I might have gotten Opie—but I would have been set up for the second guy. It's a knife fight in a phone booth at that point. No man has an advantage. You want to get the guy in the spleen or the kidney or the heart—something. If it had gone another thirty seconds, they may have gotten me—but I may have taken one with me."

In the end, the missed bomb runs and the second attack proved fatal—leading to the probable destruction of the whole flight. "It would have been completely different had all four of us been together coming off the target," says Rage. "But we also couldn't just wait to rejoin over the target. You make yourself vulnerable when you orbit up there—not just to threats from the air, but threats from the ground. So you really can't loiter in the target area. It's dangerous enough just to do the re-attack."

The confusion between the Viper pilots and the AWACS controller proved fatal. First, Punch missed the call alerting him to the danger he was in. Second, the AWACS controller's mistake about the altitude of the enemy fighters left Rage and Beaker fatally vulnerable as they closed in—denying them the safe, missile kill at a distance.

On the other hand, it proved an excellent object lesson for the punks, about to launch into the real world. "The goal of the mission is for the wingman to drop the correct bombs and stay with his flight lead," says Punch. "If you go blind—if you lose sight—then you have to do everything to get back together as quickly as possible. When you get separated, you learn how uncovered you are. You learn how valuable it is to have everybody together. You don't ever want—in the real world out there—you don't ever want to be alone. The hair on the back of your neck starts to stand up—you go, 'Oh shit, where's the rest of my flight?' "

Suddenly, the seemingly obsessive emphasis on getting to briefings precisely on time, merging at precisely the right altitude, and dropping the bombs on the target within five seconds of the planned moment makes sense. Sloppy habits have fatal consequences in the bewildering confusion of a real-world orchestration of bombers, fighters, Wild Weasels, and AWACS planes.

"What we're really trying to produce here is smart wingmen—with initiative and aggressiveness and discipline," says Rage. "Fighter pilots always get the shaft about being cocky—it's like a stigma—but really it's a quiet meekness and confidence you have to demonstrate in your skills. When you fly across into Bad Guy Land for the first time, it's a completely different ball game. These guys haven't seen it. But 99 percent of the IPs here in the last fifteen years have flown in situations like that—where you see SAMs coming up, you see triple-A, you go drop bombs for real on real targets. When these guys get to those combat units, you don't want your bros out there to go, 'What are you guys doing out there at Luke? You're sending us guys that aren't prepared.' We want these guys to be prepared to go out and do their job and come home alive."

For the B-coursers, the mission is a revelation—the closest they've come to real combat conditions—with the din of confusion. "We've done everything in pieces," says Beaker. "You flow from one thing to the next. We did intercepts. We dropped bombs. It's like the whole package of everything they teach us here. But putting it all together is different. You're pumped up for the whole time—your senses are always heightened and you're looking out more. But you're so focused on what you're doing that you don't really notice it. If I had taken a second missile shot—one of the guys that Rage merged with might have been dead. If I had stayed visual with them, we would have been two versus two. I thought my first missile shot was good, so I didn't take another. When I looked at the tape, I saw that I should have taken a second shot."

Rage shrugs. "You don't just view it as either-or—good or bad. If it's good, it could have been better."

Mostly, Beaker did great. He got his bombs on target, stayed with his flight lead, and didn't crash into any other planes. Killing the enemy fighters would have been an unexpected bonus. "He had great awareness and great procedures to shoot the first missile. The bandit just happened to maneuver through no awareness of the missile being shot in a way that required a second shot. Still, in the real world the first missile might have hit."

That's nice.

Lessons learned and all.

But the destruction of Rage's flight now creates major problems for the second four-ship led by Gilligan, hurrying to their assistance. As Gilligan's four Vipers approach, they try to decipher the din of radio calls spurred by the battle, which include more than a few pieces of crucially bad information.

Clearly, their picture-perfect mission has turned to crap. Gilligan leads the formation, with Pap on his wing. Several miles back and offset, Crash has Gimmie on his wing.

Their bomb run went flawlessly, so they're together on the way out—slung out about 30 miles from Punch's two-ship fragment. When the bandits jump Punch, Gilligan's Vipers turn back to help, already confused by the AWACS's miscues.

By the time they get within range, Punch and Jack are already dead and the AWACS has terminated Rage and Beaker's fights—which also takes Old Man out of the fight. This leaves Opic and Ozone free now to turn to face the new threat.

Aboard the AWACS plane, the controller tosses a coin. Bad news for Gilligan's guys: no hostile declaration at a safe distance. So they must close to visual range to kill the approaching fighters, while Opie and Ozone have no such restriction—a lethal advantage despite the two-to-one odds against them.

Gilligan now needs to get close enough to determine whether the approaching jets have orange missiles marking them as hostile, and then stay alive long enough for Pap to get off a shot. As they approach to within 5 miles, Pap shifts his radar lock back and forth between the two approaching enemy Red Air jets—keeping both in his HUD. But when they get to within 5 miles—at a closing speed of 15 miles a minute—Gilligan sorts Pap to the southernmost approaching bogey. As Pap shifts his attention and narrows his radar beam in the air-to-air mode, he completely loses track of the second approaching enemy fighter. He still cannot actually see either of the enemy jets.

If he'd been a veteran, Pap would have kept that unseen, unlocked fighter in mind. He would have been able to fly his jet, decipher the bewildering chatter from the AWACS, keep track of Gilligan, keep locked on his target, and still continually shift his radar mode to scan the sky for that other fighter—all the while looking over his shoulder for a backstab. Instead, Pap focuses solely on his assigned fighter—and his desperate desire to kill him. As a result, Pap locks up Ozone, but holds his shot, waiting for Gilligan to call "hostile."

"I should have supported my flight lead through the notch," says Pap of the moment Gilligan hurtled into range of the enemy fighter. "I had a lock on both of them at 14 miles, but when I got in close I lost my lock. I didn't have the situational awareness. I wasn't locked, so I didn't shoot. I could have taken the shot. Hopefully, it's not like that in war—because I'll be dead."

So Pap isn't watching Gilligan when Opie suddenly locks him and the two spin into a swirling fight. If he'd seen them start fighting, he would have known they were facing hostile jets. Instead, he continues to watch Ozone. But he's concentrating so hard that he actually misses Gilligan's declaration on the radio that the jets are hostile. Moreover, although Pap can now see Ozone's jet, he can't see the orange markings.

So Gilligan flashes through his merge with Opie, assuming Pap will take the shot—unaware that Pap still doesn't realize he's cleared to kill Opie.

Even in the midst of his turn toward Gilligan, Opie notes that Pap is pivoting away from the fight in the air—turning toward Ozone. With a glance he reads the complex geometry of the speeding jets, and he locks and fires at Gilligan as he hurtles through the merge. A hit. But he wants more. So Opie holds his turn after the shot, aligning himself perfectly on Pap, who continues to maneuver to deny Ozone a shot—oblivious to Gilligan's death and his own sudden danger. Opie gets them both.

Meanwhile, Crash and Gimmie have come within range. Acting like wingmen for Pap and Gilligan, they have positioned themselves above and south of the fight. So while Gimmie concentrates on watching for a backstab from some unexpected quarter, Crash shifts his attention to the battle below—looking for a chance to pick off Ozone or Opie as they maneuver for advantages. He had assumed Gilligan would stay alive long enough to force them into an ambush. Guess again. Opie and Ozone's game plan called for forcing the fight quickly—gambling on killing both Pap and Gilligan before the second two-ship could get into position. So far, the plan's working.

But then, no plan's perfect. And sometimes, you can't beat the odds.

So although Crash and Gimmie get into position too late to save either Pap or Gilligan, they come upon Opie and Ozone at the end of a fight that has cost them much of their energy—that vital combination of speed and altitude that largely determines who has the upper hand in a dogfight. Cursing inwardly, Crash tells Gimmie to target Ozone, but to hold off shooting. Now Crash fires all four of his missiles in quick succession. Opie and Ozone maneuver to defeat the shot, but they've lost too much energy. By contrast, Crash has time to line up the shot, a huge energy advantage, and a high perch. He kills them both.

But the engagement has been a disaster for Rage's contingent of Blue Air. In effect, they lost six of the eight jets in the flight. In return, they killed two Red Air fighters—three if you count Rage's probable kill in the terminated fight—all despite an eight-to-three advantage. By contrast, on the way in they killed all the Red Air fighters with no losses—thanks to the AWACS's hostile calls beyond visual range. The outcome perfectly illustrates the basis of U.S. air supremacy in every conflict since Vietnam:

a huge advantage in detecting the enemy and coordinating the attacks of two, four, and eight-ship units scattered across the sky.

Now it's Doughboy's turn to run the gauntlet, leading his Blue Air group of eight fighters in two flights. Doughboy leads Rex, AWOL, and Pong in a flight named "Snoopy." Bongoo leads Igor, Ship, and Stihl in "Clam."

Buster and Festus are waiting for them.

In theory, the Good Guys should have a good day. They'll have the advantage of four-to-one odds—with eight Vipers facing just two enemy fighters. But the enemy fighters are flown by Buster and Festus, veteran assassins.

Doughboy's four-ship will head for the target at 30,000 feet, with Bongoo's four-ship following. However, the first problem develops before they leave the ground. Pong's jet develops instrument problems awaiting takeoff and he has to switch jets. They can't delay the whole formation to wait for one jet, or they'll run out of airspace time. So they take off as Pong switches jets and he goes to afterburners to catch up. He links up before they get to the airspace—but now Pong has less fuel than the rest of the flight.

Fortunately, on the way in the AWACS makes it easy. The distant controller warns Doughboy of the approach of Buster and Festus in a loose two-ship before the radar blips appear on the Vipers' screens. Doughboy spreads out his formation and splits them so they're in the perfect alignment by the time the glowing icons representing Buster and Festus appear on the screen. With the advantage of knowing Red Air's position before the veteran pilots ever spot his flight, Doughboy arranges it so that he and Rex appear on Buster's radar screen at extreme range, while AWOL and Pong split for a flanking move. Just as Doughboy hoped, Festus and Buster immediately turn toward him, not knowing AWOL and Pong have now outflanked them. Buster and Festus die quickly, perfectly set up by Doughboy's adroit ambush, which was made possible by the early warning from the AWACS.

The fight seems but a brief flurry. Only later does it seem significant.

The original plan called for Doughboy's four-ship and Bongoo's four-ship to hit the same target from different directions. That's not unusual. Attackers often try to overwhelm air defenses and bewilder enemy air controllers by following different paths to a target. So Doughboy re-forms his four fighters after the intercept and repositions his flight to approach from a different heading.

But as they approach the target, life gets fatally more complicated.

Bongoo's flight finds the path to the target blocked by medium-level clouds. In the real world, they would drop GPS bombs which laugh at clouds. But since they're dropping gravity-driven dumb bombs—and fake ones at that—Bongoo decides to go to the low show backup plan at about 500 feet to stay under the clouds. Doughboy stays high, since he has no clouds on his path.

In combat, the controllers would not have let two flights approach the same target area at different altitudes—even though the precisely timed separation between the two flights should prevent the lower-level jets from flying into the fragments of the bombs dropped by the higher flight. But a combat plan wouldn't rely on timing alone for the vital purpose of deconfliction; it would also make sure the flights were at deconflicted altitudes.

Sure enough, in the role-switch resulting from the dogfight, the flight schedules get screwed up. By the time the two flights separate and make their attacks, Doughboy's flight is a little behind schedule. Meanwhile, Bongoo's flight has gotten a few seconds ahead of schedule on the way in. A few seconds. Like being just barely late to a briefing. This turns out to be a big deal.

Bongoo, Igor, Ship, and Stihl go screaming in at 500 feet, pop up, roll, line up, drop their bombs, bank, veer, and pull away. Their programmed defensive maneuver takes them over Doughboy's target. In the plan, Doughboy's flight should have finished off that target a minute earlier. Instead, the last ship in Bongoo's flight—Stihl—flies past just as the first bombs from Doughboy's flight hit their target. If Doughboy had been dropping real bombs, the fragments from the explosion could have riddled Stihl's Viper with shrapnel.

But it gets worse. Coming off the target, Pong sees the approaching jets of Bongoo's flight and improvises, rolling off in the opposite direction from the plan. That's good. He avoids bombing the Good Guys. But by the time he comes around, finishes the jinks intended to frustrate any triple-A fire or SAM shots from the ground, and looks around to locate the rest of the flight for the rejoin, he's astonished to find himself alone in the sky. A minute ago, he was on a bombing run with four buddies. Now, suddenly, he's completely alone and faintly disoriented. Fresh meat—as in sitting duck.

Now, Pong should roll out the instant he realizes he's a lost sheep. He should make a beeline for the rendezvous point. Instead, he flies in circles, looking for the rest of the flight—painfully aware that he won't last more than an eyeblink if Buster and Festus happen upon him, wandering around over the desert like some freaking tourist.

The rest of Doughboy's flight has recovered from its brush with Bongoo's flight, only to discover Pong's missing when they link up. So they circle around, eventually picking him up, but opening a sizable gap between Doughboy's flight and Bongoo's, since Bongoo's boys have headed for home without waiting for Doughboy's flight to reassemble itself.

This ain't going well.

Moreover, by the time they link up with Pong, they discover he's low on gas as a result of having used afterburners to catch up on the way to the bomb run. In the real world, he'd go back with the others—and they'd put him in the middle of a protected circle, to minimize the chance that he'd have to maneuver to avoid getting shot down. But there's no sense in messing with running out of gas on a training mission, so Pong heads for the barn and the AWACS takes him off its list.

Suddenly, the odds have improved significantly for Buster and Festus—waiting in the deadly blue yonder. The staggered wall of eight jets has now become Bongoo's four-ship element out front, trailed at a distance by Doughboy's three-ship element.

Still, good odds for the good guys. Even if you grant that Festus and Buster are two of the best Viper pilots on the planet, Doughboy and Bongoo's guys should dice them and serve them on crackers.

Except, the AWACS controller is still in training.

Festus and Buster spot Bongoo's approaching four-ship first.

So they split.

Here's where the AWACS's directions gets dicey.

The AWACS controller warns Bongoo about Buster, splayed out to the south and trying to loop in behind. But the controller fails to mention Festus, outflanking them to the north.

Naturally enough, Bongoo's four-ship turns to face Buster—who the AWACS initially reports as two ships. In the process, they turn their backs on Festus, who they still can't see on their own radars. This is shaping up to be a case of "Death by AWACS."

This is the moment fighter pilots live for—leastwise if you're Festus, grinning and closing on four fat targets from behind.

On the other hand, if you're one of Bongoo's guys suddenly hearing the missile lockup warning tone out of nowhere—it's the moment that wakes you up in the middle of the night in a cold sweat.

Let Festus walk up behind you with a stiletto and you're just plain dead. You'll never even feel the tip of the blade.

Festus snaps off two missile shots—killing Ship and Stihl before they could say half a Hail Mary.

Suddenly, Bongoo and Igor find themselves the only survivors of a four-ship element, getting backstabbed. They throw their jets into defensive maneuvers as Festus targets them from behind. As soon as they turn to deal with Festus, Buster shifts from bait to hunter. He whips around and kills Igor, easily anticipating the pattern of his jinks. But it costs him: Bongoo pounces, abruptly re-reversing himself. He comes around a beat too late to save Igor, but fires two missiles in quick succession.

Buster dodges the first missile, but squanders so much energy in the maneuver that he's an easy kill for the second.

Bongoo enjoys a split second of triumph.

But it costs him too.

Festus's legendary sixth sense for the geometry of an air-to-air battle serves him well now. He has an uncanny ability to predict the flow of the battle—and somehow to keep several jets in his peripheral vision at the same time. So as Bongoo dispatches Buster, Festus repositions and kills Bongoo an instant after Buster dies.

Suddenly, it's one to three.

Now all Festus has to worry about is Doughboy, AWOL, and Rex hurrying toward the fight on afterburners, trying to decipher the chaos of radio calls the short, lethal fight has generated. Pong is already on his way home, low on gas.

Doughboy has both Festus and Buster on his radar, with Bongoo's flight scattered.

Only problem is, the AWACS controller forgets to call Buster dead.

So Doughboy focuses on Buster, the Red Air bastard who just killed off a whole flight of Good Guys and now flying along like he doesn't have a care in the world. Doughboy sorts Rex and AWOL to Festus, to make sure Festus can't stab him in the back. Then he goes after Buster.

Naturally, Buster is easy to kill, since he's already dead and not dodg-ing the attack. Doughboy's legend will surely grow—killing dead people. This is gonna cost at least a six-pack.

Now Festus faces two-to-one odds in a head-on fight with the veteran AWOL and the hapless Rex.

AWOL and Rex follow standard doctrine approaching the merge. Rex offsets from the fight, positioning himself on the perch and taking care to find an angle that lets him keep AWOL, Doughboy, and Festus in sight at the same time.

Festus gets a fleeting lock and takes a wild shot as he heads into his merge with AWOL—a veteran's tactic. The key to winning a turning fight is to force the other guy into a jink at the merge, throwing him on the defensive. It's Festus's fourth missile, which leaves him just two more. It doesn't look like he's going to survive—but he'd be happy with one more kill. Killing four Vipers is a good day's work for anyone.

Festus sees that if he turns upside down and pulls through the turn on AWOL's tail, he'll line up on Doughboy, just disengaging from killing the already dead Buster. Perhaps Festus could outturn AWOL—but once Doughboy gets into the fight, Festus doesn't have a chance. So Festus fig-ures he can backstab the confused Doughboy if he just for a moment ignores Rex, who is cluelessly circling above the fray. Festus figures Rex will expect him to go after AWOL. After all, Rex has been drilled on the responsibilities of the wingman, so he's no doubt lining up for a shot at the slow point of the turn Festus would have to make to chase down AWOL. Rex isn't one for freelancing. So Festus figures he'll do the unex-pected—and kill Doughboy first.

It's a perfect plan—vintage Festus.

It should have worked.

But, unaccountably, Rex sees it all unfolding in an instant. It's strange. Freaky. Everything slows down. The twisting specks of the three planes—AWOL, Doughboy, and Festus—suddenly seemed etched with detail. Rex can see the firing solutions, the angles, the relationships—like it was drawn in red and blue on the briefing room whiteboard. He sees what Festus is doing the instant Festus breaks out of the turn that would have brought him around on AWOL's tail.

So Rex presses the stick to the side, throws in a little rudder, and pulls in the throttle so he's hanging there with the little target squares of the HUD lined up on where Festus is going instead of trailing along behind where he actually is—instead of trailing behind the jet as he's been these last six nightmarish months.

And sure enough, Festus flies right into the little target circle in the center of Rex's HUD.

And Rex kills him. Right there, with the press of a button. He kills Festus, who killed Ship—and God knows who else.

Kills him dead.

And best yet, Rex kills him in the split second before Festus's own targeting circle settles on Doughboy, hanging like a bull's-eye in his turn back to the battle.

Well. Who'd have figured?

Someone owes that boy a beer.

Epilogue: The Eye of the Viper

AND SO, FINALLY, they have finished.

Punks no more.

They have graduated.

Every freaking one.

And in a treasured extravagance of ceremony and solemnity, their families gather for the graduation ceremony in the officers' club. They have journeyed from all over the country to see their children transformed now, in dress blues and gleaming shoes, into something different.

They are fighter pilots, precisely machined cogs in the most expensive and capable military force ever created. The eye of the Viper.

But they are also Emerald Knights—fighter jocks in a long line of descent stretching back to the Red Baron.

And one of them will soon be the distinguished graduate—the Top Gun—the most lethal son-of-a-bitch in the bunch.

With its dinner and speeches, the event has that combination of sentimentality and humor that distinguishes the fighter pilot culture—when they're dressed up and serious. Out of their flight suits and in their dress uniforms for the first time in months, the pilots seem crisp and fatal and interchangeable. Each B-courser presides over a tableful of friends and family, close packed in the big room.

At the front of the room stands an empty table, with fine silver—empty. It's set for the pilots missing in action, glass inverted, salt beside the plate for their tears, lemon for their bitter fate.

Punch presides, introducing the B-coursers as "single-engine, ass-kicking American fighter pilots," drawing a raucous cheer from the beaming families.

Next they offer a slide show recapping the course. Pap took the pictures with his digital camera. Each one of the B-coursers posed in some self-mocking parody of their nicknames, and Pap digitally edited them for effect. Rex's picture shows him towed behind the jet—which gets a laugh. He's a good sport, that Rex. And a Viper pilot. It concludes with spectacular aerial photos of F-16s blowing up stuff—great, mushrooming fireballs of destruction. Dogfights from the HUD. Everyone loves it. Although, here and there around the room, the mothers purse their lips and brave a thin smile.

Old Man isn't there. He decided to retire. The Air Force insists that its colonels transfer ceaselessly—in the name of cross training. After nearly twenty years of putting his family second, he decided to take his retirement pay and bail. He has a couple of teenagers. They would have moved again if he'd asked them. But he couldn't quite bring himself to do it. So he's gone, along with those 3,000 hours of flight time, that killer instinct, that three-dimensional understanding of both a dogfight and a B-courser's confusion.

The slide show continues, with candid shots from throughout the last six months. They're scattering now across the planet—novice F-16 pilots for the world's only superpower, spread thin. Gimmie and Stihl are heading for South Korea. Igor's going to Germany, Rex to New Mexico.

They drink toasts—to the Knights, to friends and family—but not to the French.

A general gets up to give a speech—one of those Blue Suits the Fighter Mafia loved to torment, except he's got a lot of combat experience. He's an old F-16 fighter jock. He talks fondly of blowing the hell out of the Iraqi Republican Guard—a long line of tanks obliterated one by one in the darkness by Viper pilots wearing night-vision goggles, and nighttime targeting pods—dropping bombs from so high up that the tank crews never even heard the engines. He later talked to the Special Forces guys who crept out into the desert to locate the targets, radioing in coordinates in a whisper. The general talks fondly about the planned upgrades to the Viper, the helmet-mounted sights connected to missiles that will continuously correct in midair to hit whatever the pilot's looking at, the planned "sniper pod."

"I'd do anything to trade places with you guys right now," says the general fondly. He's chained to a desk in the bowels of the bureaucracy, but still a fighter pilot when he dreams.

He tells them to keep their hair short, their shoes spit-shined. He tells them to volunteer for everything and never complain. He tells them to expect the long hours—and make sure their families understand and their wives know that dinner will be cold and she'll put the kids to bed alone.

He tells them to never quit learning and to always pay attention to the veterans—and never balk at asking the question. He tells them to have faith in themselves and to ready themselves for that day when they advance from wingman to flight lead. He tells them to spend ninety minutes a day running and working out, or the g-forces will beat the stuffing out of them. He tells them to befriend the maintenance crews—to know their names and the names of their wives and children.

Then—oddly enough—he tells them to balance their role as high-tech killers in a plane that can never be mastered with their roles as husbands and wives and parents.

Yeah. Right.

He tells them to leave the jet behind when they turn toward home, although you can hear in his voice the undiminished longing for the cockpit and a 9-g turn and a twirl that turns the earth into the sky and back again.

And in the end he says again, "I'll tell you right now, I'd trade with you in a heartbeat."

Because the Viper's like heroin or cocaine: it builds up in your blood and leaves you insatiable.

Now, finally, the awards start coming.

First the B-coursers recognize their favorite IPs.

They vote Ship the top IP.

They vote Rage the greatest contributor to morale.

They hand out roses to all the spouses—fragrant but frail compensation.

The maintenance crews name their favorite student pilot: Gimmie. Of course. She gets a real sword. Very cool.

Beaker gets the award as the top student in academics—with a 95.69 percent average on tests.

Igor gets the air-to-air "Turkey Shoot" award.

Gimmie wins the one-day "Duke of Nuke" competition, for missing a target by a mere five feet with a simulated nuclear bomb.

Stihl gets the award for the most accurate bomber overall. He also gets the air-to-air Top Gun award.

Pap gets the class leadership award, for being there for everyone all the time.

Igor gets the "outstanding officer award," for displaying all those modest, officer-and-a-gentleman-type qualities.

And when all the scores have been totaled, all across the board in the relentless competition, Stihl earns top graduate.

The Zen of the Surfer Dude.

They all linger when it's over, impressive in their dress blues—distinguished by their awards. Rex is grinning. Granted, he scraped through. But he's a Viper pilot now—just like Stihl.

The world waits out there in the darkness. The North Korean MiGs are fueled and waiting in the cold, just across the bristling line. The Taliban are creeping back toward Kabul. Iraq remains in chaos. The Israelis just bombed the Syrians—with their purchased American F-16s. The freshly minted Viper pilots could be in the deep muck next month. They might get a quick crack at their war—to atone for the bad timing of having missed the chance to go after Saddam. They're ready, although the IPs will tell you with a shake of their heads that they'll still be baby seals for at least six months after they get to their operational squadrons. They've got nicknames to earn. Technology to master.

And maybe they're even The Last of Their Kind, the last honest-to-God, hotshot, single-seat, single-engine, Lord of Creation fighter pilots—making their last stand against evil empires and evildoers before the computer-driven drones push them aside.

But in truth, they're not thinking about that now.

Tonight, they're no-kidding, shit-hot fighter pilots in their dress blues, the envy of the known world, the flutter in every woman's heart. Right now, in the bar, a ground-pounder couldn't tell Rex from Ship.

So they head for the bar. They've got parents and brothers and sisters and girlfriends. And those without girlfriends have gotten very interested in the sisters of their buddies.

They'll do some serious celebrating tonight—and nurse some serious hangovers in the morning.

After all, they're fighter jocks. And sometimes, you've just got to let a fighter pilot be a fighter pilot.

Doughboy and Rage and Gilligan stand around in the empty meeting room for a little bit after the B-coursers have gone. They exchange a couple of fond and mocking stories about Rex and Gimmie and Beaker and Igor.

Doughboy's the last to leave, laughing at the memory of the day that good old Top Gun Stihl pulled a perfect, Syrian lead turn in air-to-air.

That's a story Chips would enjoy.

Afterword: Turning Writers into Pukes

<hr />

"WANT TO PULL SOME G'S?" asks Major Jamie Scofield, a combat-veteran fighter jock who normally trains fresh-meat rookies at Luke Air Force Base, but who tomorrow will afterburn my media butt into the Wild Blue Yonder—strapped nervously into the backseat of a training-adopted F-16 with 25,000 pounds of thrust devoted to revealing whether I have even a dollop of the right stuff.

Pull some g's. Sounds harmless.

But he's talking about a turn so sharp that my body will seem to weigh 1,800 pounds—including about 100 pounds worth of head and helmet should I want to turn my head and take in the upside-down scenery. And if I forget to tighten every muscle in my body and gasp for air once every three seconds in the turn, the blood will drain out of my head and I'll pass out like a putz. "Curly" wants to pull 9 g's—the limit set by the shipboard computer, which worries constantly about pilots passing out and flying their silly selves into the ground.

Oh God, I think. *Please no. I'm gonna whimper. Faint. Vomit.*

"Absolutely," I say. "Sounds like fun."

After all, for years I've secretly wanted to take this ultimate test of macho, so I can be like a fighter pilot. After all, they're real men, oozing the right stuff. They know it—much as they try not to swagger. I know it—much as I try not to whimper. That's why the lantern-jawed fighter is always the hero of the movie, while the reporters scramble around in sweating, squealing little scrums. Besides, my dad was a test pilot in World War II, and all my life I noticed how he sometimes tilted his head to watch the cloud-scudded sky with a certain fond yearning. I wondered what he saw.

But now that the event looms, I just don't want to puke or pass out.

Curly made it sound easy—a lark. Yeah. Easy for him. He's got thousands of hours in the air, including combat missions over Bosnia and Iraq. One night over Bosnia, while he was flying around with four F-16s trying to get SAM missile batteries to shoot at them so they could bomb them, he got a warning from a patrolling AWACS plane that two mystery jets were approaching—probably Serbian MiG 29s. The AWACs couldn't give clearance to shoot, so instead the F-16s had to turn tail and run to stay out of the MiGs' missile range. The ever-so-lucky MiG pilots chased them for a few heady moments, then hightailed it. Curly still fumes when he even thinks about running from a couple of raggedy MiGs.

So they send me to Life Support for my cool zippered flight suit, snugged-on helmet, spiffy black boots, and computer-inflated anti-g suit for the high-g turns, not to mention a discreet package of barf bags. The idea of unbuckling my oxygen mask quickly enough to use my barf bag inspires a wave of resolutely suppressed anxiety. Next they bundle me off to a simulator to show me how to pull the ejection seat lever. They also show me the sticks and buttons I ABSOLUTELY, DEFINITELY SHOULD NOT TOUCH.

Finally, retired Marine Corps Master Gunner Sergeant Bill Smith drives us out to the runway, where our heart-stoppingly sleek jet awaits. Later I learn that Bill spent thirty years in the Marines as a helicopter door gunner and was shot down three times and broken in many different places. He retired from the Marines and has spent the last sixteen years driving people around Luke.

The crew chief—a seemingly nice enough fellow—cannot resist a final, "Have fun. Don't puke."

A few minutes later, we spring lightly into the air, on a hurtle and a prayer.

The ground drops away, the sky opens up. On our wing, another F-16 climbs with us—all grace and power and threat. We sit near the arrow-sharp nose, high on the body of the jet in front of the short, angled wings. The frameless canopy offers a terrifying, exhilarating view. But for the consuming roar of the great engine, it would seem like we were flying free.

We fly in formation with the other F-16 for the 60 miles to the aerial range. The HUD screen offers a stream of information, most of it meaningless to me. With his seat reclined at a comfortable 30 degrees to resist g-forces and all of the controls built into the stick and throttle, a Viper pilot can perform any imaginable maneuver without ever looking down or taking his hands off the stick.

It scares the hell out of me.

But then Viper Euphoria begins to seep out of the jet and into my bones.

Standing on the stolid, stodgy ground, I have watched ravens cavorting through the sky and wondered what it must be like to live free in three dimensions. I remember watching Carl Sagan's *Cosmos,* in which he tried to explain the "fourth dimension" by asking his viewers to imagine themselves stick people sketched in two dimensions mystified by the concept of "up." I remember the wonder of snorkeling over brilliantly corrugated reefs, floating in that third dimension as a giant manta ray glided soundlessly past—heartbreakingly beautiful.

This is better.

I quickly lose control—but not like I thought.

Swooping between earth and heaven, I gasp, swear, and laugh manically. The sky stretches on forever and the desert tilts to the far horizon as the F-16 obliterates any notion of up and down. In a turn the g-forces overwhelm gravity, so the canopy defines "up" and the g-force of the turn creates "down." The scorched browns and reds of the desert serve as sky as easily as the white-streaked blue of the atmosphere.

Encouraged by my gasps and expletives, Curly puts the Viper through an escalating series of maneuvers. He twirls the F-16 on its axis, the ground flashes past the canopy. We climb straight up and then he pulls back into a loop, holding the arc of the turn so I hang in my straps as I crane my neck to look straight up at the earth below. He waggles, veers, and swoops—simulating the twists needed to bring the "death dot" to bear on another jet or to shake off a SAM's radar lock. Then he flips the jet on edge for a series of tightening turns, maxing out finally at 9 g's. My g-suit inflates explosively—squeezing my legs and chest. I sink into the hard seat, gasping for breath every two or three seconds, my cheeks sagging, my arms leaden, my head enormous as I struggle to look up through the canopy. The horizon tumbles crazily; the g-forces make it seem that the jet is holding its position and the earth is wobbling drunkenly out of its orbit.

Reassured by my demented laughter and perhaps remembering my wistful remark about how my dad loved to fly through clouds, Curly dives toward the ground, pulls up in a 9-g turn, and points the heart-piercing nose of the Viper at the only cloud he can find—a lonely wisp drifting above the sun-seared desert at about 10,000 feet. He pierces the cloud, which streams past the window in a blur of steam and yearning.

"Oh. God. That's incredible," I gush.

"Afraid that's the only cloud up here," says Curly, sounding disappointed.

That's when the nausea hits me—like a pothole at 60 miles per hour.

"Now, you'll like this," says Curly, determined to show me a good time. "Take off your glove and put it in your lap. We'll do the astronaut thing—I'll go into a big loop that makes you weightless. Your glove will float up off your lap. It's cool."

"Uh. Oh. Well. Hang on a second," I say, fumbling with my oxygen mask until I find the little release catch, rip it away, and grope for the airsickness bag stuffed into the chest strap of my shoulder harness. Miraculously, I get the bag open in time. Mercifully, Curly flies the plane very carefully and calmly for the next few minutes. "You OK back there?" he asks pleasantly, after a decent interval.

"Oh, yeah. Fine. Fine. Just kind of came over me. Out of nowhere, really," I say, wiping my face clumsily.

He flies on—dead level, absolutely calm.

"Well, we could head back," he offers.

Yeah. And I could shoot myself.

"Thought you said we were going to bomb a SAM site," says I.

"We can if you want to," says Curly, dubiously.

"Why not?" says I, tying off my little bag of humiliation, since I can't find the attached twisty tie.

So we bomb a couple of simulated SAM sites—which involves coming in low, popping up sharply, plunging toward the SAMs, releasing a missile, and then rolling out in a 6-g turn designed to evade small arms fire and any hasty radar locks. I emit a couple of grunted "wows," although I've been exposed as a mere reporter.

We get back to Luke with about ten minutes of fuel in the tank.

I figure I'll wait until dark before getting out of the Viper with my little plastic bag. But they all stand there, looking at me. So I climb out, bag dangling delicately. The ground crew smile. Well, actually, they smirk.

Driving away from the air base, I finger the mottled, black-and-blue bruise on my pride.

But then a Viper passes overhead and I lean forward to watch it slice through the sky. For just a moment, the earth shifts and lifts and I must stifle an urge to pull back on the stick shift of my battered jeep, to lift the nose and forsake the pavement and return to life in the third dimension. And for a long while, the sight of the earth wheeling beyond the canopy has lingered in my mind like the retinal burn of the sun on the inside of a blink—and I dimly understand the yearning in my father when he tilted his head to watch the drift of a single cloud, alone in the sky.

And hey.

I didn't pass out.

One out of two ain't bad—for a *writer.*

BIBLIOGRAPHY

Boyne, Walter. *Beyond the Wild Blue: A History of the U.S. Air Force 1947–1997.* New York: St. Martin's Press, 1997.

Coram, Robert. *Boyd: The Fighter Pilot Who Changed the Art of War.* Boston: Little, Brown and Company, 2002.

Darling, Kev. *Combat Legend: F-16 Fighting Falcon.* London: Airlife. 2003

Friedman, George and Meredith. *The Future of War: Power, Technology and American World Dominance in the Twenty-First Century.* New York: St. Martin's Press, 1996.

Gandt, Robert. *Bogeys and Bandits: The Making of a Fighter Pilot.* New York: Penguin, 1997.

O'Grady, Scott. *Basher Five-Two: The True Story of an F-16 Pilot.* New York: Bantam Doubleday, 1997.

Peacock, Lindsay. *On Falcon Wings: The F-16 Story.* Hong Kong: The Royal Air Force Benevolent Fund Enterprises, 1997.

Rendall, Ivan. *Splash One: The Story of Jet Combat.* London: Weidenfeld & Nicholson, 1997.

Rosenkranz, Keith. *Vipers in the Storm: Diary of a Gulf War Fighter Pilot*. New York: McGraw-Hill, 2002.

Shaw, Robert. *Fighter Combat: Tactics and Maneuvering*. Annapolis: Naval Institute Press, 1985.

Smallwood, William. *Strike Eagle: Flying the F-15E in the Gulf War*. McLean, Virginia: Brassey's, 1996.

Spick, Mike. *The Great Book of Modern Warplanes*. London: Salamander Books, 2002.

Thompson, Warren. *Bandits over Baghdad: Personal Stories of Flying the F117 Over Iraq*. North Branch, Minnesota: 1996.

Toliver, Raymond and Constable, Trevor. *Fighter Aces of the U.S.A.* Fallbrook: Aero Publishers, Inc., 1979.

Wilcox, Robert. *Black Aces High*. New York: Thomas Dunn Books/St. Martin's Press, 2002.

Wilcox, Robert. *Wings of Fury: From Vietnam to the Gulf War*. New York: Pocket Books, 1996.